THE POLITICAL POWER OF THE WORD: PRESS AND ORATORY IN NINETEENTH-CENTURY LATIN AMERICA

Nineteenth-Century Latin America Series
General Editor Eduardo Posada-Carbó

The Institute's Nineteenth-Century Latin America Series results from the annual workshop on nineteenth-century Latin American history held at the Institute, and is aimed at encouraging the study of various aspects of what has largely been a neglected period in the modern historiography of the region.

Publications in the Series

1. *Wars, Parties and Nationalism: Essays on the Politics and Society of Nineteenth-Century Latin America*
Eduardo Posada-Carbó (ed.) – 1995

2. *In Search of a New Order: Essays on the Politics and Society of Nineteenth-Century Latin America*
Eduardo Posada-Carbó (ed.) – 1998

3. *Independence and Revolution in Spanish America: Perspectives and Problems*
Anthony McFarlane and Eduardo Posada-Carbó (eds.) – 1999

4. *Law, Justice and State-Building: Judicial Institutions in Nineteenth-Century Latin America*
Eduardo Zimmermann (ed.) – 1999

5. *The Politics of Religion in an Age of Revival*
Austen Ivereigh (ed.) – 2000

6. *Rumours of Wars: Civil Conflict in Nineteenth-Century Latin America*
Rebecca Earle (ed.) – 2000

7. *The European Revolutions of 1848 and the Americas*
Guy Thomson (ed.) – 2000

Institute of Latin American Studies
School of Advanced Study
University of London

The Political Power of the Word:

Press and Oratory in Nineteenth-Century Latin America

Edited by
Iván Jaksić

Institute of Latin American Studies
31 Tavistock Square, London WC1H 9HA
http://www.sas.ac.uk/ilas/publicat.htm

Institute of Latin American Studies
School of Advanced Study
University of London

British Library Cataloguing-in-Publication Data
A catalogue record for this book is available from the British Library

ISBN 1 900039 46 X

Institute of Latin American Studies
University of London, 2002

CONTENTS

Notes on Contributors

Rebecca Earle teaches Latin American History at the University of Warwick. Her research concerns the social and political history of late colonial and early national Colombia; letters print and modernity; and the role of the past in shaping national identity in nineteenth-century Spanish America. She is editor of *Epistolary Selves: Letters and Letter Writers, 1600-1945* (1999) and *Rumours of Wars: Civil Conflict in Nineteenth-Century Latin America* (2000) and she is currently working on a book entitled *The Return of the Native: Indians and Mythmaking in Spanish America.*

Charles A. Hale is Emeritus Professor of History at the University of Iowa. He is the author of *Mexican Liberalism in the Age of Mora, 1821–1853* (1968) and *The Transformation of Liberalism in Late Nineteenth–Century Mexico* (1989).

Iván Jaksić is Associate Professor of History and Faculty Fellow of the Helen Kellog Institute for International Studies at the University of Notre Dame. His is author of *Academic Rebels in Chile: The Role of Philosophy in Higher Education and Politics* (1989) and co-editor of *The Struggle for Democracy in Chile, 1982–1990* (1991) and *Sarmiento: Author of a Nation* (California,1994). His most recent publication is *Andrés Bello: Scholarship and Nation-Building in Nineteenth-Century Latin America* (2001).

Carlos Malamud is Professor of History of the Americas at the Universidad Nacional de Educación a Distancia in Spain and Director of the Latin American Department at the Instituto Universitario Ortega y Gasset, where he also heads the Latin American Security and Defense Observatory (OSAL). He has written widely on Latin American history, including *Juan Manuel de Rosas, América Latina. Siglo XX. La búsqueda de la democracia* and *Partidos políticos y elecciones en la Argentina: la Liga del Sur (1908–1916)*, and he edited, with Elizabeth Joyce, *Latin America and the Multinational Drug Trade.*

Carmen McEvoy is Assistant Professor of History at Sewanee, The University of the South, Tennessee. She has written widely on Peruvian and Latin American politics and culture. Her study of political culture in Peru at the turn of the nineteenth century is being prepared for publication by Pontificia Universidad Católica del Perú. Her work on Latin

American republicanism: 'Power, Identity and Republicanism in the Andean Region, 1817-1878' will be part of the nine volume *History of the Andean Region* edited by Juan Maiguashca and sponsored by University Simón Bolivar and Pacto Andino.

Eduardo Posada-Carbó is a historian, currently a Senior Teaching Fellow at the University of Warwick. He has published extensively on the history and politics of Colombia, including *The Colombian Caribbean: A Regional History, 1870–1950* (1996) and *¿Guerra civil? El lenguaje del conflicto en Colombia* (2001). He is the general editor of this series.

Sol Serrano teaches at the Instituto de Historia, Pontificia Universidad Católica de Chile. She is the author of *Universidad y nación: Chile en el siglo XIX* (1994) and *Vírgenes viajeras. Diarios de religiosas francesas en su ruta a Chile, 1837–1874* (2000).

Douglass Sullivan-González is an associate professor of history at the University of Mississippi. He is a specialist on religion and nation formation in nineteenth-century Guatemala and is the author of *Piety, Power, and Politics: Religion and Nation Formation in Guatemala, 1821–1871* (1998), he is the editor, with Charles Reagan Wilson, of *The South and the Caribbean* (2001).

Introduction

In a rare moment of despondency Domingo Faustino Sarmiento stated in 1841 that 'without complete freedom of the press there can be neither liberty nor progress'. At the same time, he lamented, 'with it one can barely maintain public order'. He had every reason to be dismayed, for even the stable Chile in the 1840s had become the scene of tumultuous gatherings and riots resulting from the intemperate tone of the press. Journalists, including himself, became vociferous, offensive to their opponents and willing to engage in the most outrageous allegations. The press, it would appear, was an instrument of disorder, a far cry from the vehicle of civilisation that he and others expected it to be.

There is much evidence to confirm Sarmiento's gloomy assessment. The post-Independence press in Latin America was openly partisan, reflecting the narrow interests of competing political forces, groups and even individuals. Although many papers became well established in the nineteenth century, and survive to this day, most did not, often confining their life span to the agitation of a particular issue, or to elections. In fact, elections were the surest means to spawn a wide variety of papers, but they vanished with the same speed with which they appeared in the first place. Circulation was limited, quality uneven and balanced information uniformly lacking.

These are certainly rather disheartening facts, albeit not unique to Latin America, for such was also the predicament of the press in Europe and the United States. What is more surprising is the relative shortage of serious study of the press in the historiography of nineteenth-century Latin America. Scholars have traditionally used the press as a source rather than as a subject of study, but that is now changing, especially in the last decade or so. This is partly related to the degree of sophistication and novelty shown in the historiography of other areas, especially Europe and the United States, which has had a positive effect on the study of Latin America. In addition, scholars no longer see the press as only a temporary consequence of elections and political struggles, but as a component of larger transformations brought about by the age of Atlantic revolutions. They view the press as a manifestation of what some may term 'modernity', 'written culture', or the set of changes resulting from the creation of national systems of education, expanded literacy, citizenship requirements and technological innovations. In addition, 'press' has come to mean more than 'newspapers', to comprise a wide spectrum of printed materials, from leaflets, pamphlets and broadsheets, to journals and books. Scholars now recognise the effects of the press in shaping a public sphere, expanding readership and contributing to the formation of political and national cultures.

Another significant development in the historiography is the increasing interest in oratory. Clearly, the growth in the circulation of written materials involved enormous transformations in reading and communication practices, but recent scholarship reminds us of the substantial overlap between orality and literacy. The word was written (and printed) not only to be read but also to be heard. This was a well-established tradition in the Catholic Church, especially through the delivery of sermons, but the post-Independence period opened new opportunities for other institutions and political groups. As Latin American nations mostly adopted a republican political model, parliaments now provided a significant venue of political debate. Such debates were oral, but often based on written statements, or soon to become written as papers published transcripts of congressional interventions. The successful politician could be a gifted natural speaker, but more often than not he would have a clear awareness of the techniques of writing and delivery. Oratory, now seen in relationship to writing, and in the context of an expanding periodical press, constitutes a significant new development in the field. Both the press and oratory, and their relationship, are the subject of this volume.

In the opening chapter Rebecca Earle examines the question of the influence and impact of print on the process of Spanish American Independence. While the historiography of other areas, primarily that of the United States and France, posits a direct link between the emergence of the press and revolutionary activity, Earle finds that such was not necessarily the case in Spanish America. Although the argument has been made for Mexico that high levels of literacy, in addition to the abundant circulation of printed materials, provided the basis for both Independence and the country's entrance into the larger phenomenon of modernity, Earle argues that other Spanish American cases invite a completely different conclusion. By looking at the experiences of New Granada, Peru and Chile she asserts that not only is there no causal linkage between the press and revolution (it could also serve the interests of reaction) but also the press in these areas often came *after* the imperial crisis, thus confirming Alexander von Humboldt's statement to the effect that the printing press 'has followed and not preceded a political revolution'. High levels of illiteracy, especially in New Granada and Chile, limited the reading public to very small numbers of people who relied heavily on book imports which were often of a religious nature. As a result, printed materials that discussed or advocated independence did not precede but rather became a part of the process itself. As Earle puts it 'We ought to search, not for evidence that the press "caused" the Spanish American wars for independence, but rather for examples of how (if at all) the spread of information transformed during the revolutionary period.'

Such a call is heeded by Carmen McEvoy in chapter two, where she examines the transformations of the press in Lima from the 1790s to the 1820s. Unlike Chile, or Venezuela, the press in the capital of the Viceroyalty of Peru was well established. *El Mercurio Peruano*, published between 1791 and 1795, advanced some central notions of republicanism, such as virtue, order and citizenship, yet it was not in any way an advocate of independence. Its significance, argues McEvoy, resided in the awareness of its writers of what constituted the public sphere, and of the role of the press in defining and building an educated readership. Journalistic practices, along with discussions of the key concepts of republicanism, would acquire new connotations as the larger political landscape changed. A critical moment came with the constitutionalist regime of 1811–14, which, among other things, introduced a policy, however limited, of freedom of the press sanctioned by the Constitution of 1812. The principal paper of the time, *El Verdadero Peruano*, built on the practices of *El Mercurio*, but adopted a critical stance, especially with regard to economic policy, that soon translated into a locus of anti-colonial opposition. It was closed as a result, on charges of sedition, but its more militant republican stances endured, and would flourish into an unabashedly political press during the Protectorate of José de San Martín. McEvoy explains the centrality of republicanism as a response to the monarchical stances of the Argentine general, but makes clear that it built on decades of press discussions. The press provided the space to explore republican views, while responding to the larger phenomena of viceregal policy, imperial crisis and foreign occupation. In fact, no sooner did San Martín leave Peru than advocates of republicanism abandoned the more militant aspects of their stance in favour of a pragmatic version typical, in its emphasis on property and security, of nineteenth-century Latin American liberalism.

The contrasting approaches of liberal and ecclesiastical circles with regards to the press, and written culture more generally, occupy Serrano and Jaksić in chapter three. They argue that liberal appropriation of the medium of print went far beyond the typical foundation of newspapers for the advancement of the movement's political goals. Rather, it encompassed the entire spectrum of publications and the establishment of a national educational system designed to spread literacy. It went further into the elaboration of a written style for government documents and international negotiations and treaties, the establishment of written law as the juridical basis of the nation and a sophisticated analysis of the field of rhetoric. The Church, on the other hand, was slow to react, due in large measure to its very nature: literate at the top, but oral at the grass-roots. The Church relied heavily on ritual rather than on a religiosity informed by doctrine and the written documents of the institution. However, the regalist tendencies of the government, and the increasingly secular and anticlerical stances of Chilean liberalism, forced the Church to enter into public debate on the same terms as its opponents, through periodicals and other printed materials. As the century progressed the Church embraced a series of other ways to oppose liberalism, but it remained sceptical, if not hostile, to written culture. The clearest example comes from the rejection of Protestantism, which was tellingly based on this religion's reliance on books, especially the Bible. The combined effect of such Church policies allowed liberals to dominate political culture for most of the century and effectively use print to propagate their views. However reluctantly at first, the Church eventually caught up with its opponents, and thus contributed to the richness and intensity of political debate.

In contrast, the Guatemalan case discussed by Douglass Sullivan-González in chapter four shows how the Church took a series of earlier initiatives to consolidate and legitimise the national state after the demise of the liberal-inspired Central American Federation in the early 1840s. That they did so through carefully crafted sermons delivered on the yearly Independence Day celebration is of central relevance to this volume. The hierarchy proved willing to embrace independent nationhood now that the nation, under Rafael Carrera, fully embraced Catholicism. This still required theological foundations, which the Church found in the form of covenant theology: God had chosen Guatemala in a way that mirrored God's covenant with Israel — a covenant that, as Sullivan-González reminds us, was also invoked in the colonial United States and in nineteenth-century South Africa. The message proved to be quite powerful, helping Carrera to maintain his conservative regime through the mid-1860s (in fact, until his death in 1865), successfully responding to liberal challenges from neighbouring republics and internal unrest. But the symbiotic relationship between the conservative regime and the Catholic Church could not survive the death of Carrera, and the institution once again became the target of liberal regimes after the successful revolution led by Justo Rufino Barrios in 1871. The success of the Church in conveying and disseminating its message, however, should not be ignored. Sermons were prepared for reading, delivered with the pomp and circumstance of Independence Day celebrations and printed for dissemination across the country. Sullivan-González documents and discusses both the sermons and their press coverage, to suggest that the Guatemalan Church was not alien, indeed quite skilful, in realising the potential of print and oratory.

The following three chapters are chiefly concerned with political oratory in nineteenth- and early twentieth-century Latin America. Chapter five by Eduardo Posada-Carbó discusses the enormous influence of the Spanish liberal Emilio Castelar on the politics, politicians and press of the region. A prolific, yet not particularly brilliant, thinker, Castelar was nevertheless a powerful figure who could move and persuade through both his journalistic writings and, most significantly, his electrifying speeches. His articles (*correspondencias*) appeared regularly in Argentina, Uruguay, Chile, Peru, Cuba and Mexico during the last third of the nineteenth century. A steady stream of politicians visited him to express their admiration and later boast of their meetings with him. As Posada-Carbó argues, there was some substance behind the skilful rhetoric of Castelar, which resonated particularly strongly among Spanish Americans: his defence of republicanism (which could be quite conservative) and his staunch support for the independence of the region. The 1860s, it should be recalled, had witnessed a monarchical experiment in Mexico and a failed, but worrisome, Spanish incursion on the Pacific coast. Such events invited a flood of republican nationalist sentiment, and Castelar was adept at providing the rhetoric to express it. To have such validation from a *peninsular* who would soon preside over the Spanish Republic (in the 1870s) proved to be a singularly powerful reason for claiming kinship with his views. Liberals and reformers found additional ammunition in Castelar's support for the abolition of slavery and his defence of individual freedoms. However, Posada-Carbó invites us to look beyond political and intellectual commonalities and into the very craft that made Castelar's reputation. His oratory, we learn, was based on a careful script. The speeches could be histrionic, but they were based on a thorough command of writing techniques. Furthermore, he understood the overlap and mastered both forms of delivery. As Posada-Carbó puts it, Castelar 'was an orator who could be read', and his powerful statements were 'written to be heard'. Writing and speech were used by Castelar as parts of the same rhetorical spectrum.

Charles A. Hale further explores the influence of Emilio Castelar in chapter six, in this case on Mexico. There his influence was very directly associated with the emergence of 'scientific politics', an ideology advocated by a group of younger intellectuals who clustered around the periodical *La Libertad*, and who would come to dominate politics under the *Porfiriato*. What attracted them to Castelar was his 'conservative-liberalism', which was compatible with their own positivist views regarding order, strong government and economic development. They were keenly aware of Castelar's rejection of both monarchy and 'cantonalism' (an extreme form of federalism), as well as the politics of the Third French Republic. These Mexican positivists tried to find a similar path between left and right, between liberty and order. Castelar not only led by example, but became a sort of disseminator of the French experience in his *correspondencias* to Mexico. His influence was in many ways due to the similarities and dilemmas of the European and Mexican political situations, but in this latter country the influence was also due to personal ties, including those with two of the leading lights of the positivist movement: Justo Sierra and Telésforo García. Charles Hale does not neglect to mention another element of his influence, his 'mesmerising rhetoric', which became 'a fixture in Mexican public life'. Castelar inspired a great deal of it among the positivists themselves. Justo Sierra, for one, celebrated Castelar 'in grandiloquent prose that was truly Castelarian'. Quite aside from the substantive message of the Spanish republican, and there was one, Hale reminds us of the impressive power of his rhetoric, which came to characterise a significant part of Mexican political discourse during the *Porfiariato*.

The closing chapter in this volume, by Carlos Malamud, focuses on Lisandro de la Torre, the Argentine politician (and presidential candidate) who was the prime force behind the Liga del Sur and the principal leader of the Partido Demócrata Progresista during the early decades of the twentieth century. At the time he was perhaps the most formidable opponent of Hipólito Yrigoyen and the emerging Radical Party. Now largely forgotten, Lisandro de la Torre nevertheless represented a style of politics that was unusually effective and which required great oratorical gifts. Malamud provides an analysis of De la Torre's parliamentary debates, focusing not only on the substance — as for instance on the Constitution of Santa Fe and the so-called 'debate de las carnes' — but also on his rhetorical techniques. Just as Castelar was the master of the long-winded speech, De la Torre thrived on the contentious give-and-take of parliamentary discussions. His mastery of minutia, sarcastic commentary and dismissive counterargument was utterly devastating, as was his frequent resort to chicanery and rude interruptions. Malamud illustrates the rivalry between De la Torre and Yrigoyen (a famous one, which once led to a duel) by contrasting the 'informed and direct rhetoric' of the former to the 'ornate yet vacuous' rhetoric of the latter. Such arts — or lack thereof — made sense in a parliamentary context and were indeed essential for anyone with political ambitions. But they could not have much influence without the press. Malamud makes clear how politicians and journalists functioned in a mutually dependent relationship which was not devoid of conflict, especially as the Argentine press moved from being primarily partisan to increasingly independent.

The essays in this volume provide important examples of the rich ramifications of a focus on the press and political oratory — and their relationship — in modern Latin American history. While they do not exhaust the topic, they raise significant issues, unearth new evidence and offer methodological and critical insights, which will hopefully be extended to other national cases. The field will be all the richer for understanding not just what Latin Americans in the post-Independence period saw fit to print, but how they used words, both spoken and written, to advance their political ends.

Chapter I

The Role of Print in the Spanish American Wars of Independence

Rebecca Earle

In 1814 Baron Alexander von Humboldt, the great German traveller and explorer of the Americas, drew attention to an unusual feature of the movement for independence from Spain in parts of Spanish America. This was that the establishment of printing presses and newspapers generally followed, rather than preceded, the outbreak of war: 'It's quite extraordinary to see in modern times that an establishment of this sort [the printing press], which offers the best means of communication between men, has followed and not preceded a political revolution.'[1] Humboldt was struck by the contrast this offered with the two more famous political revolutions of the age: the American and French revolutions. A great proliferation of printed pamphlets, periodicals and books had preceded the outbreak of revolution in both British North America and France. How curious, Humboldt commented, to find the process reversed in Spanish America.

Humboldt is not alone in viewing the newspaper as the expected harbinger of change in the age of Atlantic revolutions. While the precise role played by the printed word in the American and French revolutions remains a subject of debate, the study of the press's impact on the French and American revolutions has a venerable history.

It has long been claimed that the printing press played a central role in rousing anti-British feeling in colonial America. During the revolutionary years themselves Tory observers of the developing conflict complained that the revolutionary press was 'poisoning the minds of the people'. Within decades of the Treaty of Paris, American printers were claiming for themselves the honour of having brought about Independence.[2] This view was amplified in this century by studies that focused on the propagandis-

1 Alexander von Humboldt, *Alejandro de Humboldt por Tierras de Venezuela* (Caracas, 1969), pp. 80–1.

2 Stephen Botein, 'Printers and the American Revolution,' in Bernard Bailyn and John Hench (eds), *The Press and the American Revolution* (Worcester, 1980). See pp. 49 and 55 for quotations.

ing role of the revolutionary press. Works such as Arthur Schlesinger's *Prelude to Independence: The Newspaper War on Britain* (1958) maintained that the revolutionary leaders had consciously used the press as a propagandising tool, while at the same time affirming that ultimately this had served to educate the public.[3] Similarly, Philip Davidson's *Propaganda and the American Revolution* (1941) argued that propaganda, both written and oral, played a vital role in articulating popular attitudes.[4] 'Without their work Independence would not have been declared in 1776 nor recognised in 1783 ... It was the propagandists who made inchoate feelings articulate opinion and provided the compulsive ideals which led to concrete action.'[5]

This view of the revolutionary press as a propagandising tool cum echo-chamber of opinion was laid aside by Bernard Bailyn's classic study of the ideological origins of the American Revolution, published in 1967. While not an explicit examination of the role of the press, Bailyn's work implicitly evaluates the importance of the press in the American Revolution. The book, which is based on extensive study of revolutionary pamphlets, sets forth Bailyn's view that the 'American Revolution was above all else an ideological, constitutional, political struggle and not primarily a controversy between social groups undertaken to force changes in the organisation of the society or the economy'.[6] Within this setting the revolutionary pamphlet occupies a central position: it provides 'evidence of a transformation that overtook the inheritance of political and social thought as it had been received in the colonies by the early 1760s'.[7] The printed pamphlet, in other words, reflected underlying transformations in colonial society. It was a mirror, not an agent of change. Bailyn saw the pamphlet, and, by extension, the printed media as a whole, as a means for reflecting opinion, rather than shaping it. His work is a 'study of the ... colonists' thoughts as expressed ... in documents'.[8] Bailyn did not see the press as a distinctive agent for change; it was merely a medium for articulating pre-existing opinion.

3 Arthur Schlesinger, *Prelude to Independence: the Newspaper War on Britain, 1764–1776* (New York, 1958), p. 266.

4 Philip Davidson, *Propaganda and the American Revolution* (Chapel Hill, 1941). The historiography is surveyed in Robert Weir, 'The Role of the Newspaper Press in the Southern Colonies on the Eve of Revolution: an Interpretation,' in Bailyn and Hench (eds.), *The Press and the American Revolution.*

5 Davidson, *Propaganda and the American Revolution*, p. 410.

6 Bernard Bailyn, *The Ideological Origins of the American Revolution* (Cambridge, MA, 1967), p. vi.

7 *Ibid.*, p. ix

8 *Ibid.*, p. 23.

The subsequent trend in the historiography has been away from an explicit consideration of how and whether the press 'caused' the American Revolution.[9] Gordon Wood's *The Radicalism of the American Revolution* (1991), although based largely on printed sources, does not even devote an index entry to printing, or the press.[10] Indeed, the overall emphasis has shifted dramatically from a consideration of whether the press helped develop revolutionary sentiment to a broader examination of the role of printing, reading and literacy in colonial and post-colonial society. Works such as Richard Brown's *Knowledge is Power. The Diffusion of Information in Early America* (1987) focus on the dramatic rise in literacy and the growth of the press in the eighteenth century.[11] Brown is concerned to uncover the changing ways in which information was acquired from the colonial period to the mid-nineteenth century. In other words, rather than fixating on whether the press caused the American Revolution, this more recent writing sees the growth of the press as symptomatic of broader changes in American society, which spanned the revolutionary period. A changing press is a symptom of broader transformations, not necessarily a force for change in itself.

As works such as Brown's make clear, the more recent historiography of the American Revolution has begun to interact much more deliberately with the historiography of the French Revolution. Historians searching for the roots of the French Revolution have long considered whether the revolution was 'la faute à Voltaire, la faute à Rousseau'.[12] Starting with Daniel Mornet's classic study, many works have attempted to locate the origins of the French Revolution in the world of the Enlightenment, and, more specifically, in its books. The novels and political writings of individuals such as Jean-Jacques Rousseau or the *encyclopédistes*, it was suggested, destroyed the legitimacy of the Old Regime and ushered in the era of science and democracy. Since then the historiography has painted a complex and contradictory picture of the role of the press in creating revolu-

9 Bailyn and Hench (eds), *The Press and the American Revolution*, provides a good example. This work focuses largely on the development of printing as an industry and on the careers of individual printers.

10 Gordon Wood, *The Radicalism of the American Revolution* (New York, 1991).

11 See Richard Brown, *Knowledge is Power: the Diffusion of Information in Early America, 1700–1865* (Oxford, 1987); and William Gilmore, *Reading Becomes a Necessity of Life: Material and Cultural Life in Rural New England, 1780–1823* (Knoxville, 1989).

12 See Robert Darnton, *The Forbidden Best-sellers of Pre-Revolutionary France* (London, 1996) for a lucid discussion of the French historiography. Further comments may be found in Joan Landes, 'More than Words: the Printing Press and the French Revolution,' *Eighteenth-Century Studies*, vol. 25 (1991).

tionary sentiment. Roger Chartier's works on the history of the book have argued that the growth in publishing and reading was merely one aspect of a broad change in cultural orientation, which in turn destroyed the legitimacy of the French monarchy. Changes in reading practices were but one strand of a larger set of changes, which also included secularisation and declining participation in public ritual. The French Revolution, Chartier argues, was certainly not caused by Rousseau and Voltaire's writings.[13] These printed works could not claim credit for the downfall of the monarchy. Robert Darnton, on the other hand, believes that ultimately, books do make revolutions.[14] He merely claims that historians have been looking at the wrong books. He argues that, if one wants to understand the role of the press in the French Revolution, one must consider a wholly different genre of book from the writings of Voltaire or Rousseau. In his 1996 study of the underground literature of eighteenth century France he argues that so-called 'philosophical' novels — i.e. pornographic novels which often revolved around the sexual depravity of the French aristocracy — were as important as the works of Rousseau in causing the French Revolution. Such novels, Darnton argues, contributed to destroying the aristocracy's attachment to the old regime, and further weakened the monarchy's legitimacy. According to Darnton print and the press played a central role in the French Revolution, although not in precisely the same way that historians such as Schlesinger would have recognised.

Darnton is careful to situate the press within a wider communications network. The printed word, he argues, while important, should not be unduly separated from the complex interactions between gossip, rumour, song, newspapers, the salon and the book. What Darnton does not do is examine the relationship between the press and the revolutionary governments themselves. The works which do examine this relationship have charted the unprecedented freedom of the press that obtained from the

13 See, in particular, Roger Chartier, *The Cultural Origins of the French Revolution* (Durham, NC, 1991); and Daniel Mornet, 'Les enseignements des bibliothèques privées (1750–1780),' *Revue d'histoire littéraire de la France*, vol. 17 (1910).

14 Darnton, *The Forbidden Best-sellers*. Darnton has explored this thesis in many publications. For an early example, see Robert Darnton, 'Reading, Writing and Publishing in Eighteenth-Century France: a Case Study in the Sociology of Literature,' *Daedalus*, vol. 100, no. 1 (1971); or see his introduction to the edited collection by Robert Darnton and Daniel Roche (eds.), *Revolution in Print: the Press in France, 1775–1800* (Berkeley, 1989).

fall of the Bastille to the abolition of the monarchy in 1792.[15] While not considering whether the printed word in any sense caused the revolution, historians such as Jeremy Popkin stress that, once the revolutionary process was underway, the press formed an 'indispensable link between the government and the public'.[16] Newspapers, which perhaps had helped to delegitimise the Ancien Regime, now served to legitimate the revolution. Nor was the newspaper merely one part of a larger revolutionary culture; it was, according to Popkin, that culture's central feature. The development of the press was part of what made the French Revolution revolutionary.

This brings us back to the historiography of the American Revolution. There too, as I noted earlier, the more recent studies have viewed the evolution of the press as but one feature of the revolutionary period, rather than as a cause of the revolution. This more recent historiography of both the American and French Revolutions has other common features. In particular, I want to draw attention to the link that is made between the growth of printing and the press, on the one hand, and modernity, on the other. This connection has been highlighted not only in relation to the French and American Revolutions, but also by such works as Jürgen Habermas's classic account of the rise of the bourgeois public sphere in Europe, which focuses very explicitly on the importance of the press in creating this 'modern' public space.[17] In sum, the current historiography of the American and French Revolutions suggests that any thorough account of the move from Ancien Regime to modernity, from colony to republic, must consider the role of the press.

*

Historians of Latin America's Wars of Independence have picked up the link between the press, modernity and revolution. A number of very insightful and imaginative historians have been examining the role of the press in Spanish America's revolutionary period, from 1810 to 1830. Much of the interesting work on the development of the press focuses on Mexico. I want to look in particular at François Xavier-Guerra's *Modernidad e independencias*,

15 Jeremy Popkin, *Revolutionary News: the Press in France, 1789–1799* (Durham, NC, 1990). Also see the lengthy introduction to J. Gilchrist and W. J. Murray, *The Press in the French Revolution: a Selection of Documents Taken from the Press of the Revolution from the Years 1789 to 1794* (London, 1971).

16 Popkin, *Revolutionary News*, p. 2.

17 Jürgen Habermas, *The Structural Transformation of the Public Sphere. An Enquiry into a Category of Bourgeois Society* (Cambridge, 1994).

which was published in 1992.[18] Guerra's very title makes explicit his concerns and his position in relation to the historiography of the French Revolution. Guerra sees Mexico's War of Independence from Spain as part of a larger move towards modernity in Mexico. Modernity, loosely defined as the creation of the nation-state, a public sphere and public opinion, began to develop in Mexico, according to Guerra, in the mid-eighteenth century. Guerra is clear about the role the press played in this modernisation process. Guerra insists that Mexico's progress towards modernity required both widespread literacy and an active press, and he finds evidence for both of these in eighteenth-century Mexico. Guerra charts a dramatic rise in both literacy levels in late eighteenth-century Mexico and in the volume of printed material available to Mexican readers. Let's consider a few examples drawn from both Guerra and other histories of education, in particular those of Dorothy Tanck de Estrada. In the Valley of Mexico in the 1780s perhaps one in six inhabitants attended school. Even in the distant reaches of the viceroyalty Bourbon-inspired educational schemes had brought literacy to the unlettered. In 1791 there were 175 schools in the Yucatán peninsula catering to nearly 36,000 students. In 1809 there were calls to open the capital's three public libraries on holidays and in the evenings, so as to allow greater public access. By 1810 some 200 books were published annually in Mexico City. On a single day in 1811 the *Diario de México*, the capital's premier newspaper, had a print-run of 7,000 copies. This equates to one copy for every 20 people in Mexico City.[19]

This explosion in Mexico's print culture, Guerra argues, both illustrates Mexico's move towards modernity and also illuminates our understanding of

18 François-Xavier Guerra, *Modernidad e independencias. Ensayos sobre las revoluciones hispánicas* (Madrid, 1992), pp. 275–318.

19 A few more examples: in the two years from 1754 to 1756 the number of 'escuelas de castellano' in the Archbishopric of Mexico City increased from 84 to 262. In the 1820s the US diplomat Joel Poinsett noted that 'Most of the people in the cities can read and write. I would not be understood as including the *léperos*; but I have frequently remarked men, clothed in the garb of extreme poverty, reading the Gazettes in the streets.' See Joel Roberts Poinsett, *Notes on Mexico Made in the Autumn of 1822* [1824] (New York, 1969), p. 83 (or see p. 121); Guerra, *Modernidad e independencias*, pp. 275–318; Jaime Rodríguez, *The Independence of Spanish America* (Cambridge, 1996), p. 41; Dorothy Tanck de Estrada, 'La enseñanza de la lectura y de la escritura en la Nueva España, 1700–1821,' in Seminario de la Historia de la Educación en México (ed.), *Historia de la lectura en Mexico* (Mexico City, 1997); and Dorothy Tanck de Estrada, *La Educación Ilustrada (1786–1836)* (Mexico City, 1977). The purpose and impact of the Bourbon educational reforms are also discussed in Serge Gruzinski, 'La "Segunda Aculturación": el estado ilustrado y la religiosidad indígena en Nueva España (1775–1800),' *Estudios de Historia Novohispana*, vol. 8 (Mexico, 1985), from which the 1754–56 figures are drawn.

the revolutionary period. He documents the vast literature of ephemeral pamphlets, underground publications and anonymous flybills that circulated immediately before and during the conflict with Spain. Guerra speaks not only of a 'war of words' that mirrored and shaped the armed conflict, but also of the rise of 'opinion', as Mexicans of all classes devoured the hundreds of books, pamphlets and periodicals published each year during the war. The Mexican War of Independence from Spain, in other words, shows the importance of the press in shaping Mexican opinion, and also illustrates the dramatic changes that had occurred in Mexican society in the last decades of the eighteenth century. The press, Guerra argues, was at the centre of these changes.

Other scholars have shared Guerra's view that the Mexican press played an important role in the revolution. Manuel Chust, for example, has argued that the press in early national Mexico played a key role in shaping the new liberal, bourgeois nation through the transmission of opinion, ideology and practical knowledge. In addition, he argues, the transformation of the press is emblematic of the profound changes that were underway in Mexico as a whole: 'The colony became the nation. Subjects became citizens. The *Gazeta* became the daily paper.'[20] In other words, Chust, like Guerra, sees the revolutionary press as an indicator of social change as much as an agent of that change.

Guerra and the other advocates of 'modernity' are ambitious in their analysis of Mexican society in the Age of Revolution. Not everyone would agree with the estimate of 62 per cent literacy levels in Mexico City in 1820. However, Guerra is not over-ambitious in geographic terms. He does not make claims about the applicability of his observations to other parts of Spanish America. But the Mexican case offers an enticing model to the scholar of Independence. To what extent was the Mexican experience, assuming that one agrees that it occurred in the first place, repeated in other parts of Spanish America? Did the press play a similar role in the revolutionary conflicts in Peru or Chile? The remainder of this chapter will explore this question. Tempting though it may be to do so, the Mexican case cannot automatically be taken as representative of the whole of Spanish America.[21]

20 Manuel Chust, 'Construir y difundir. La prensa en la formación del estado nacional mexicano, 1821–1835,' *Caravelle*, no. 68 (1997), pp. 19–42. The quotation is from p. 20.

21 Others have not been as cautious. See, for example, Jaime E. Rodríguez O., *La Independencia de la América española* (Mexico, 1996).

Let us begin by enquiring into the nature of publishing in late colonial and independence era Spanish America in regions other than Mexico. We have already seen that eighteenth-century New Spain experienced a tremendous growth in publishing. Moreover, the importation of books augmented the supply of locally published texts. As we have seen, this development in itself may be taken as evidence for the rise of modernity in eighteenth-century Mexico. Moreover, not only was there an increase in the volume of published material; it is argued that there was also a change in the nature of the material being published. In Mexico the period from 1808 to 1814 saw a dramatic increase in the publication of political works, and a drop in the publication of religious or liturgical works. For the preceding three centuries the overwhelming majority of the reading material printed and sold in the Americas had been religious or judicial in nature. Between 1808 and 1814 political publications, rather than religious works, came to dominate in Mexico. This situation lasted until 1814, when Ferdinand VII revoked the freedom of the press granted by the Cortes.[22]

22 The dominance of religious books during the whole of the colonial period has been asserted by many scholars. Helga Kropfinger von Kügelgen, for example, has calculated that approximately 70% of the printed matter imported into the Americas was theological and liturgical (cited in Teodoro Hampe Martínez, 'The Diffusion of Books and Ideas in Colonial Peru: a Study of Private Libraries in the Sixteenth and Seventeenth Centuries,' *Hispanic American Historical Review*, vol. 73, no. 2 (1993), p. 216.) However, Hampe, along with a number of other scholars, argues that legal texts concerned with jurisprudence, rather than religious works, made up the majority of many colonial libraries. For further discussion of the colonial book trade and of colonial libraries, see Irving Leonard, *Books of the Brave, Being an Account of Books and of Men in the Spanish Conquest and Settlement of the Sixteenth-Century New World* (Berkeley, 1992); Guillermo Ovando-Sanz, 'Dos Bibliotecas Coloniales de Potosí,' *Journal of Inter-American Studies*, vol. 3, no. 1 (1961); Ildefonso Leal, *Libros y bibliotecas en Venezuela Colonial (1633–1767)*, 2 vols. (Caracas, 1978); Josefina Plá, 'La cultura paraguaya y el libro,' *Estudios Paraguayos*, vol. 8, no. 2 (1980); Carlos Alberto González Sánchez, 'Los libros de los españoles en el Virreinato del Perú, siglos XVI y XVII,' *Revista de Indias*, vol. 56, no. 206 (1996); Bernardo Gallegos, *Literacy, Education and Society in New Mexico, 1693–1821* (Albuquerque, 1992); and Teodoro Hampe Martínez, *Bibliotecas privadas en el mundo colonial. La difusión de libros e ideas en el virreinato del Perú (siglos XVI–XVII)* (Frankfurt, 1996), which also contains full references to the dozens of studies of individual libraries made by Hampe.

Table 1: Titles Published in Mexico by Type, 1804–20 (Excluding Newspapers)

	Religious	Political	Literary	Other
1804	90	0	5	12
1805	62	1	1	18
1806	52	4	1	14
1807	72	1	5	14
1808	69	67	3	14
1809	78	114	40	12
1810	69	184	5	17
1811	42	91	23	12
1812	46	71	11	9
1813	15	35	6	19
1814	28	29	1	12
1815	77	33	3	18
1816	99	11	1	13
1817	68	6	2	11
1818	64	3	7	18
1819	94	0	6	9
1820	75	341	12	26

Source: Based on Table 1: Títulos publicados en México (excluidos los periódicos), François-Xavier Guerra, *Modernidad e independencias*, p. 289.

The temporary eclipse of religious works is striking, and seems clearly to indicate the growth of political sentiment that characterised the capital during these years.[23] But also striking is the persistent vitality of religious publications, which made a comeback both in 1815 and, according to Anne Staples, in the 1820s.[24] Ought the resurgence of religious works to temper the view that the expanding press marked the end of the old regime? Suppose the majority of works published in Independence-era Spanish America proved to be not merely non-revolutionary but indeed positively conservative. Would we then need to reassess the role of the press in the revolution? Must an expanding press necessarily serve the interests of revolution, or might it instead serve the forces of reaction? In other words, does it matter *what* was published, or does it matter only that publishing flourished?[25]

Consider an analogous chart from Lima.

23 The participation of the capital's population in elections, for example, has attracted considerable attention. See, for example, Nettie Lee Benson (ed.), *Mexico and the Spanish Cortes: 1810–1822. Eight Essays* (Austin, 1968); Antonio Annino, 'Pratiche creole e liberalismo nella crisis dello spazio urbano coloniale: el 29 novembre 1812 a Città del Messico', *Quaderni storici: notabili elettori elezioni*, no. 69 (1988); François-Xavier Guerra, 'La independencia de México y las revoluciones hispánicas,' in Antonio Annino and Raymond Buve (eds), *El liberalismo en México: cuadernos de historia latinoamericana*, no. 1 (1993), pp. 15–48; Antonio Annino (ed.), *Historia de las elecciones en Iberoamérica, siglo XIX* (Mexico City, 1995); and Rodríguez, *The Independence of Spanish America.*

24 For the revival of religious publishing in the early national period see Anne Staples, 'La lectura y los lectores en los primeros años de vida independiente,' in *Historia de la Lectura en Mexico*, pp. 94–6. Religious works dominated in revolutionary North America. See G. Thomas Tanselle, 'Some Statistics on American Printing, 1764–1783,' in Bailyn and Hench (eds), *The Press and the American Revolution.* For a contrasting example of a Spanish-American public library from the 1860s that apparently contained no religious works whatsoever, see María Magdalena Guerrero, 'La biblioteca de la Secretaría del Gobierno Superior Civil de Santo Domingo (1862–1864),' *Anuario de Estudios Americanos*, vol. 45 (1988).

25 Of course, books without an explicit political content may nonetheless contribute, not only to the experience of modernity, but also to political change. For example, Jay Fliegelman's 1982 study of educational theory and reading habits in eighteenth-century North America reveals well the significance of 'non-political' novels, plays, and parenting manuals in shaping the political space of pre-revolutionary America. The tremendous popularity of works such as Samuel Richardson's *Pamela* or Daniel Defoe's *Robinson Crusoe*, works which condemn parental 'tyranny' and celebrate middle-class democracy, suggests much about the concerns of America's revolutionary generation. Thus, it is surely not necessary to search solely for works of explicitly political content in our attempt to assess the importance of the press to revolutionary ideology. See Jay Fliegelman, *Prodigals and Pilgrims: the American Revolution against Patriarchal Authority, 1750–1800* (Cambridge, 1982).

Table 2: Titles Published in Lima by Type, 1800–1816

	Religious	Political	Literary	Journals
1800	5	0	1	0
1801	7	0	3	0
1802	12	2	5	0
1803	7	0	2	0
1804	10	0	1	0
1805	13	1	1	1
1806	13	4	1	1
1807	9	4	0	1
1808	30	25	0	1
1809	24	16	1	1
1810	24	13	1	1
1811	22	27	8	2
1812	21	26	12	5
1813	16	25	13	9
1814	22	29	10	3
1815	23	5	10	1
1816	18	1	16	1

Source: Table labelled 'La circulación de la lectura en Lima,' Víctor Peralta, 'La revolución silenciada,' p. 20.

This chart would appear to suggest that a very similar process of politicisation was underway in Lima during the same period. In Lima, too, the volume of religious publications declined from 1808 to 1814, while political publications increased correspondingly. But in fact, the political context for this development differed considerably from that in Mexico.

This context has been explored by Víctor Peralta in a recent study of reading and publishing in Independence-era Peru.[26] Peralta documents the development of a new, literate culture in Lima in the 1790s, linked to cafes

26 Víctor Peralta, 'La revolución silenciada. Hábitos de lectura y pedagogía política en el Perú, 1790-1814,' *Anuario de Estudios Americanos*, vol. 54 (1997). See also Pablo Macera, 'El periodismo en la independencia,' in *Trabajos de historia*, 4 vols (Lima, 1977), vol. 2; and Ascensión Martínez Riaza, *La prensa doctrinal en la independencia del Perú, 1811–1824* (Madrid, 1985), for detailed discussion of the different political papers published during the Independence period.

and salons, which differs from Habermas's bourgeois public sphere only in that it was not in any sense bourgeois. According to Peralta, Lima's cafes and *tertulias* were aristocratic venues, not the democratic zones imagined by Habermas. This was a conservative world. The private libraries of Lima's book-owning elite contained very few prohibited books, and heavy viceregal censorship prevented the spread of printed works deemed subversive. The developing 'public opinion' in Lima was thus aristocratic opinion, and it was tightly controlled by the colonial government. Thus, it is not surprising that the first explicitly political sentiments to appear in print in Lima's newspapers were royalist. During the early years of the War of Independence, the viceregal government made effective use of the press to disseminate royalist opinion, introducing such innovations as official disinformation.[27] During this period religious works ceased to dominate the field of publishing, because of the growth in *royalist* political propaganda. In Lima the burgeoning political publications consisted primarily of royalist texts, rather than the more liberal printings in circulation in Mexico.

This Lima both resembles and differs from Mexico City. The similarities are striking. In both regions political publications flourished during the years of the Cortes, at the expense of religious publications. Moreover, both regions experienced an almost identical increase in the per capita volume of publications. In 1812, for example, 137 titles were published in Mexico City with its population of 140,000. In the same year 59 works appeared in Lima, a city with perhaps 55,000 inhabitants. But in Lima this increase consisted of counter-revolutionary, rather than revolutionary, publications. In other words, the press in Lima, as in Mexico, did change dramatically in the early years of the War of Independence, but in Lima that change was not in the direction of greater democracy.

*

I would like at this point to return to the remarks by Humboldt with which this chapter began. Humboldt, the de Tocqueville of Spanish America, commented in 1814 that the press, far from representing the vanguard of the revolution, in fact marched in the rear, well behind the main army: 'It's quite extraordinary to see in modern times that an establishment of this sort [the printing press], which offers the best means of communication between men, has followed and not preceded a political revolution.'

27 Royalist and republican disinformation in New Granada is discussed in Rebecca Earle, 'Information and Disinformation in Late Colonial New Granada,' *The Americas*, vol. 54, no. 2 (1997).

Humboldt's remarks about the late development of the periodical press do not appear to square with the Mexican scenario, in which a flourishing press marks the move towards modernity. How are we to interpret this?

Humboldt was speaking of the Viceroyalty of New Granada, so let us look in a bit more detail at the New Granadan case. New Granada simply did not experience the sort of 'information revolution' that scholars are now locating in colonial Mexico. Let us consider first the question of literacy levels. New Granada's population remained largely illiterate during the years of the war. Figures for school attendance, while only indirect indicators of literacy, do point to a striking difference between Mexico and New Granada. Unlike Mexico, where it is claimed that a large percentage of the eighteenth century population enjoyed primary education, in New Granada only a minority had access to any sort of schooling. José Manuel Restrepo, a republican politician and the author of a monumental history of Colombia's revolution, claimed that the shortage of primary schools left at least 80 per cent of New Granada's population illiterate.[28] Even in 1835, a decade after President Francisco de Paula Santander's mammoth effort to alphabetise the population, only a tiny percentage of Colombia's inhabitants attended primary school. According to Frank Safford in 1835 the percentage of the population attending primary school hovered at about one per cent. Using a conservative estimate that children of school age constituted only one quarter of the population, Safford's figures indicate that at most four per cent of children attended primary school in early republican Colombia. Safford's figures indicate that school attendance in the national capital was, if anything, slightly lower. In contrast, historians now estimate that in 1820 roughly half the children in Mexico City attended school.[29] The small size of Colombia's literate population is further indicated by the fact that even in 1825 the capital reportedly had only one small book-

28 José Manuel Restrepo, *Historia de la Revolución de Colombia* (Medellín, 1974), 6 vols, vol. 1, pp. 37–45.

29 Frank Safford, *The Ideal of the Practical: Colombia's Struggle to Form a Technical Elite* (Austin, 1976), p. 32; and Carlos Newland, 'La educación en Hispanoamérica desde la independencia hasta la centralización de los sistemas educativos nacionales,' *Hispanic American Historical Review*, vol. 71, no. 2 (1991). For the striking Mexican figures, see Guerra, *Modernidad e independencias*, p. 279; and Tanck de Estrada, *La Educación Ilustrada*, p.. 196–202. For a very rough indication of the percentage of Neogranadan children of school age, see, for example, the census of the Province of Ríohacha from 1825 in the microfilm collection of nineteenth century census material in the Archivo Histórico Nacional de Bogotá, Colombia; and also the estimates in Pablo Rodríguez, *Sentimientos y vida familiar en el Nuevo Reino de Granada* (Santa Fe de Bogotá, 1997), p. 97.

shop, which did poor business.[30] As Humboldt had lamented, the region apparently contained few 'persons who felt the need to read'.[31]

Beyond widespread illiteracy, the number of printing presses itself imposed severe limitations on the reach of printed material in New Granada. There were dramatic differences between the provision of printing presses in Mexico and in regions such as New Granada. This is significant because, as Roger Chartier has shown, the quantity of printed material is very important in shaping the nature of a country's print culture. In regions saturated with printing, the medium can exert great influence even among the illiterate. Moreover, the quantity of printed matter is also important in determining the experience of literacy. Literacy, as Lawrence Cremin has noted, is a technical ability to interact with a particular literary environment. For literacy to be meaningful there must be things to read.[32] Early nineteenth-century Mexico, with its 300-year tradition of printing and publishing, stands in stark contrast with regions such as New Granada. Mexico's privileged position can be appreciated from a glance at the dates for the arrival of the first printing press in different parts of Spanish America.

Table 3: First Printing Presses in Spanish America, 1539–1830[33]

Viceroyalty of New Spain

1539	**Mexico City**
	By 1600 there were 6 print-shops, each containing multiple presses
1640	Puebla
1660	Guatemala
	By 1800 there were 4–5 presses
1720	Oaxaca
1793	Guadalajara

30 William Duane, 'Viaje a la Gran Colombia en los años 1822–1823,' in David Sowell (ed.), *Santander y la opinión anglo-americana. Visión de viajeros y periódicos, 1821–1840* (Bogotá, 1991), p. 141. Also see Renán Silva, *Prensa y revolución a finales del siglo XVIII. Contribución a un análisis de la formación de la ideología de independencia nacional* (Bogotá, 1989) for comments on the small number of books available in late colonial New Granada.

31 Humboldt, *Alejandro de Humboldt*, p. 80; and Silva, *Prensa y revolución*, p. 39.

32 Lawrence Cremin, *American Education: the Colonial Experience, 1607–1783* (New York, 1970), pp. 548–9.

33 There is debate about some of these dates. For comparison, note that in late eighteenth century Madrid there were 193 printing presses, divided between 25 printshops and employing over 1,000 artisans. (Madrid's population was roughly 167,000.) See Diana Thomas, 'The Book Trade in Ibarra's Madrid,' *The Library*, vol. 5, no. 4 (1983).

1794	Veracruz
1812	Sultepec
1813	Mérida
1813	Acapulco
1821	Querétaro
1821	Campeche
by 1821	Iguala
by 1824	Chilpancingo
by 1824	San Salvador
by 1824	Jalapa
by 1824	Tampico
by 1827	San Cristóbal
by 1827	Monterrey
by 1828	San Luis Potosí
by 1829	Morelia
by 1829	Tegucigalpa
by 1829	Villahermosa

Viceroyalty of Peru

1584	**Lima**
	By 1800 there were 4 presses
1610–12	Julí
1811	Santiago de Chile[34]
1821	Arequipa
1822	Cuzco
1823	Trujillo
by 1824	Humachuco
by 1824	Santiago de Chuco
by 1826	Chuquisaca
by 1826	Valparaíso
by 1829	Huánuco
by 1829	Puno
by 1830	Coquimbo

Viceroyalty of Río de la Plata

1700	**Paraguay**
1764	Córdoba

34 The first press arrived in 1748, but in practical terms was not used until 1811.

1780	Buenos Aires[35]
	By 1819 there were 3 print shops
1807	Montevideo
by 1824	Mendoza

Caribbean

1707	**Havana**
	By 1800 there were 3–4 presses
1796	Puerto España
1796	Santiago de Cuba
1821	Santo Domingo[36]
1808	Puerto Rico
1813	Matanzas

Viceroyalty of New Granada

1738	**Santa Fe**
	By 1800 there were 4 presses
1754	Ambato
1760	Quito[37]
1776	Cartagena
1808	Caracas
1810	Guayaquil
1810/12	Cumaná
1812	Valencia
1812	Maracaibo
1813	Guiria
1813	Tunja
1814	Medellín
1814	Popayán
1816	Santa Marta
1816	Margarita/Ocumare
1918	Angostura
1820	Panama
1821	Maracaibo

35 This consisted of the 1764 Cordoba press.

36 Moreau de Saint-Méry claimed that there was a small press in the 1790s, which he said was used 'only to print newspapers, registers, reviews and other things of this sort for the various branches of the administration'. See Médéric-Louis-Élie Moreau de Saint-Méry, *Descripción de la parte española de Santo Domingo* [1796] (Ciudad Trujillo, 1944), p. 349.

37 This consisted of the 1754 Ambato press.

1821	Rosario de Cúcuta
1822	Puerto Cabello
1824	Guanare
1829	Barinas

Sources: 'The Report of Mr. C.A. Rodney, commissioner sent by the U.S. government to inquire into the state of the Republic of Río de la Plata,' in *Messrs Rodney and Graham's Reports on the Present State of the United Provinces of South America* (London, 1819), pp. 108–110; José Toribio Medina, *La imprenta de Cartagena de Indias (1809–1820)* (Santiago de Chile: 1904); José Toribio Medina, *Notas bibliográficas sobre la imprenta en Bogotá, 1739–1821* (Santiago de Chile, 1904); José Torre Revello, *Los orígenes de la imprenta en la América española* (Madrid, 1927); José Torre Revello, *Orígenes de la imprenta en España y su desarrollo en América española* (Buenos Aires, 1940); Juan de Bautista Pérez Galaz, *La introducción de la imprenta en Campeche* (Campeche, 1942); José Toribio Medina, *Historia de la imprenta en los antiguos dominios españoles de América y Oceanía*, 2 vols. (Santiago de Chile, 1958); José Toribio Medina, *La imprenta en algunas ciudades de la América española, 1754–1823* [1904] (Amsterdam, 1964); Julio Febres Cordero, *Historia de la imprenta y del periodismo en Venezuela, 1800–1830* (Caracas, 1974); Hensley Woodbridge and Lawrence Thompson, *Printing in Colonial Spanish America* (Troy, 1976); Manuel Pérez Vila, 'Andrés Bello y los comienzos de la imprenta en Venezuela,' *Bello y Caracas* (Caracas, 1979); Sergio Martínez Baeza, 'La introducción de la imprenta en el nuevo mundo,' *Atenea*, vol. 451 (Chile, 1985); and María Isabel Grañén Porrúa, 'El ámbito socio-laboral de las imprentas novohispanas, siglo XVI,' *Anuario de Estudios Americanos*, vol. 48 (1991).

Mexico City had six separate print shops before most other regions had a single printing press. More titles were printed in seventeenth-century Mexico City than in many European cities, despite the fact that paper had to be imported from Europe.[38] Yet, with the exception of Lima, virtually no other region enjoyed an active press until the eighteenth century, and many not until the nineteenth century.

To return to our example, at the start of the independence process in 1810, New Granada as a whole had only three poorly equipped printing workshops, located in the capital and in Cartagena. These three print shops

38 Lucien Febvre and Henri-Jean Martin, *The Coming of the Book. The Impact of Printing, 1450–1800* (London, 1998), pp. 207–9.

shared a mere five printing presses, one of which dated all the way back to 1738.[39] This antique collection constituted New Granada's entire stock of printing presses on the eve of Independence. Moreover, their geographical concentration in only two cities denied access to print to those outside the environs of Cartagena and the capital. Thus, at the start of the War of Independence in New Granada, the potential influence of print was limited. Even Viceroy Francisco Montalvo had no printing press between 1813 and 1816.[40] So, prior to the War of Independence in New Granada, there were few readers and fewer printing presses. In other words, there is no evidence that New Granada experienced either a burst of literacy or rapid development of the press in the years preceding war with Spain. If these are essential characteristics of modernity, then New Granada was not on the road to modernity in 1780, or in 1810, when the conflict with Spain began.

This is not to deny that the periodical press in New Granada played any role in shaping a climate conducive to revolutionary challenge. After breaking with Spain, a number of regional juntas made efforts to acquire printing presses in order to disseminate news and propaganda. Moreover, as Renán Silva has shown in his fine study of the *Papel Periódico de Santafé de Bogotá*, a newspaper published in the Granadine capital of Santa Fe in the 1790s, it is possible to speak of a 'public' in late colonial New Granada.[41] The pages of the *Papel Periódico* itself provided a meeting-place for a community of readers who identified themselves as educated and patriotic. Individuals exchanged opinions and corresponded through the pages of the *Papel Periódico* in a way reminiscent of Habermas's public sphere. It is possible to trace some connections between the individuals who participated in this community of letters and in the movement for independence. However, we are talking about a very small community. At its peak the *Papel Periódico* had perhaps 150 subscribers in a region with a

39 For this and the subsequent discussion of Neogranadan publishing, see Gustavo Otero Muñoz, *Historia del periodismo en Colombia* (Bogotá, 1936); José Torre Revello, *Los orígenes de la imprenta en la América española*; José Torre Revello, *Orígenes de la imprenta en España*; and the many works of José Toribio Medina, particularly his *Historia de la imprenta.*

40 See Francisco Montalvo to Ministry of Grace and Justice, Santa Marta, 22 August 1813, Archivo General de Indias, Seville (henceforth AGI), Audiencia de Santa Fe, legajo 746.

41 Silva, *Prensa y revolución.*

total population of perhaps 1.8 million.[42] Participation in this sphere of letters was confined to a very small minority of well-educated members of the colonial elite. Moreover, it is unclear whether it was participating in this Habermasian sphere of letters that served to propel individuals into breaking with Spain. Silva asserts that the *Papel Periódico* contributed to, but by no means caused, the ideology of independence.

But this, as the historiography of the American and French Revolutions has suggested, is probably the wrong question. We ought to search, not for evidence that the press 'caused' the Spanish American Wars of Independence, but rather for examples of how (if at all) the spread of information was transformed during the revolutionary period. Although no dramatic transformation in information networks occurred in late eighteenth century New Granada, printing did experience considerable growth during the early years of the war. The number of printing presses virtually doubled, and a number of new newspapers emerged, even if their numbers did not remotely approach those being published in Mexico. Approximately 18 new journals were created during the first years of the war, seven outside of the old capital, Santa Fe. The increase in periodicals, most dramatic for the period after 1820, and the importation of printing presses in the years after 1810 suggest that the war transformed printing, rather than the reverse.

An examination of the situation in Independence-era Chile reinforces the view that the war transformed the medium of print, rather than print transforming the war. Chile's insurgents had read European (specifically French) writers such as Mercier or Rousseau, and they employed the press to circulate their views and opinions. Nonetheless, in the earlier years of the war the press formed but one element in a much larger information network. This is not surprising, as Chile was effectively without a single printing press until 1811. (At this time Chile had a population of perhaps

42 *Ibid.*, pp. 29–31. Nor, as Silva notes, was the paper 'libre y barata' (pp. 16–17). I am also sceptical about assertions that issues of colonial newspapers were routinely shared among dozens, or, as it is sometimes claimed, hundreds of readers. In contrast to such claims, consider the complaint of one inhabitant of the Puerto Rican town of Utuado in 1813. Pedro Antolín de Ribera claimed that the town's *alcalde constitucional* monopolised the sole copy of the *Gaceta*. The *alcalde* getting hold of the *Gaceta*, Ribera complained, 'is the same as the *Gaceta* falling into the depths of the ocean, and the alcalde being washed by the waters of the River Lethe, with the result that the inhabitants of this town cannot gain the slightest information even from his conversations' (Pedro Antolín de Ribera to the Captain General of Puerto Rico, Utuado, 22 April 1813, Archivo de Puerto Rico, San Juan (henceforth APR), Gobernadores Españoles, asuntos políticos y civiles, caja 118, exp. 1379).

900,000.)[43] Thus, prior to that date, Chileans wishing to ventilate their ideas were obliged to rely on the spoken word, or, failing that, hand-written manuscripts. As Simon Collier has noted, in Chile 'the spread of autonomist proposals was largely by word of mouth, [although] political manuscripts plainly passed from hand to hand as well'.[44] When describing the political atmosphere in the years before 1810, contemporaries cited the opinions expressed in 'conversaciones públicas', rather than 'papeles públicos'.[45] Thus, in Chile as in New Granada a transformation in information networks did not precede revolution.

The transformation in the role of print occurred after the first splits with Spain, rather than before. As we have noted, the printing press itself was not employed until 1811, after the initial break with Spain. Thus Chilean journalism was intimately linked to the revolutionary project from the very moment of its birth. The first newspaper, the *Aurora de Chile*, was founded in 1812 by José Miguel Carrera specifically to encourage the spread of revolutionary ideas. After that, a veritable flood of insurgent publications presented themselves to the Chilean public, with the explicit aim of educating the public. 'We now have in our possession the great and precious instrument of universal enlightenment: the printing press', proclaimed Camilo Henríquez, the most prolific of these early insurgent journalists.[46] This optimistic view of printing's potential seems to have been shared by the newspapers' readers. One contemporary recalled the reception of the first issues of the *Aurora de Chile*:

> Words cannot describe the delight that this caused. Men rushed down the street with a copy of the 'Aurora' in their hand, stopping anyone they found in order to read and re-read them its contents, all the while congratulating themselves on their great good fortune and insisting that by this means they would banish the ignorance in which they had hitherto lived, which would be replaced by enlightenment and culture that would transform Chile into a kingdom of the wise.[47]

Printing, and the newspaper in particular, was thus identified with a national project that would transform Chile into a modern, enlightened realm.

43 Francisco A. Encina, *Historia de Chile desde la prehistoria hasta 1891* (Santiago, 1970), vol. 5, pp. 159–62.

44 Simon Collier, *Ideas and Politics of Chilean Independence* (Cambridge, 1967), p. 46. See also Sergio Villalobos, *Tradición y reforma en 1810* (Santiago, 1961), p. 35.

45 Villalobos, *Tradición y reforma*, p. 98

46 Collier, *Ideas and Politics*. The quotation from Henríquez is from p. 97.

47 Encina, *Historia de Chile*, vol. 5, p. 384, quoting from Martínez, *Memorial histórica.*

The newspaper was the medium whereby the population would be informed and educated. This emphasis on the printing press as the prime disseminator of progress is striking, given its recent introduction into Chile. It seems that the press was accorded an importance in the revolutionary project that was entirely disproportionate with its actual role in the spread of information. It is likely that for many years after 1811 information spread by word of mouth and by the written (not printed) word far more than by the press. As in New Granada, in Chile literacy levels alone would have barred the press from serving as the primary source of information. In the early nineteenth century even in the capital only perhaps eight per cent of children attended primary school.[48]

The period of the war thus elevated the Chilean press to an important, indeed disproportionate, position. To what extent was the culture of reading transformed by this change? Newspapers certainly flourished in the first decade of Independence, which saw the appearance of dozens of new publications. The allegedly spectacular growth of the book trade in the years after 1820 also suggests that reading practices were transformed. With the collapse of the Spanish colony came a great increase in the number of books, particularly political books, imported into the region. Included in this burgeoning trade were many works that, while not entirely absent from the colony, had been officially prohibited by the crown. In the early 1820s the traveller Gilbert Farquhar Mathison commented on the 'shiploads of French deistical books [which] are freely imported, and bought up with great avidity' in Santiago.[49] The vogue for books of all sorts was satirised in 1828 by one newspaper, which reported, under the heading of 'Shipping News', that an Argentine ship had arrived in port laden with:

> a trunk containing the following works: Parliamentary tactics, compilation of laws, the *Tauromaquía*, Buchan and the Art of Cooking. Passengers include Messrs Rousseau, Hobbes, Vossius, Cottu, Bentham,

48 *Ibid.*, pp. 545–97. The somewhat arbitrary figure of 8% is based on Collier's report that 400 children attended Santiago's nine lay schools. I have doubled this figure to take into account the various church-run schools, and estimate that school-age children constituted one third of the city's total population of 36,000. See Collier, *Ideas and Politics*, p. 9. For a less optimistic estimate, see Newland, 'La educación en Hispanoamérica,' p. 360. (Newland's figures suggest that in Santiago only 4% of all school age children attended primary school in 1813.)

49 Collier, *Ideas and Politics*, p. 170. Or see the comments of Captain Basil Hall, *Extracts from a Journal written on the Coasts of Chili, Peru, and Mexico in the Years 1820–1821, 1822* [1824] (Upper Saddle River, 1968), vol. 1, p. 89.

> Constant, Montesquieu, Machiavelli, Voltaire, Say, Puffendorf, Grotius, Sully and Genovesi, with their wives and a couple of nieces.[50]

Chile had certainly not been without books before 1810; the monastic and private libraries of late colonial Santiago contained over 20,000 volumes.[51] Thus, the frequent complaint of Chilean patriots that the Spanish had barred all learning from the colonies was not entirely justified. But there seems little evidence that these libraries had contained the works of 'Rousseau, Hobbes, Vossius, Cottu, Bentham, Constant, Montesquieu, Machiavelli, Voltaire, Say, Puffendorf, Grotius, Sully and Genovesi'. (Whether they consisted entirely, as Sergio Villalobos asserts, of saints' lives and works of theology and jurisprudence, or whether, as Francisco Encina claims, they offered a balanced and up-to-date selection of law texts, historical studies, Graeco-Roman classics and other literary works is not yet clear.)[52] The vogue for the works of writers such as Montesquieu, and for cookery books, seems to be a new feature of life in the early republic.

Did the Press Cause Revolution in Spanish America?

No, not even in Mexico. Rather, the transformation of printing, where it occurred, was but one aspect of a broader transformation in political culture. The press emerged from the wars strengthened and equipped to embark on a period of rapid growth. In New Granada the press emerged from the Wars of Independence profoundly transformed. David Bushnell and Eduardo Posada-Carbó have described the flourishing world of political journalism that developed in the 1820s as a number of new printing presses were imported into the republic, allowing a corresponding growth in newspaper and pamphlet production. Venezuela, in which no newspapers of any sort had been printed prior to 1808, experienced a comparable growth. Between 1809 and 1819, 16 journals were published. The following decade saw the publication of 82 different titles, a five-fold

50 Collier, *Ideas and Politics*, p. 170.

51 Colonial Chilean society lacked not the products of the press, but the printing press itself. Colonial Spanish America was thus not strictly comparable to pre-Gutenberg Europe, which lacked the printed book altogether. This distinction is significant because scholars have argued that the advent of printed books in early modern Europe made possible new ways of thinking. See Elizabeth Eisenstein, *The Printing Press as an Agent of Change. Communications and Cultural Transformations in Early-Modern Europe* (Cambridge, 1980).

52 Villalobos, *Tradición y reforma*, p. 69; and Encina, *Historia de Chile*, vol. 5, pp. 596–7.

increase over the previous decade.[53] In Chile too the 1820s was the period of most exuberant periodical growth. Between 1811 and 1820 some 18 newspapers were published; from 1821 to 1830 over 73 different titles appeared.[54] This phenomenon was repeated across Spanish America: in the region as a whole approximately 45 different newspapers were published prior to 1810, the earliest in 1679. From 1810 to 1819 some 125 new titles were printed. The subsequent decade saw the publication of nearly 400 new newspapers. Renán Silva has claimed that, in Colombia, by the mid-nineteenth century the press was the principle source of information for the literate on political affairs.[55] This had not been the case even at the start of the war in 1810. At that time, as in Chile, the press had been but one source of information, and was not necessarily even the preferred source. Individuals were quite prepared to doubt the veracity of press reports, preferring to trust news delivered in person, or by letter.[56] Information spread by rumour, by letters and by public announcement, as well as by newspapers and other printed sources. The importance of these alternative, non-printed means of spreading information was acknowledged by the Consulado de Caracas in 1815 when they proposed the creation of a publicly-funded official journal. Such a journal would be useful, the *consulado* believed, as it would provide information to the public, 'accustomed for years to *hearing* only the most horrific language of disorder emanating from the *mouths and pens* of evil-doers'.[57] Information, or, as the *consulado* believed, misinformation, was spread by word of mouth and by the written (not printed) word. It was heard, not read. The tremendous vitality of oral communication is well-illustrated by Richard Boyer's study of bigamists in colonial Mexico, which reveals that information about the private affairs of obscure individuals could and did spread from Spanish port cities to the most remote towns in the Mexican interior with

53 For the press after 1820, see Bushnell, 'The Development of the Press'; and Eduardo Posada-Carbó, 'The Role of Newspapers and Leaflets in Electoral Campaigns in Colombia, 1830–1930,' presented at the Latin American Studies Association 1995 conference in Washington, DC. The statistics for Venezuela are taken from the appendix of Julio Febres Cordero, *Historia de la imprenta y del periodismo*.

54 Collier, *Ideas and Politics*, pp. 372–6. This is not a complete count of all Chilean newspapers during this period.

55 Silva, *Prensa y revolución*, p. 16.

56 See Earle, 'Information and Disinformation'; or, List of the Principal Insurgents in Popayán, 1811, AGI, Audiencia de Quito, 235.

57 *Gaceta de Gobierno*, 27 January 1815, Caracas, in Eduardo Arcila (ed.), *Documentos del Real Consulado de Caracas* (Caracas, 1964), pp. 181–2, my emphasis.

amazing accuracy.[58] The transformation of this vibrant oral culture into the print-based culture of modernity did not *precede* the outbreak of the War of Independence in regions such as New Granada. Rather, it developed after Independence.[59] It seems that Independence transformed the ways that information spread, rather than the reverse. Periodicals flourished in regions where there had been none, and began to play a central role in the spread of news and opinion. Reading practices were opened to the influence of a growing book trade. New educational systems were introduced; the enthusiastic reception of Jeremy Bentham's Lancasterian system has been discussed in a number of studies. Although one can find embryonic traces of these changes in some regions in the late colonial period, and although Mexico perhaps led Spanish America in its adoption of 'modernity', the real growth occurred after, not before, Independence.

By way of conclusion, we need to ask more questions about the spread of information in the decades after Independence. Did public oratory take on a new political meaning, with politicians employing forms of rhetoric previously used by the clergy, as Richard Brown has suggested occurred in North America after Independence? Certainly Anne Staples has noted the extraordinary popularity of the printed speech in post-Independence Mexico; printed speeches outstrip printed sermons by ten to one in the early national period.[60] Was this the case in other parts of Spanish America? Did letters move from the public to the private sphere, as their contents ceased to provide the sort of information increasingly available in newspapers? Elsewhere, the nineteenth century was a period of transition for letters, which came increasingly to be viewed as a form of private, rather than public writing, as had often been the case previously. Did the letter come to reside in the feminised domestic, private realm of the household, in the

58 Richard Boyer, *The Lives of the Bigamists: Marriage, Family and Community in Colonial Mexico* (Albuquerque, 1995), especially Chapter 5: 'The Flow of Information'.

59 This is shown with particular clarity by the situation of those regions remaining in Spanish hands after 1820. In Puerto Rico, for example, Spanish officials continued to prevent the importation of printing presses until well into the 1840s. Thus, in 1841 a request to import a small hand-press into Ponce was declined because, as one official explained, 'there are already two presses on this island [both in San Juan] and if I am to speak frankly I believe that given our present state we have more than we need'. Spanish opposition to a proliferation of printing presses was based primarily on fears that they would fall into the hands of anti-colonial agitators. (See Consulta de José Silvestre Sanlatir, Puerto Rico, 7 January 1841, APR, Gobernadores Españoles, asuntos políticos y civiles, caja 118, exp. 1379.)

60 Staples, 'Lectura y lectores,' pp. 97–9.

same way that women themselves were urged to do by the nineteenth-century state? Did newspapers themselves move towards reporting 'news', rather than simply discussing information already circulating in the public domain? To what extent, if at all, did literacy increase during this period? Finally, how did these changes intersect with that other great indication of modernity: commerce? How did the printed word combine with the growth of consumer goods during the nineteenth century? In 1810 government officials in Lima detained a number of individuals for the possession of handkerchiefs printed with the subversive slogan 'personas, conciencia y comercio libre'.[61] Someone, it seems, had decided to market revolutionary handkerchiefs with a printed motto. Here, in these handkerchiefs, revolution, commerce and print combine in a way that seems distinctly modern. This, it seems to me, says as much about the transformations under way in the revolutionary era as the publication of any newspaper.

61 Peralta, 'La revolución silenciada', pp. 121–2. Or see Hall, *Extracts from a Journal*, vol. 2, p. 265, for patriotic mottoes stamped onto pieces of gingerbread in 1822.

CHAPTER 2

'Seríamos excelentes vasallos, y nunca ciudadanos': prensa republicana y cambio social en Lima, 1791–1822

Carmen McEvoy

El escaso interés, salvo casos excepcionales, por articular un argumento que explique la correlación entre la activa discusión en la prensa y las intensas transformaciones socioculturales que las reformas ilustradas, primero, y el derrumbe del orden colonial, después, provocaron en Lima, ha colaborado en modelar la visión sesgada que tenemos de la Independencia peruana.[1] En Lima, las palabras, las que remplazaron a las balas en el proceso de ruptura con el orden colonial, ejercieron un importante papel en la definición de las configuraciones políticas y del rumbo ideológico a seguir en el período republicano. A diferencia de otros países de la América Española, en el Perú la definición del rumbo político y la hegemonización de los diversos grupos involucrados en dicha tarea no se forjó en el espacio de las juntas o en el de la guerra. En Lima el acontecer político y la temática que lo acompañó se fue decantando en la discusión periodística. En efecto, la crisis de legitimidad del imperio se manifestó en el discurso escrito. Es por ello que resulta muy útil establecer para el caso peruano la metodología usada por J.G.A. Pocock para otras latitudes: el mostrar que la historia del pensamiento político es la historia del idioma o de los idiomas políticos desarrollados a través del tiempo.[2]

1 Uno de los esfuerzos más notables por proseguir con el análisis, iniciado hace varios años en el Perú por Alberto Tauro del Pino y Raúl Porras Barrenechea, es el de Ascensión Martínez Riaza, *La prensa doctrinal en la Independencia del Perú, 1811–1824* (Madrid, 1985). Recientemente se ha dado un importante esfuerzo para rescatar el papel de la esfera pública en Latino América. Para este punto véase, François-Xavier Guerra et al., *Los espacios públicos en Iberoamérica. Ambigüedades y problemas. Siglos XVIII–XIX* (México, 1998).

2 Pocock señala que las ideas y el lenguaje en el que son expresadas son una parte fundamental tanto de la realidad social como de sus instituciones y su estructura. El lenguaje es al mismo tiempo un producto de la historia y tiene una historia propia. Una de las claves para entender el cambio social es seguirle la pista a los cambios en la naturaleza del lenguaje tanto en el surgimiento de nuevas palabras como en los nuevos significados dados a las viejas. Véase J.G.A. Pocock, *Politics, Language and Time* (Chicago, 1989), pp. 12, 38 y 105. También, su 'El trabajo sobre las ideas en el tiempo,' en L.P. Curtis (ed.), *El taller del historiador* (México, 1975), pp. 171–85. Para una reelaboración reciente sobre el mismo tema y para la discusión del lenguaje como 'matriz cultural' véase Michael Wagner, *The Letters of the Republic: Publication and the Public Sphere in Eighteenth-Century America* (Cambridge, MA, 1990).

En la remoción del todopoderoso secretario del protectorado, Bernardo Monteagudo, la prensa limeña desempeñó un papel fundamental. El 'motín de las palabras' que culminó con la deportación de Bernardo Monteagudo a Panamá se gestó en las páginas de los diarios limeños que como *El Republicano* organizaron la reacción de 'la comunidad de Lima' contra la política autoritaria del gobierno protectoral.[3] No es una coincidencia entonces que en un contexto que significó el punto de inflexión de la discusión entre la propuesta monárquica y la republicana, el detonante para el levantamiento de 'la Ciudad de los Libres' contra Monteagudo fuera el rumor que circuló en la capital del ex-virreinato español respecto al apresamiento y deportación de un periodista republicano ampliamente conocido, el limeño Mariano Tramarria.

La evolución, entre un sector del periodismo limeño, de un discurso de corte clásico a otro en que la simpleza conceptual intentó conquistar, como lo hizo en 1822, la imaginación de los sectores menos ilustrados de la ciudad estuvo íntimamente relacionado con la hegemonización en el campo intelectual de un grupo de letrados limeños y provincianos. Los mismos, convertidos debido a las reformas ilustradas primero y al desplazamiento violento de la nobleza después en actores protagónicos en la transición entre la colonia y la república, elaboraron una retórica que a más de alejarlos de la vocinglería de la plebe, los identificó con la elocuencia, el decoro y la simpleza del republicanismo clásico. El análisis del uso que el periodismo limeño dio a los escritos del panfletario inglés Thomas Paine resulta fundamental en un contexto en el que el concepto de nación varió de una sociabilidad, ligada a los valores de una cultura urbana, a uno, que sin dejar de lado lo anterior, abogó por la defensa de un sistema en el que primara la defensa de los derechos ciudadanos, entre ellos el de la representación y el de la libre expresión. La existencia en Lima de un republicanismo simple y directo en el cual los periodistas peruanos, Faustino Sánchez Carrión el más reconocido, creyeron encontrar su voz, su lugar y su público en el nuevo orden de cosas, dan cuenta de las profundas transformaciones socioculturales ocurridas en la capital peruana entre 1791 y 1822.

Este capítulo está dividido en tres partes. En la primera analizo el surgimiento del *Mercurio Peruano* (1791–95) y su influencia en la articulación de ciertos conceptos que como orden, virtud, mérito, república y ciudadanía reaparecerán en las discusiones de los años posteriores. En la

3 Un recuento pormenorizado de este suceso es el provisto en mi ensayo 'El motín de las palabras: la caída de Bernardo Monteagudo y la forja de una cultura política en Lima, 1821–1822,' en *Forjando la nación: ensayos de historia republicana* (Lima, 1999), pp. 1–60.

segunda parte exploro los decisivos años de la administración Abascal, especialmente la etapa constitucionalista, 1811–14, en la que surge una prensa de opinión. El acercamiento a la difícil relación entre el letrado ilustrado y el poder colonial, cuyo patronazgo lo favoreció, permite explorar las estrategias del periodismo disidente, que como la enmascarada apropiación del espacio cultural, le permitió convivir con la censura oficial. El estudio de la pedagogía política de la que hizo gala el periodismo limeño, especialmente el periódico *El Peruano*, permite entender ciertas constantes en el pensamiento político peruano, las que se remontan, como he observado anteriormente, a los años de edición del *Mercurio Peruano*. La parte central del capítulo está dedicada a discutir el rol que la prensa limeña desempeñó luego de obtenida la independencia, especialmente en el debate entre monarquistas y republicanos. La apelación por parte de los republicanos a los escritos de Thomas Paine (cuyo 'Common Sense' fue traducido en 1821 al español por Anselmo Nateiu, 'indígena del Perú')[4] muestra la difusión del republicanismo radical entre los periodistas y el público lector limeño.[5] La conexión del periodismo limeño, especialmente el representado por *La Abeja Republicana*, con la obra de Paine, que se trasunta en la estructura de los escritos de varios de sus redactores, entre ellos Faustino Sánchez Carrión, permite descubrir una desconocida dimensión del republicanismo peruano, a la vez que posibilita explorar la recreación, en la capital del ex-virreinato español, del debate paradigmático que sostuvo el autor de 'Common Sense' con Edmund Burke. En la parte final del capitulo evidencio la maduración política de la prensa limeña y del sector letrado a la que estuvo asociada. Él mismo será capaz de encontrar una voz original en las cartas del 'Tribuno de la República', Faustino Sánchez Carrión, así como una fuerza política que culminará el 26 de julio de 1822 en la remoción del secretario del régimen protectoral, el tucumano Bernardo Monteagudo. A manera de epílogo examino los desafíos políticos que la Independencia significó para la élite intelectual peruana.

4 Alberto Tauro del Pino opina, aunque no está comprobado, que el nombre es una elisión anagramática que corresponde al diputado Manuel José de Amunátegui. Para este punto véase: *La Abeja Republicana, 1822–1823* (Lima, 1971), p. 167.

5 Para el análisis del mismo proceso para los Estados Unidos, véase: Michael Durey, *Transatlantic Radicals and the Early American Republic* (Kansas, 1997).

El *Mercurio Peruano* y la forja de la 'República de las Letras' (1791–95)

La etapa previa a la disolución de los vínculos imperiales, con su punto de inflexión durante la 'primavera gaditana', es única por la posibilidad de percibir la transformación cultural que la puesta en marcha de las reformas borbónicas provocó en el tejido social limeño.[6] De aquellos intensos años de producción cultural nativa data la publicación del *Mercurio Peruano* (1791–95), uno de los esfuerzos intelectuales más ricos y consistentes en el Perú.[7] La propuesta del *Mercurio*, que analizaremos seguidamente, significó una reconceptualización de la esfera pública. Tímidamente, los mercuristas esbozaron una nueva representación del orden político, al articular un discurso que además de reformular las relaciones de poder (letrados-autoridad colonial), fue capaz de proveer de nuevos significados al acto de escribir, de imprimir y de publicar. El discurso del *Mercurio* rompió con el estilo deferente del pasado e introdujo la tendencia al debate con todos los riesgos que ello significó. Sin embargo, los redactores del *Mercurio* debieron de manejarse con sumo cuidado ya que el debate, que se promovió desde sus páginas, debió de tomar en consideración el hecho de que sus escritos podían percibirse como una amenaza no sólo contra el espíritu público, sino contra el principio de la autoridad virreinal de la cual sus autores recibían el subsidio. Los constreñimientos de habitar una sociedad de 'Antiguo Régimen' obligó a los periodistas del *Mercurio* a guardar las formas, incluido un respeto deferencial por la autoridad de turno. Eso aunque los periodistas del *Mercurio* disputasen con esa misma autoridad el control sobre la esfera cultural limeña.

6 Juan Carlos Estenssoro ha explorado las transformaciones culturales que las Reformas Borbónicas provocaron entre las clases populares limeñas. No existe, sin embargo, un trabajo que explique cómo dichas transformaciones afectaron a los sectores intelectuales nativos. Para la propuesta de Estenssoro véase, 'La plebe ilustrada: el pueblo en las fronteras de la razón,' en C. Walker (comp.), *Entre la retórica y la insurgencia* (Cuzco, 1996).

7 La idea del *Mercurio Peruano* comienza en 1787 cuando un grupo de jóvenes, José María Egaña, José Rossi y Rubí, Hipólito Unanue, Demetrio Guasque y otros dos más, cuyos nombres se desconocen, constituyeron la Sociedad Filarmónica. Después de 22 meses se reencontraron para fundar la Sociedad Amantes del País, la que publicó el *Mercurio Peruano de Historia, Literatura y Noticias Públicas* que apareció periódicamente los jueves y domingos de cada semana y que constó de un pliego entero cuya subscripción era de 14 reales mensuales. Uno de los mejores estudios sobre el *Mercurio* es el de Jean Pierre Clement, *Índices del Mercurio Peruano, 1790–1795* (Lima, 1979).

En el prospecto de presentación del *Mercurio*, publicado el 2 de enero de 1791, Jacinto Calero y Moreira, su editor, señaló claramente la importancia que los periódicos desempeñaban en el proceso de pensar a la nación.[8] En 'Idea general del Perú', el artículo con el que se inauguró el periódico, su autor, José Rossi Rubí, señaló la necesidad de hacer conocido al país 'contra el qual los autores estrangeros' habían publicado 'tanto paralogismo'.[9] La noción manejada por el cuerpo de redactores del periódico, el cual aparecía los jueves y domingos de cada semana, era que la publicación debía subsanar dichos errores, abriendo la discusión intelectual a un público más amplio que el meramente erudito.[10] Es decir, a lo que los mercuristas apuntaron fue a crear una esfera pública donde las ideas podían ser intercambiadas. La meta principal fue romper el aislamiento en el que, a decir uno de sus articulistas, se encontraban los intelectuales nativos.[11] Era obvio, sin embargo, que una sociedad colonial como la peruana tenía serias dificultades en articular aquel espacio deseado por su 'intelligentzia'.[12] Otro de los riesgos a contemplar por los mercuristas era que la literatura tradicional 'inteligible por demasiado profunda' se podía convertir en 'fútil' y 'vacía' a fuerza de querer ser, en palabras de Calero, meramente 'agradable'.[13] Así, el gran reto del periódico fue el desarrollar un lenguaje que sin alejarse de la solidez académica, que sus redactores respetaban, tomara en consideración la nueva audiencia, personalidad y orden social que reinaba en la ciudad de

8 Jacinto Calero y Moreira, *Prospecto del papel periódico intitulado el Mercurio Peruano de Historia, Literatura y Noticias Públicas que a nombre de una Sociedad Amantes del País, y como uno de ellos promete dar a luz Don Jacinto Calero y Moreira con Superior Permiso* (Lima, 1790).

9 José Rossi Rubí, 'Idea General del Perú,' en *Mercurio Peruano*, no. 1, 2 de enero de 1791.

10 Calero y Moreira, *Prospecto.*

11 Para la condena del aislamiento intelectual y para la celebración del establecimiento de vínculos sociales véase 'Tertulia poética remitida a la sociedad,' en *Mercurio Peruano*, no. 35, 1 de Mayo de 1791 y 'Historia de la Sociedad Académica de Amantes del País, y principios del Mercurio Peruano,' en *Mercurio Peruano*, no. 7, 23 de enero de 1791 respectivamente.

12 Keith Baker, en una reelaboración en torno la esfera pública habermiana, ha señalado como unas sólidas bases económicas son fundamentales para el desarrollo de la misma. La existencia de la esfera pública depende de la comercialización de la cultura dentro de una sociedad capitalista, en la que el sustento de sus escritores y críticos depende de la producción de la cultura como mercancía. Una situación que distaba de ocurrir en el Perú de 1791. Para este punto véase Keith Baker, 'Defining the Public Sphere in Eighteenth-Century France: Variation on a theme by Habermas,' en Craig Calhoun (ed.), *Habermas and the Public Sphere* (Cambridge, MA, 1996). pp. 181–211.

13 Calero y Moreira, *Prospecto.*

Lima.[14] A ella había que educar con elegancia pero también con claridad sobre las grandezas del Perú.

Los cambios en el discurso literario plasmado en el *Mercurio Peruano* fueron un reflejo de las profundas transformaciones que atravesó la capital del virreinato peruano.[15] En efecto 1791, año en el que aparece el *Mercurio*, coincidió no sólo con la puesta en marcha del censo ordenado por Francisco Gil de Taboada, que arrojó una población de 52,627 habitantes para Lima, sino con la inauguración del hermoso Jardín Botánico capitalino. Unos años antes, en 1787, el Intendente Jorge Escobedo, siguiendo la tendencia, de reorganizar a la ciudad, inaugurada por Teodoro de Croix en 1784, ordenó la confección de un mapa de la capital del virreinato.[16] En uno de los artículos más reveladores por los cuadros estadísticos que insertó, 'Reflexiones históricas y políticas sobre el estado de la población de esta capital, que se acompaña por suplemento', se subrayó cómo 'con la libertad de comercio' la capital virreinal ganó en 'recursos para la manutención y comodidades de la vida'. La proliferación de nuevos espacios de sociabilidad, 'cafés, fondas y peluquerías', era el síntoma claro de 'la prosperidad' que disfrutaba, según el redactor del *Mercurio*, 'el estado medio de los ciudadanos'. El bienestar de este novísimo estrato social compuesto del 'artesano, el pequeño mercader,

14 La elocuencia era percibida por los mercuristas como una característica cívica. En la mejor tradición clásica, de la que habían bebido sus miembros fundadores, 'el homo rethor' debía vivir en el forum persiguiendo activamente la vida pública. El 'homo rethor' debía de exhibir, asimismo, un lenguaje claro y simple. Para este punto véase, por ejemplo, 'Epístola escrita por Anticyro a Lucipo, criticando la intolerable y perniciosa Philaucia de los eruditos,' en *Mercurio Peruano*, no. 72, 1 de setiembre de 1791. La naturaleza cívica de la retórica, analizada por Kenneth Cmiel, asume que el verdaderamente elocuente era el capaz de llegar a una audiencia amplia. Para un análisis sobre este punto véase Kenneth Cmiel, *Democratic Eloquence: The Fight over Popular Speech in Nineteenth-Century America* (Berkeley y Los Angeles, 1992). Para una reelaboración del tema para Colombia, Malcom Deas, *Del poder y la gramática y otros ensayos de historia política y literatura colombiana* (Bogotá, 1993).

15 Aunque, como anota John Lynch, las reformas borbónicas obedecieron más a necesidades concretas que a nuevas ideas, no por ello dejaron de ejercer una influencia transformadora que se sintió en el Perú desde la economía hasta la cultura. Para este punto véase John Lynch, 'El reformismo borbónico en Hispanoamérica,' en Agustín Guiméra (comp.), *El reformismo borbónico* (Madrid, 1996) y Scarlett O'Phelan (comp.), *El Perú en el siglo XIX: la era borbónica* (Lima, 1999).

16 Para los cambios en la arquitectura de la ciudad que fueron evidencia de cambios sociales más profundos véase Gabriel Ramón, 'Urbe y orden: evidencias del reformismo borbónico en el tejido limeño'; y Jesús Cosamalón, 'Amistades peligrosas: matrimonios indígenas y espacios de convivencia interracial (1795–1820),' en O'Phelan, *El Perú en el siglo XVIII*, pp. 295–394 y 345–68, respectivamente.

el menestral y el traficante' se vio favorecido por cambios económicos muy puntuales. La 'navegación directa, la creación de la Aduana, la amplificación del Estanco de Tabaco y el aumento de la tropa' multiplicaron, en palabras del mercurista, 'los caudales de la circulación'.[17]

Las variaciones en la estructura y en la demografía urbana, que hablan de un proceso de movilidad social que discutiremos más adelante, fueron de la mano con intensas transformaciones en las percepciones y en las reglas de convivencia social. En 1790 aparecieron nuevas categorías raciales y se intensificó una sociabilidad plebeya, cuyo centro de expresión fue una intensa vida barrial. Una en la que el ocio y la diversión se constituyeron en valores fundamentales de la cultura plebeya.[18] En torno a ello José Ignacio de Lequanda señaló, en uno de los artículos publicados en el *Mercurio*, cómo la falta de empleo, causa fundamental de la vagancia en Lima, unida a las pretensiones sociales de las clases menos privilegiadas de la ciudad eran responsables de los daños morales y políticos que exhibía el virreinato peruano. Las disquisiciones de Lequanda querían, en sus palabras, llamar la atención sobre los defectos sociales que estaban llevando a 'la República a su propia ruina'.[19]

Más allá de los pobres y los menesterosos que tanto preocupaban a Lequanda, las transformaciones socioeconómicas, anotadas en el *Mercurio*, provocaron el surgimiento de ese 'estrato medio', al que se refirió uno de sus redactores. Del mismo, compuesto por profesionales, comerciantes y servidores públicos, dio cuenta uno de los cuadros publicados por el periódico en 1791.[20] Es interesante observar cómo dentro del cuerpo de redactores del *Mercurio* una gran mayoría puede considerarse como perteneciente a la categoría de servidor público.[21] A excepción de José Baquíjano y Carrillo, ninguno de los mercuristas formó parte de la sociedad cortesana y aristocrática limeña. En efecto, los voceros de este

17 'Reflexiones históricas y políticas sobre el estado de la población de esta capital, que se acompaña por suplemento,' en *Mercurio Peruano*, no. 10, 3 de febrero de 1791.

18 Jesús Cosamalón, 'Amistades peligrosas,' pp. 360–5.

19 Joseph Ignacio de Lequanda, 'Discurso sobre el destino que debe darse a la gente vaga que tiene Lima,' en *Mercurio Peruano*, no. 325, 13 de febrero de 1794.

20 'Plan demostrativo de la población comprehendida en el recinto de la ciudad de Lima con distinción de clases y Estados,' en *Mercurio Peruano*, no. 10, 3 de febrero de 1791.

21 Del grupo fundador, Egaña era teniente de policía; Rossi y Rubí, consultor del Tribunal de Minería; Unanue, catedrático de Medicina; Guasque, archivero en la Secretaría de Cámara y Virreinato y Calero y Moreira, abogado en la Real Audiencia de Lima (Jean Pierre Clement, *Indices*, p. 11). En uno de los artículos uno de los redactores anotaba como 'absorbidos por los empleos y destinos que los alimentan' a los mercuristas les faltaba 'aquel dulce sosiego indispensable a las meditaciones filosóficas' ('Introducción al Tomo X del Mercurio Peruano,' en *Mercurio Peruano*, no. 313, 2 de enero de 1794).

frágil estrato social, que el *Mercurio* descubrió para sus lectores, eran un grupo de intelectuales sin los valores propios de una clase burguesa, aunque con el interés y la voluntad suficiente para promover ciertas reformas en las costumbres tradicionales.[22] La clase media comercial que podría haber servido de público a los escritores no estaba aún desarrollada en Lima.[23] Es por ello que el subsidio estatal fue fundamental para la sobrevivencia de una publicación cuyo destino, en palabras de uno de sus redactores, fluctuó 'entre la ruina y la esperanza'.[24]

En 1794 el *Mercurio* se vio obligado a cerrar cuando perdió el apoyo político y económico del virrey.[25] Y es que los escritores del *Mercurio* estaban atrapados en una suerte de limbo social, a pesar de que se percibían a sí mismos como los líderes de la revolución cultural cuyo epicentro era Lima. Entre una aristocracia de cuyo subsidio vivían, pero a la que poco o nada le interesaba el discurso crítico del *Mercurio*, y una plebe, cuyas formas de expresión aquellos despreciaban, la 'república de las letras' se constituyó en el único refugio de los mercuristas.[26] Es importante observar cómo el enmascaramiento del que hicieron gala en los números iniciales y del que se alejaron posteriormente, al punto de revelar públicamente sus respectivas identidades, muestra la fragilidad de aquellos estratos medios ilustrados de los que el *Mercurio*

22 'El objeto de este periódico sólo es manifestar los males que padece esta capital' cediendo a 'mayores talentos y poder' la solución a 'envejecidos y arraigados principios' que deben de ser exterminados (*Mercurio Peruano*, no. 325, 13 de febrero de 1794).

23 A pesar de los intentos que se dieron por liberalizar el sistema económico, del que dan cuenta muchos de los artículos que publicó el *Mercurio*, el mercantilismo era aún muy vital en el virreinato peruano. Una aproximación al impacto del Comercio Libre y a los reacomodos que supuso es la provista por Cristina Mazzeo, 'El Comercio Libre en 1778 y sus repercusiones en el mercado limeño,' en O'Phelan, *El Perú en el siglo XVIII*, pp. 127–45.

24 'Introducción al Tomo X del Mercurio Peruano,' en *Mercurio Peruano*, no. 313, 2 de enero de 1794.

25 Las quejas sobre las penurias económicas que atravesaron los editores del *Mercurio*, cuyos subscriptores bajaron de 398 a 257, se hace evidente en la mayoría de los balances cuatrimestrales. Para este punto véase, por ejemplo, 'Introducción al Tomo X y al Tomo XI del Mercurio,' en *Mercurio Peruano*, no. 313, 2 de enero de 1794 y no. 347, 1 de mayo de 1794.

26 'Tertulia poética remitida a la sociedad,' *Mercurio Peruano*, no. 35, 1 de mayo de 1791. Uno de los primeros ilustrados peruanos que utilizó el término 'república de las letras' fue Eusebio de Llano y Zapata, cuando se refirió a la biblioteca y a los periódicos como espacios donde la construcción de la misma debía de llevarse a cabo. Para este punto véase Alberto Tauro del Pino, 'Fundación de la Biblioteca Nacional,' en *Anuario Bibliográfico de 1948* (Lima, 1951), pp. ix–xvii.

fue vocero.[27] La impotencia política de la 'intelligentzia' criolla[28] por su pertenencia a un mundo que a pesar del maquillaje ilustrado aún seguía reproduciendo sus formas despóticas, llevó a los mercuristas a buscar sustitutos en sus logros intelectuales. Así, la celebración de 'la carrera de las letras', única capaz de proveer al hombre con las cualidades suficientes para acceder al mundo de 'la verdad', de 'la elocuencia' y de 'la elegancia' fue un tema que se repitió a menudo en las páginas del periódico limeño.[29]

La constante apelación a encontrarse operando en una esfera que estaba más allá de la política proveyó de legitimidad a la 'intelligentzia' criolla, cuya plataforma fue el *Mercurio.* El tema que más les interesó desarrollar a los mercuristas estuvo relacionado con la construcción de espacios de sociabilidad urbana. Dentro de ese contexto, la celebración de lo cotidiano adquirió una especial relevancia. La sociabilidad limeña, donde el escritor, según confesión propia, se veía 'absolutamente aislado', sufría a fines del siglo XVIII de graves defectos. Por ello el periódico se propuso colaborar en la construcción de una esfera pública capaz de absorber las ideas expuestas en el periódico.[30] En el artículo 'Rasgo histórico y filosófico de los cafés', por ejemplo, el autor analizó 'el origen de los cafés de Lima' y el 'enlace' que éste tenía con 'el sistema civil de la República'. El articulista percibió con optimismo la posibilidad de que 'algún día' Lima apreciase más la noticia sobre la proliferación de más cafés que la historia de 'sus guerras y sus conquistas'.[31]

El concepto de 'República' que manejaron los redactores del *Mercurio* exhibe un aire de familia con el republicanismo clásico de estirpe florentina.

27 Refiriéndose a la 'mascarilla de los nombres griegos' con los que los ocultaron durante un par de años sus respectivas identidades, los mercuristas afirmaron que 'al abrigo' de ese 'disfraz enigmático' aspiraron a conseguir 'el triunfo inaúdito' de ser profetas en su Patria. Todo ello porque habían ayudado a desenvolver la educación, a 'rasgar' la 'dolosa cortina' que cubría el tocador y las recámaras de las peruanas y por hacer 'una demostración anatómica de los vicios del Perú' ('Introducción al Tomo VII del Mercurio Peruano,' en *Mercurio Peruano*, no. 209, 3 de enero de 1793).

28 El caso paradigmático fue el de Baquíjano y Carrillo, quién ejemplifica las ambiciones y frustraciones de la elite criolla. Véase Mark Burkholder, *Politics of a Colonial Career. José Baquíjano and the Audiencia of Lima* (Wilmington, DE, 1990).

29 'Introducción al Tomo XI del Mercurio Peruano,' en *Mercurio Peruano*, no. 347, 1 de mayo de 1794.

30 'Introducción al Tomo VII del Mercurio Peruano,' en *Mercurio Peruano*, no. 210, 6 de enero de 1793.

31 'Rasgo histórico y filosófico de los cafés,' en *Mercurio Peruano*, no. 12, 10 de febrero de 1791. Para la defensa de 'la tertulia' como forma de sociabilidad capaz de neutralizar 'la división y el tumulto' véase 'Historia de la Sociedad Académica Amantes del País, y principios del Mercurio Peruano,' en *Mercurio Peruano*, no. 7, 23 de enero de 1791. Una aproximación a la manera como se divertían los limeños: 'Idea de las diversiones públicas de Lima,' en *Mercurio Peruano*, no. 4, 13 de enero de 1791.

Para él mismo, el orden, la virtud y el espíritu ciudadano debían de constituirse en fundamentos de toda sociedad civilizada.[32] Las alusiones constantes, como veremos más adelante, a elementos de la historia clásica y el uso, por parte de los redactores, de nombres con claras resonancias griegas y romanas, permiten incorporar a los mercuristas dentro de una tradición occidental que ellos conocían muy bien. Sin embargo, este incipiente discurso republicano distó de ser monolítico. Para entenderlo debemos tomar en consideración, también, la existencia en el virreinato del Perú de una tradición republicana de corte hispánico. La que al igual que el republicanismo clásico, pero contraponiéndose a su tendencia de hacer prevalecer 'la razón de Estado' por sobre todas las demás,[33] intentó fomentar el accionar en la esfera pública del 'hombre virtuoso, cristiano y de buena opinión'. Él mismo debía de sentir su trabajo como una verdadera obligación en pos del 'bien común de la República'. Lo anterior implicaba, básicamente, una permanente preocupación por 'la salvación de todos sus miembros'. No ser 'un buen republicano', es decir despreocuparse de la cosa pública, podía acarrear, como afirmaba Juan de Matienzo, 'la confusión de todo el cuerpo social'.[34]

La ausencia, entre la burguesía limeña, de lo que para otras latitudes Norbert Elias denominó un 'hinterland social',[35] determinó que la intelectualidad urbana se encargara de proveerse de su propio espacio en esa suerte de 'república de las letras' que fue el *Mercurio.* El combate intelectual de la 'intelligentzia' peruana contra el régimen virreinal, que se inicia en 1791, y del que se ha explorado muy poco, tuvo como objetivo hegemonizar el campo de la sociedad y de la cultura. Desde allí los productores culturales nativos fueron capaces de poner en funcionamiento una suerte de infra-política cuya estrategia fundamental fue evidenciar y con-

32 J.G.A. Pocock, *The Machiavellian Moment: Florentine Thought and the Atlantic Republican Tradition* (Princeton, 1975) y *Virtue, Commerce and History: Essays on Political Thought and History, Chiefly in the XVIIIth Century* (Cambridge, 1985).

33 Quentin Skinner, *The Foundations of Modern Political Thought. The Age of Reformation*, vol. II (Cambridge, 1988), pp. 142–3.

34 Rafael Sánchez Concha-Barrios, 'La tradición política y el concepto de "cuerpo de República" en el Virreinato,' en Teodoro Hampe, *La tradición clásica en el Perú virreinal* (Lima, 1999), pp. 112–14.

35 La comparación entre el comportamiento de la 'burguesía limeña' y la analizada por Elias, para el caso alemán, resulta muy sugerente. Norbert Elias, *The Civilizing Process: Sociogenetic and Psychogenetic Investigations* (Londres, 1998), pp. 5–35.

frontar la conducta poco aceptable de sus dos claros enemigos: 'la nobleza desarreglada y la plebe despreciada'.[36]

Un ejemplo muy claro de la situación anteriormente anotada nos la provee el ensayo que con el título 'Apólogo histórico sobre la concepción de las colonias romanas en África' salió publicado en uno de los primeros números del *Mercurio.* Dejando muy claro que el mismo no era 'una sátira metafórica' de la sociedad limeña, lo que a todas luces era, el autor de la pieza se permitió analizar el proceso de destrucción de las virtudes republicanas entre los romanos, quienes las abandonaron debido a 'la riqueza y la molicie'.[37] La sencillez, la sobriedad, el valor y la constancia fueron valores que poco a poco 'se relaxaron' en la Roma colonial para dar lugar 'al enredo, al regalo, al ocio y a las frioleras'. La 'enervación' de la sociedad romana, continuaba el articulista, trascendió a sus mujeres. Las que miraban con desdén 'la noble ocupación de amamantar y educar a sus hijos'. La infidelidad, que se volvió una práctica generalizada entre los romanos, favoreció a 'la mezcla de especies'. Así, 'las diversas subdivisiones' provocadas por las relaciones adúlteras crearon 'frutos espurios' que trastocaron, continuaba el relato, las jerarquías sociales. Este trastocamiento que se sintió también en Lima, donde en palabras de otro mercurista, la servidumbre llevaba las riendas de los hogares de las clases acomodadas era causa directa del socavamiento de los cimientos sociales.[38] Es interesante observar que los artículos señalados fueron escritos en el mismo año en que la 'mezcla racial', evidenciada en el censo limeño, y la presencia de una activa cultura plebeya, a la que incluso se le acusó de introducir la costumbre del tuteo entre las élites,[39] se convirtieron en el mayor desafío para el monopolio cultural y los cánones de la sociedad armónica y ordenada a la que aspiraban los ilustrados limeños

En el espacio cultural concedido a la 'intelligentzia' criolla por las autoridades ilustradas fue posible que aquella articulara sus sueños, sus temores y sus ideas. En el contexto de apertura provisto por la

36 Para una elaboración sobre la dicotomía aristocracia-plebe y sobre las formas de destruirla véase: 'Carta remitida a la sociedad que publica con algunas notas', en *Mercurio Peruano*, 20, 24 y 27 de abril de 1794. Para el concepto de infrapolítica véase James Scott, *Domination and the Arts of Resistance: Hidden Transcripts* (New Haven y Londres, 1990).

37 'Apólogo histórico sobre la concepción de las colonias romanas en África,' en *Mercurio Peruano*, no. 5, 16 de enero de 1791.

38 'Amas de leche. Segunda carta de Filomates sobre la educación,' en *Mercurio Peruano*, no. 8, 27 de enero de 1791.

39 La introducción de la costumbre plebeya del tuteo fue vista con disgusto en uno de los artículos. Véase 'Educación. Carta escrita a la Sociedad sobre el abuso de que los hijos tuteen a sus padres', *Mercurio Peruano*, 16 de enero de 1791.

Ilustración, los intelectuales nativos se apropiaron de un espacio para pensar y escribir, pero no para actuar. En el mismo fueron forjando muchos de los conceptos que como república, ciudadanía, patria, nación o virtud reaparecerán nuevamente y con más fuerza durante la 'primavera gaditana', primero, y en la discusión en favor del sistema republicano, luego. En infinidad de artículos los mercuristas supieron introducir sus críticas a la cultura vigente. En gran parte de aquellos, escondidos entre los tratados económicos o las disquisiciones filosóficas, contrapusieron valores antitéticos como virtud-vicio, honestidad-falsedad, razón-pasión, mérito-favor, consumo-austeridad, civilidad-barbarie, autenticidad-falsedad, humanismo generoso-erudición vana o claridad-confusión, intentando llamar la atención en torno a, lo que ellos consideraban, el deterioro cultural y social que atravesaba Lima.[40] Los ataques dirigidos a la conducta de una aristocracia renuente a ejercer su función directriz, lo que había ocasionado el relajamiento de las costumbres entre las clases populares, no significó, sin embargo, que los redactores del *Mercurio* no exhibieran las mismas tendencias hacia la ambigüedad, la cortesanía y el disimulo que tanto criticaban.[41] Dichas formas fueron recreadas, también, con algunas variables, durante los años de la prensa constitucionalista. La libertad de imprenta que la Constitución de Cádiz sancionó permitió, sin embargo, que la prensa que inauguró el siglo XIX ventilara con más detenimiento y sin tanto doblez los temas que los mercuristas tímidamente sugirieron.

40 Para estas discusiones véase 'Manías particulares,' en *Mercurio Peruano*, no. 5, 16 de enero de 1791; 'Medicina práctica. Carta escrita a la sociedad sobre el origen de las enfermedades, que regularmente padecen los que desde esta capital vuelven a la sierra y modo de preservarlas,' en *Mercurio Peruano*, no. 6, 20 de enero de 1791; 'Historia de la Sociedad Académica de Amantes del País, y principios del Mercurio Peruano,' en *Mercurio Peruano*, no. 7, 23 de enero de 1791; 'Carta escrita a la sociedad sobre los gastos excesivos de una tapada,' en *Mercurio Peruano*, no. 12, 10 de febrero de 1791; 'Tertulia política remitida a la sociedad,' en *Mercurio Peruano*, no. 35, 1 de mayo de 1791; 'Carta escrita a la sociedad sobre la vana ambición de algunas personas que procurando imitar a los grandes se hacen de tan pequeños ridículos,' en *Mercurio Peruano*, no. 72, 11 de setiembre de 1791; 'Progresos del papel periódico que se publica en Santa Fe de Bogotá anunciado en el Mercurio Peruano, T.I, p. 306,' en *Mercurio Peruano*, no. 87, 3 de noviembre de 1791; 'Epístola escrita por Anticyro a Lucipo, criticando la intolerable y perniciosa Philaucia de los eruditos,' en *Mercurio Peruano*, no. 72, 1 de setiembre de 1791.

41 Para una crítica a las ambigüedades de los mercuristas véase 'Carta recibida por la sociedad en el último correo del Cuzco criticando los cinco primeros Mercurios,' en *Mercurio Peruano*, no. 17, 27 de febrero de 1791. Sobre las limitaciones de las críticas que podía aspirar a formular el *Mercurio* véase 'Carta remitida a la sociedad que publica con algunas notas,' en *Mercurio Peruano*, no. 255, 20 de abril de 1794. En la misma se sugería integrar ambas repúblicas, la de Indios y la de Españoles, en una sola.

El interregno constitucionalista: 1811–14

En 1811, en pleno auge de la libertad de imprenta,[42] Manuel Villalta, un criollo relegado por una política de ascensos que consideraba injusta con los americanos, se quejó públicamente del tratamiento recibido por la administración colonial. Sus quejas fueron censuradas por la junta que para tal efecto controlaba el virrey José de Abascal. En su defensa a ejercer el derecho de opinión Villalta señaló como 'el despotismo' no tenía 'mayor enemigo que la libertad de hablar y escribir'. Hablar, subrayaba Villata, 'gritar y clamar para ser oído' era 'el voto general sancionado por las Cortes, y la obligación primera de todo ciudadano'. El argumento principal de Villalta apuntó a denunciar como 'la Junta Censoria de Lima' además de destruir el 'sacrosanto' derecho de la opinión, dio golpes funestos en 'la raíz misma del espíritu público'. Abascal no podía ni debía atentar, según Villalta, contra la libertad de prensa. Los dominios españoles en ambos hemisferios formaban 'una sola monarquía, una misma y sola Nación y una sola familia' y por lo mismo 'los naturales' que fueran originarios de ambos dominios europeos y de ultramar, poseían 'iguales derechos'.[43]

El peligro que la Constitución jurada en Cádiz representó para la estructura del poder colonial es innegable.[44] Antonio Annino ha observado, por ejemplo, cómo la difusión del término ciudadanía, ampliamente discutido en Cádiz, no fue extraña ni fue negada en las colonias españolas. Su difusión dio lugar a significados diversos y articuló otros tantos derechos. Para Annino fue esta pluralidad la que creó los mayores problemas a

42 El 18 de abril de 1811 se publicó en Lima el decreto de las Cortes de Cádiz que declaraba la libertad de imprenta y de publicar sin licencia previa. Se abolían los Juzgados de Imprenta pero se reglamentaban las Juntas de Censura. Las que debían examinar los escritos que fueran denunciados como 'libelos infamatorios, calumniosos, subversivos de las leyes fundamentales de la monarquía, licenciosos y contrarios a la decencia y a las buenas costumbres'.

43 Manuel Villalta, *Breves reflexiones sobre la censura de los oficios dirigidos al Excmo Ayuntamiento de esta capital* (Lima, 1811), pp. 2–3 y 17–36. Para una biografía de Villalta que a decir de Ascensión Martínez 'hizo saltar los mecanismos de la relación que establecía la prensa con los poderes públicos' véase Martínez Riaza, *La prensa doctrinal*, pp. 78–79.

44 Las Cortes de Cádiz, su legislación y la Constitución de 1812 contemplaron la igualdad de representación y de derechos a los territorios y a los ciudadanos americanos. Este acontecimiento, inédito en el parlamentarismo y constitucionalismo europeo, se convirtió en el punto de partida para el constitucionalismo americano. Para la influencia gaditana en la política americana véase Demetrio Ramos, 'Las Cortes de Cádiz y América,' en *Revista de Estudios Políticos* (Madrid, 1962), pp. 433–635.

la gobernabilidad republicana en México.[45] En el caso de la libertad de imprenta, otro aporte de la legislación gaditana, ni bien el decreto fue publicado, Lima se vio inundada de periódicos, y de innumerables hojas sueltas, que reimprimían publicaciones extranjeras, que comentaban sobre sucesos políticos del momento o que, simplemente, ventilaban las enemistades personales de los criollos.[46] La esfera pública por la que lucharon tenazmente los mercuristas logró hacerse de un espacio mucho más sólido y consistente durante el interregno constitucionalista. Dicha esfera, la de los 'ciudadanos lectores' se corporizó para todo el que fue capaz de asumir, por cuenta propia, los gastos de impresión. 'No hay,' se decía por esos días, 'amanuense de abogado, ni amanuense de amanuense que no diserte sobre el estado y cuyas palabras no sean comentadas en calles y cafés'.[47]

Durante la etapa constitucionalista el espacio periodístico limeño exhibió dos grupos definidos. De un lado, el de los críticos del gobierno, en su mayoría bajo el liderazgo de periodistas y editores extranjeros (Gaspar Rico y Fernando López Aldana los más reconocidos) y de otro el periodismo pro-gobiernista subsidiado por la administración Abascal.[48] En este último grupo destacan las figuras de importante letrados criollos — Hipólito Unanue, José Joaquín Larriva, José Baquíjano y Carrillo, Félix Devoti, José Manuel Valdez — todos ellos redactores de *El Verdadero Peruano* y conectados de diversas maneras a la Universidad de San Marcos y al Colegio de San Carlos.[49] Si prestamos atención a la anterior lista de nombres observaremos la presencia en ella de un par de mercuristas. Lo que podría estar sugiriendo

45 Antonio Annino, 'Ciudadanía versus gobernabilidad republicana en México: los orígenes de un dilema,' en Hilda Sabato (ed.), *Ciudadanía política y formación de las naciones: perspectivas históricas de América Latina* (México, 1999), pp. 62–93.

46 Los periódicos que aparecieron en Lima durante la etapa constitucionalista fueron: *Diario Secreto de Lima* (9 números); *El Peruano* (86 números); *El Satélite Peruano* (4 números); *El Verdadero Peruano* (45 números); *El Argos Constitucional* (7 números); *El Cometa* (6 números); *El Investigador* (60 números); *El Peruano Liberal* (18 números).

47 *Colección documental de la Independencia del Perú. T. XXIII. Periódicos. Vol. 2. El Peruano*, edición y prólogo de Carmen Villanueva (Lima, 1971 (en adelante *El Peruano*)).

48 José Fernando de Abascal (1806–16) un funcionario colonial formado en la tradición del despotismo ilustrado de Carlos III, aceptó a regañadientes la solución liberal al impase político que la invasión napoleónica provocó en España. En las memorias que escribió sobre su experiencia en el virreinato peruano Abascal evidenció su desagrado frente a una libertad de imprenta que 'conspiraba contra la ilustración de los pueblos'. La propuesta de Abascal fue encargar a 'las clases más recomendables del Estado' la difusión de las luces. Fernando de Abascal, Memoria de Gobierno (Sevilla, 1944) T. I, pp. 431–8.

49 Para una aproximación biográfica de cada uno de ellos véase Martínez Riaza, *La prensa doctrinal*, pp. 68–93.

que ante el cierre definitivo del *Mercurio*, en 1795, intelectuales como Unanue y Baquíjano optaron por cerrar filas con una administración virreinal, que fue capaz de procurarles una serie de prebendas y beneficios. La fragilidad de un mercurismo a la deriva habría permitido la cooptación de algunos de sus miembros por el gobierno. Sin embargo, las cosas no fueron tan simples como parecían. La existencia en Lima de un grupo de criollos, entre ellos, Jaime Bausate y Mesa, Juan Freyre y Miguel Eyzaguirre, editando a partir de 1811 y por cuenta propia 'El Peruano' o el caso de Bernardino Ruiz, antiguo director de la imprenta del *Mercurio* fungiendo como editor y prologuista de los 'Derechos y deberes del ciudadano',[50] podría estar señalando a la existencia de nuevas tribunas que, al margen del patrocinio estatal, se abrieron a los sectores disidentes de la 'intelligentzia' criolla.

La presencia de Ruiz editando, en su propia imprenta y con su propio dinero, una obra tan importante como los 'Derechos y deberes del ciudadano' evidencia la presencia en la esfera pública limeña de un nuevo sector profesional, el de los impresores. La labor fundamental que ejerció, durante los años del constitucionalismo, el 'impresor y el librero' fue altamente reconocida en el prológo de los 'Derechos y deberes', editado por Ruiz. El impresor, con la finalidad de 'ganar el sustento a costa de su trabajo', acogió con interés los escritos de los periodistas y 'folletistas' republicanos.[51] Los impresores de Lima, entre los que se encontraban Guillermo del Río, Pedro Oyague y el mismo Bernardino Ruiz, se constituyeron en los motores de una activa vida cultural disidente que al no contar con un apoyo oficial absoluto debió de procurarse de su propia autonomía económica.[52] Bernard Baylin ha señalado, para el caso norteamericano, que por ser intermediarios entre el autor y la audiencia, los impresores jugaron un importante papel en el proceso de modelar la cultura republicana. Los impresores, cuyo poder en la formación de la opinión pública en las colonias norteamericanas es sólo comparable a la influencia que ejercieron los curas, desempeñaron al mismo tiempo las funciones de artesanos, empre-

50 Bernardino Ruiz, uno de los impresores más requeridos a partir del período constitucional, fue el encargado de la impresión del *Mercurio* entre los años 1791–94. Para una aproximación a su vida: Clement, *Índices*, p. 211; Carmen Villanueva, introducción a *El Peruano* y Martínez Riaza, *La prensa doctrinal*, p. 101. La obra que Ruiz editó apareció con el título *Derechos y deberes del ciudadano. Versión del idioma oficial al castellano. Impreso en Cádiz en 1812* (Segunda vez reimpresa en Imprenta de los Huérfanos, 1813 por Bernardino Ruiz).

51 *Derechos y deberes*, p. xlvii.

52 Una aproximación al mundo de los impresores limeños es la provista por Martínez Riaza, *La prensa doctrinal*, pp. 98–104.

sarios y líderes culturales.[53] Una situación muy similar a la ocurrida en la Lima de los años del constitucionalismo gaditano.

Un acercamiento al diario *El Peruano*, impreso por Pedro Oyague a partir de setiembre de 1811, puede permitirnos ingresar al fascinante mundo de las letras limeñas durante el interregno constitucionalista.[54] Tres puntos serán tomados en consideración en nuestro análisis del *Peruano*. El primero, su continuidad en la temática y el estilo desarrollado a partir de 1791 por el *Mercurio*; el segundo, su denuncia abierta a las estructuras económicas que sostenían al sistema colonial; y el tercero, su conflictiva relación con la administración Abascal. En la introducción publicada cinco meses después de sancionada la ley de imprenta el editorialista del *Peruano* celebró la 'ruptura de las cadenas' con que la arbitrariedad había acallado a la imprenta. Lo acontecido en Cádiz, anotaba el redactor, significó la liberación del letrado criollo, quién desde ese momento fue capaz de desenvolver libremente el 'germen de sus ideas'. El trabajar en favor de la formación de la 'opinión pública' de cada uno de sus suscriptores, los que eran los únicos 'mecenas' del diario, era para los peruanistas la mayor de las satisfacciones. La libertad política y económica que la situación anterior significó, junto con lo legislado en Cádiz, permitió que los redactores del Peruano hicieran público sus esfuerzos tendientes a curar 'los males de una monarquía achacosa y desorganizada'.[55]

A pesar que el interregno constitucionalista permitió el desarrollo de una prensa más osada, una que, como veremos más adelante, no tuvo ningun reparo en denunciar los vicios estructurales del envejecido sistema colonial, los viejos temas desarrollados por el *Mercurio*, la virtud y la redención de la república mediante la participación en ella de los 'hombres de letras' por ejemplo, no fueron dejados de lado. En un ensayo sobre el

53 Bernard Baylin, *The Ideological Origins of the American Revolution* (Cambridge, MA, 1981) Cathy Davidson ha anotado, también para los Estados Unidos, la conexión entre el surgimiento de un periodismo nativo y elementos tales como el orgullo profesional y el nacionalismo. La existencia de otros factores como la innovación tecnológica, nuevos métodos de distribución, la liberalización del comercio y la voracidad del público lector colaboraron, también, en el desarrollo del periodismo nativo. Las amenazas para el mismo eran lo precario del mercado, el poco capital y la incertidumbre en los gustos del público. Véase Cathy Davidson, *Revolution and the Word: The Rise of the Novel in America* (Oxford, 1986).

54 *El Peruano* se publicó en tres tomos y sesenta y dos números, que aparecieron regularmente todos los martes y viernes hasta el 9 de junio de 1812. Su mayor enfásis estuvo en comentarios políticos y económicos. El valor de este periódico estuvo en el continuar, con mayor agudeza, el espíritu crítico inaugurado por el *Mercurio*.

55 *El Peruano*, 6 de setiembre de 1811.

teatro en Lima, publicado a los pocos días de su inauguración, el tono del artículo puso en evidencia que la disputa por el control del espacio cultural en el que se embarcaron los mercuristas prosiguió, también, entre la 'intelligentzia' criolla que se hizo de un lugar en *El Peruano*. En su análisis sobre el estado de la cultura limeña, el articulista observó cómo el teatro era 'la brújula' que permitía investigarla. El fin del teatro era 'elevar el alma, formar el corazón, excitar el horror a los grandes delitos' y fortalecer 'el amor a las virtudes sublimes'.[56] Un teatro mediocre como el que se exhibía en Lima, carente del apoyo del gobierno, sólo podía servir 'para alimentar la corrupción en los corazones depravados' y para atraer 'el gusto del populacho'.[57] Siguiendo con la vena moralizante que lo asociaba con el *Mercurio*, un redactor anónimo aludió en el mismo número del periódico a la relación entre 'la ruina de las repúblicas' y el 'egoísmo fatal' de su sector pensante. El temor ante una situación que sonaba tan familiar en Lima determinó la propuesta fundamental de *El Peruano*: el convocar a 'todo hombre de letras' con la finalidad que aportara su conocimiento para reformar las costumbres en el país.[58] Es decir, lo que se propició en Lima en 1811 fue la reapertura del diálogo que la desaparición del *Mercurio* truncó. La idea que 'todos los ciudadanos' eran iguales 'bajo el imperio de las leyes'[59] dio cuenta de la lenta transformación de una república de papel a una república política.

El aire de familia entre el *Mercurio Peruano* y su hermano menor *El Peruano* no se remitió a coincidencias en cuanto a la temática y al estilo que obviamente los emparentó. La retórica clara y simple, el apoyo a los ideales republicanos y la crítica a la cultura hegemónica, despótica y cortesana,[60] junto con la mención constante de los logros alcanzados en el pasado por su antecesor el *Mercurio* muestra las coincidencias entre sus autores.[61] El

56 *El Peruano*, 17 de setiembre de 1811.

57 Para una conexión entre el teatro y el desarrollo de las virtudes republicanas, véase Ann Mellor, *Mothers of the Nation: Women's Political Writing in England, 1780–1830* (Bloomington e Indianapolis, 2000), pp. 37–68.

58 'Los hombres de luces, los genios privilegiados, los xefes de provincia que por necesidad las conocen … en fin todo conciudadano reflexivo y pensador debe de concurrir con sus observaciones a perfeccionar quanto sea posible a nuestro Peruano' (*El Peruano*, 17 de setiembre de 1811.).

59 *El Peruano*, 24 de abril de 1812.

60 Para estos puntos véase por ejemplo 'Carta de un invisible, sobre donativos para la península', en *El Peruano*, 27 de setiembre de 1811; 'Carta remitida,' en *El Peruano*, 8 de octubre de 1811; 'El invisible,' en *El Peruano*, 11 de octubre de 1811; 'Carta de un Anciano,' en *El Peruano*, 5 de noviembre de 1811.

61 Las referencias más claras en *El Peruano*, 20 de setiembre de 1811, 8 de octubre de 1811 y 25 de octubre de 1811.

ensanchamiento de la esfera pública, cabe recordar los mecanismos de distribución de *El Peruano* el que se vendía regularmente en la mayoría de los almacenes de la ciudad,[62] el uso de un lenguaje más popular que el utilizado por el *Mercurio*,[63] su crítica aguda al sistema económico sobre el que descansaba el edificio colonial, junto con la incorporación de una visión política de la nación, son probablemente algunos de los aportes innovadores del *Peruano* a la discusión en la remozada esfera pública limeña. Su intención de desenmascarar al 'despotismo rentista', herencia directa de la contradictoria política económica ilustrada, nos permiten observar, sin embargo, cómo la propuesta de recrear una 'república de las letras' sólida debía pasar por el desmantelamiento de la cultura y de la estructura económica prevaleciente. Ésta última, al descansar sobre un sistema prebendario y de privilegios para un puñado de favoritos, era responsable de la permanente desocupación que reinaba en Lima.[64] Dentro de un contexto en el que la posición frente al comercio libre varió de un inicial entusiasmo a una gran preocupación por la suerte de los productores nacionales, *El Peruano* estableció la temprana conexión entre nacionalismo y autonomía económica.[65]

El 1 de marzo de 1812, 67 personas solicitaron la censura de todos los números de *El Peruano* publicados hasta entonces. Cincuenta y cuatro números fueron remitidos por el virrey a la junta que sólo dictaminó contra dos. El periódico fue calificado de sedicioso porque, al hacer público su desagrado de que la soberanía no residiera en América, combatía uno de los fundamentos de la monarquía, su indivisibilidad. Entre las acusaciones la junta consideró, también, sediciosa la frase que instaba a los americanos a instruirse para conocer y procurar el remedio de los males que padecían, porque indirectamente sugería que los peruanos podían buscar medios ilegales para resolver sus problemas. Ante el pedido de la junta para que el editor e impresor de *El Peruano*, Guillermo del Río, entregara los ejemplares 'sediciosos', él mismo declaró que éstos se habían vendido o regalado. El 9 de abril la junta dio a Abascal la autorización para suspender la publicación del periódico. Unos días después, ante el desacato a la autori-

62 *El Peruano*, 29 de octubre de 1811.

63 Para la dimensión popular del *Peruano* véase el tono y el lenguaje de los escritos de 'La Barahunda', 'El Invisible', 'El Anciano', 'Juan Lorenzo Matamoros y Tricio', 'El Preguntón' o 'Juan sin Tierra'.

64 *El Peruano*, 11 de octubre y 8 de noviembre de 1811

65 'Diálogo entre el Editor y el Invisible,' en *El Peruano*, 5 de noviembre de 1811. En este artículo los autores denunciaban a las autoridades responsables de otorgar a 'los extranjeros' permiso para introducir 'cincuenta millones de pesos' y de arruinar a 'los comerciantes, hacendados y artesanos …' Los que, en palabras de los autores, fueron acosados 'por alguaciles y escribanos, executores de la que ellos llaman justicia'.

dad mostrada por los redactores de *El Peruano*, la Junta Censoria acusó públicamente al periódico 'por la influencia que podía ejercer sobre el orden público'. A pesar de lo anterior el periódico no dejó de publicarse y no cedió en su intento de criticar al absolutismo de Abascal. La paciencia del virrey mostró sus límites el 23 de junio de 1814. Ese día, la junta opinó por la suspensión definitiva de *El Peruano* para 'cortar el cáncer' que al esparcirse sobre el cuerpo social peruano podía producir los efectos que se observaba en otras provincias americanas. A pesar que la Junta Suprema de Cádiz falló a favor de los periodistas peruanos estableciendo que el periódico podía volver a publicarse, *El Peruano* se despidió en junio de su público lector siendo más adelante reemplazado por *El Satélite Peruano*.[66]

En los años del constitucionalismo se discutieron muchos de los temas abordados por *El Peruano*. Un ejemplo de ello es el prólogo a la traducción de los *Deberes y derechos del ciudadano*, editado por el impresor Bernardino Ruiz. La denuncia a la corrupción y al servilismo prevaleciente, en donde 'la audiencia de un favorito, un magistrado' o un poderoso 'con aires de importancia' ocurría 'en medio de una multitud de infelices pretendientes' que esperaban 'mudos e inmóviles' y 'temblando' la contestación de sus solicitudes, y que incluso consideraban como un favor 'una sola mirada o una sola palabra' de los detentadores del poder acercó a Ruiz a la noción de que no podía haber virtud en 'almas esclavas'.[67] En efecto, a partir de 'la primavera democrática gaditana' la discusión en torno a la nación no sólo se restringió a la noción previamente enunciada por los mercuristas, la de una sociabilidad asociada a una cultura urbana, sino que apuntó a evidenciar la necesidad de crear una sociedad de derecho en la cual la moral y la virtud ciudadana pudieran ser resguardadas. En conclusión, y como afirmaba el prólogo, un gobierno sólo podía hacer felices a sus pueblos cuando junto a la ilustración era capaz de 'procurar y defender sus leyes y su constitución'.[68] Los temas desarrollados en el prólogo de la obra editada por Ruiz buscaron llamar la atención, como sus antecesores en torno a valores republicanos tan fundamentales como la virtud, la dignidad y el mérito. Virtud, estabilidad política y armonía social constituyeron conceptos indivisibles que sólo podían hacerse efectivos dentro de un régimen donde reinara la ley y no la arbitrariedad.

66 CDIP. *Periódicos*. T. XXIII. *El Peruano*, edición y prólogo Carmen Villanueva, pp. xv–xix.

67 *Derechos y deberes*, p. xiv.

68 *Ibid.*, p. lxiii; una discusión sobre el lento proceso de elaboración del concepto de ciudadanía y sus conexiones con el pensamiento político de la Ilustración es provista por José Carlos Chiaramonte, 'Ciudadanía, soberanía y representación en la genésis del Estado argentino (1810–1852),' en Sabato (comp.), *Ciudadanía política*, pp. 94–116.

El reforzamiento, durante los años del constitucionalismo, de una esfera pública en la que se articuló con más claridad el vocabulario conceptual del republicanismo, en sus dos dimensiones (el de sociabilidad y el del gobierno de la ley), es un aspecto que merece un análisis más detenido del que se le ha otorgado. Por otro lado, la existencia de un aspecto moral en el republicanismo peruano, la alusión que hace Ruiz a la dignidad humana por ejemplo o el de los peruanistas cuando señalan al 'lujo' como destructor de la unidad familiar, es un elemento que permite explorarlo más allá de los aspectos meramente políticos. El vínculo del republicanismo peruano con elementos de la Ilustración Católica[69] muestra la unidad entre ética y política existente durante esos años.[70] El lenguaje del republicanismo constitucionalista, más osado debido a la protección provista por la Constitución de Cádiz, aunque retomando la vieja discusión iniciada por los mercuristas, fue creando los cimientos intelectuales que posibilitaron la elaboración de un sinnúmero de argumentos políticos que serán continuados en la década siguiente por la prensa doctrinal. En los mismos, como veremos a continuación, la 'intelligentzia' criolla logró arribar a una teoría y a una praxis política que ni los mercuristas ni el periodismo constitucionalista fueron capaces de cristalizar.

¿Vasallos o ciudadanos?: prensa doctrinal y definición política en Lima, 1821–22

Los años que sucedieron a la 'primavera gaditana' fueron en el Perú de una brutal represión.[71] La misma se efectuó no sólo contra los focos rebeldes peruanos, sino contra la disidencia chilena y altoperuana. En la etapa post-constitucionalista el virreinato del Perú lideró la reacción conservadora, cuyo episodio más brutal fue la batalla de Rancagua. La represión militar iniciada primero por Abascal y continuada, después, por Joaquín de la Pezuela y José de la Serna, determinó el descabezamiento de todos los

69 Melchor de Jovellanos (1744–1811), representante de la Ilustración Católica española, fue uno de los primeros en denunciar la decadencia moral, política y cultural por la que atravesaba España.

70 Para una crítica a las aproximaciones que separan el mundo de la ética del mundo de la política véase Richard Morse, 'Notes towards Fresh Ideology,' en *New World Soundings* (Baltimore and London, 1989), pp. 131–69.

71 Una de las mejores aproximaciones a este punto es la provista por José de la Riva-Agüero y Sánchez Boquete, *Manifestación histórica y política de la revolución de la América y más especialmente de la parte que corresponde al Perú y Río de la Plata. Obra escrita en Lima, centro de la opresión y del despotismo en el año de 1816* (Buenos Aires, 1818).

focos rebeldes regionales peruanos.[72] Uno por uno estos fueron destruidos, siendo sus principales promotores asesinados o deportados. El efecto que la política reaccionaria tuvo sobre la configuración política del Perú post-Independencia, es un tema que aún aguarda por su historiador. La destrucción del liderazgo regional peruano, el que exhibió nombres propios como los de Mateo Pumacahua, Francisco Antonio de Zela, Mariano Melgar, José Gabriel Bejar, José Pinelo, Ildefonso Muñecas, Juan José Crespo y Castillo o los hermanos Angulo, impidió la creación, durante el período republicano, de núcleos civiles provincianos con la autonomía y la legitimidad política suficiente para convertirse en poderes autónomos.[73] Esta situación que posteriormente favoreció la hegemonía del caudillismo militar y el control político-ideológico ejercido débilmente por Lima es una entre las muchas herencias que dejó el régimen colonial a la República Peruana. La otra fue el desarrollo, entre la 'intelligentzia' nativa, de una política subterránea que derivó hacia un republicanismo radical y que, ante la ausencia de otros espacios organizativos, hizo de la prensa su más preciada morada.

Los meses previos a la llegada de la Expedición Libertadora, encabezada por José de San Martín, fueron de gran excitación en Lima.[74] Las labores de espionaje en las que se embarcaron los enviados del militar rioplatense, el activo rol de la prensa clandestina limeña, junto con los conflictos al interior del ejército realista, evidenciados en el derrocamiento del virrey Pezuela,[75] fueron algunas de las causas, otras fueron la crisis económica y las deserciones entre las burocracias civiles y militares, que aceleraron el derrumbe del edificio colonial. El bloqueo a la costa peruana, iniciado el 26 de febrero de 1818, seguido del posterior bombardeo del Callao, a cargo de las fuerzas patriotas encabezadas por el Almirante Cochrane, propinaron un duro golpe a la economía limeña, la que había venido sufriendo los embates del comercio libre y de una

72 José Fernando de Abascal partió de vuelta a España a mediados de julio de 1816. El 7 de julio de ese mismo año Joaquín de la Pezuela asumió el gobierno colonial. El 29 de enero de 1821 Pezuela fue depuesto mediante un motín militar que llevó a José de la Serna a convertirse en el último virrey del Perú.

73 Para un acercamiento a cada uno de los levantamientos rebeldes previos a la Independencia véase Félix Denegri Luna, *Antología de la Independencia del Perú* (Lima), pp. 171–213.

74 *Sesquicentenario de la Expedición Libertadora del Perú, 1820–1970* (Buenos Aires, 1970); Alberto Tauro del Pino, CDIP. T. XXXIII, *Periódicos*, vol. 1, pp. xiii–xviii; xx–xxiv.

75 Un acercamiento a este punto es el provisto por Andrés García Camba, *Memoria para la historia de las armas españolas en el Perú por el General Camba* (Madrid, 1824), T. I, pp. 334 y 343.

prolongada guerra.[76] En vísperas de la llegada de San Martín al Perú el burócrata colonial Manuel Pardo y Ribadeneyra describió a la capital del virreinato como un lugar en el que 'la confusión y el horror habían sentado sus reales'.[77] Dentro del contexto anterior, la opción por la Independencia, que generó serias dudas entre algunos miembros de la élites nativa, fue percibida como una solución pragmática al vacío de poder provocado por la huida de La Serna a la sierra. Ante el realineamiento de la élite nativa, un sector abandonó Lima con La Serna mientras que el otro negoció una salida política con San Martín, lo que dio origen al gobierno protectoral. Él mismo fue una suerte de transición política controlada que se pensó podía abrir un camino 'ordenado' a la inevitable ruptura con España.[78]

Durante los meses que antecedieron a la llegada de San Martín, la esfera pública limeña se vio inundada de panfletos que estimulaban a la rebelión, a la vez que celebraban los valores de la vida republicana.[79] La agudización de la guerra estimuló la actividad de los impresores que unos años antes fueron silenciados por Abascal. Imprentas como la Republicana, la de la Libertad, la de San Jacinto o la de Peña, se unieron a las existentes, la de Guillermo del Río, la de Bernardino Ruiz y a la de los Huérfanos, para repotencializar una 'república de las letras' seriamente dañada por la política represiva de las autoridades coloniales. Las 'tertulias patrióticas' en boticas, cafés y salones se volvieron menos clandestinas en la medida que las noticias del desembarco de San Martín en Paracas arribaron a Lima.[80] Una aproximación a la temática exhibida en los panfletos, poesías y obras de teatro publicados en el año del arribo de la Expedición Libertadora permite seguirle la pista a algunos de los temas que hemos venido analizando a lo largo de este capitulo.

76 Alberto Flores Galindo, *Aristocracia y plebe: Lima 1760–1830* (Lima, 1983), pp. 209–29.

77 Timothy Anna, 'Economic Causes of San Martín's Failure in Lima,' en *Hispanic American Historical Review*, vol. 54, no. 4 (November 1974), p. 660.

78 McEvoy, 'El motín de las palabras', pp. 12–18.

79 Para este punto hemos revisado los siguientes panfletos y obras de teatro: *Lima Libre: canción patriótica* (Lima, 1821); *Canción Lima* (Lima, 1821); *Marcha patriótica* (Lima, 1821); *El honor y la virtud: canción patriótica* (Lima, 1821); Mateo de Otero, *Poema Joco-serio* (Lima, 1821); *A Lima Libre* (Lima, 1821); *Correspondencia turca* (Lima, 1821); *Representación de América al divino tribunal* (Lima, 1821; *Los patriotas de Lima en la noche feliz: drama en dos actos* (Lima, 1821); *Para un brindis de chicha* (Lima, 1821). Para el efecto de la actividad panfletaria en la desintegración del régimen colonial en los Estados Unidos véase Baylin, *Pamphlets of the American Revolution, 1750–1776* (Cambridge, MA, 1971).

80 Los expedicionarios fueron responsables de la publicación de *El Censor de la Revolución*, *El Pacificador del Perú*, *El Americano*, *El Consolador*, *Los Andes Libres* y *El Nuevo Depositario.*

El discurso republicano dio muestras de su enorme vitalidad en Lima durante el decisivo año de 1821. Los temas que se ventilaron en los innumerables panfletos que inundaron la capital del virreinato español incidieron en conceptos como la virtud, la moralidad, el honor, el orden, la 'maternidad republicana' y las responsabilidades de los hombres de letras en el nuevo régimen que se avecinaba. El año en que se juró la Independencia peruana el *Common Sense* del inglés Thomas Paine fue publicado en Lima en la imprenta de Guillermo del Río.[81] Cabe recordar que esta obra, uno de los panfletos políticos más importantes en habla inglesa, fue traducida en Londres, en 1811, por Anselmo Natieu, 'indígena del Perú'. El *Common Sense*, constantemente citado por el periodismo limeño, fue considerado — debido a 'los principios luminosos' que comunicaba — como una pieza fundamental de teoría política republicana.[82] Y es que si aceptamos la opinión del burócrata colonial Manuel Pardo y Ribadeneyra, fue el 'ejemplo angloamericano' el que desde 1814 se encargó de sentar las pautas y de sostener 'las esperanzas de los patriotas peruanos'.[83] La conexión entre algunos de ellos con los impresores de Filadelfia es una muestra que la Independencia de los Estados Unidos, lugar donde 'la humanidad recuperó la dignidad perdida', fue seguida con interés desde el virreinato del Perú.[84] La profunda admiración por la Independencia de las trece colonias inglesas expresada en el prospecto del

81 Para la conexión del Río–Paine véase Martínez Riaza, *La prensa doctrinal*, p. 160. Thomas Paine (1737–1809) llegó a Filadelfia, procedente de Gran Bretaña, el 30 de Noviembre de 1774. Su idea inicial era inaugurar una escuela para la educación de mujeres jóvenes. En la colonia inglesa obtuvo un trabajo como editor del *Pennsylvania Magazine* donde publicó muchos de sus ensayos y poemas. En 1776 publicó el *Common Sense* y en 1791 el *Rights of Man*, como respuesta a los ataques de Edmund Burke. En 1792 fue elegido miembro de la Convención Francesa. Los escritos de Paine muestran su resentimiento con la estructura social inglesa. En muchos de sus artículos opuso la corrupción inglesa a la virtud y a la decencia norteamericana. Paine mostró un especial interés por defender los ideales de la Independencia norteamericana, articulando lo que la historiografía estadounidense ha dado en llamar el republicanismo. Para una aproximación a la vida y obra de Paine véase Thomas Paine, *Political Writings*, edited by Bruce Kuklick (Cambridge, 1998) y Eric Foner, *Tom Paine and Revolutionary America* (Londres, 1976).

82 *Los Andes Libres*, 24 de noviembre de 1821.

83 'La celébre Memoria del Regente de la Audiencia del Cuzco sobre los antecedentes y desarrollo de la Revolución de 1814,' en *Boletín del Museo Bolivariano* (Lima, Junio-Agosto, 1930), año II, no. 16, pp. 284–294).

84 Filadelfia fue el lugar que Francisco de Miranda escogió como señuelo cuando publicó en Londres 'La carta a los españoles americanos,' del peruano Juan Pablo Vizcardo y Guzmán. En 1823, Lorenzo de Vidaurre publicó en Filadelfia, *Cartas americanas, políticas y morales que contienen muchas reflexiones sobre la Guerra Civil de las Americas*, 2 vols. (Filadelfia, 1823).

diario limeño *El Republicano* estaba asociada, según su editor, al hecho que en América del Norte 'la virtud y el mérito' lograron derrotar 'al rango y a la nobleza'.[85] La constante mención a George Washington, quién usó la obra de Paine para arengar a su tropa antes de cruzar el Delaware, y a pasajes de la historia de los Estados Unidos, cuya versión concisa se vendió con bastante éxito en la librería de la Calle del Arzobispo, fue puesta de manifiesto entre los escritores republicanos limeños.[86]

Para el año en que los peruanos desenterraron el *Common Sense* y *Los derechos del hombre* su autor ya no era el ídolo popular, capaz de vender 300,000 copias de sus panfletos. Cuando en 1811 Anselmo Natieu descubre y traduce a Paine, los estadounidenses ya habían mostrado su preocupación en torno a las posibilidades de transformar al republicanismo igualitario en una administración política eficiente. Hacia 1810 el escenario europeo cambió radicalmente. Una tendencia conservadora y cautelosa posibilitó la propaganda anti-Paine no sólo en Europa sino también en los Estados Unidos.[87] Los problemas socioeconómicos en Inglaterra, unidos a los conflictos políticos fuera del país enfriaron los peligrosos radicalismos de los que Paine fue abanderado. Aquellos empezaron a moverse lentamente hacia las colonias de España. A partir de 1810 una a una éstas fueron cayendo al declarar su independencia de la Madre Patria. Fue a partir de la vuelta de un nuevo ciclo revolucionario que Paine junto con sus escritos resucitó en Latinoamérica. Ya desde 1810 el *Common Sense* y *Los derechos del hombre*, escritos por Paine, habían sido traducidos al español por la primera vez. En los años siguientes, extractos de sus trabajos circularon en los territorios de Argentina, Perú, Uruguay y Venezuela. Los escritos de Paine fueron recibidos con entusiasmo por una nueva generación de lectores que desconocían al autor.[88] Dentro de aquellos estuvieron los redactores de *La Abeja Republicana*, especialmente el preclaro representante del republicanismo peruano, Faustino Sánchez Carrión.

85 *El Republicano*, 30 de agosto de 1822.

86 Para citas sobre Washington y la experiencia norteamericana véase *La Abeja Republicana*, edición facsimilar, 1971, pp. 59, 83, 98, 101–02. El libro de historia que se vendía en Lima era *Historia concisa de los Estados Unidos desde el descubrimiento hasta el año 1807*. El dato es provisto por *Los Andes Libres*, 10 de noviembre de 1821.

87 Foner, *Tom Paine and Revolutionary America*, pp. 261–70.

88 George Spater, 'The Legacy of Thomas Paine,' en Ian Dyck (ed.), *Citizen of the World: Essays on Thomas Paine* (New York, 1988), p. 132. En 1817, en medio de la campaña reformista en Inglaterra, la colección completa de trabajos de Paine fue reeditada. Resulta probable pensar que fue durante esos años que la comunidad de exilados latinoamericanos en Londres se haya acercado más rigurosamente a Paine. Para un análisis sobre esta comunidad y sobre el papel que jugó en la elaboración de la ideología política en Hispanoamérica, véase Karen Racine, 'Imagining Independence: London's Spanish American Community, 1790–1830' (PhD Dissertation, Tulane University, 1996).

La reinstauración de la libertad de imprenta colaboró en el surgimiento de la prensa doctrinal peruana.[89] Los temas que se discutieron a partir de 1821 en la esfera pública limeña fueron una continuación, con ciertas variaciones, de aquellos desarrollados desde 1791. Entre 1821 y 1822 periódicos como el *Correo Mercantil, Político y Literario*, *El Republicano*, *La Abeja Republicana* y *El Tribuno de la República Peruana* se embarcaron en la tarea de defender el frágil republicanismo peruano frente a la opción monárquica representada por José de San Martín y Bernardo Monteagudo. En marzo de 1822 un escrito publicado por Faustino Sánchez Carrión en *El Correo Mercantil*, 'Carta sobre la inadaptabilidad del gobierno monárquico al Estado libre del Perú', dio inicio del combate político-ideológico que culminó con la derrota de la opción monárquica y con la caída del régimen protectoral.[90] Es interesante anotar cómo el republicanismo fortalecido a partir de la Independencia fue capaz de articularse políticamente y acorralar al régimen inaugurado por San Martín.[91] Sánchez Carrión fue parte activa de la 'intelligentzia' peruana que lideró la reacción republicana limeña contra la política autoritaria del gobierno protectoral. Sánchez Carrión, quien junto con otros intelectuales peruanos, fue haciéndose de un espacio en los años de la represión y de la guerra, representa la cristalización de un republicanismo que, no contento con su hegemonía en la esfera de las letras, decidió asumir un rol activo en las movilizaciones urbanas que desembocaron el 26 de julio de 1822 con la remoción del secretario de gobierno e ideólogo del protectorado, Bernardo Monteagudo. Como profesor de San Marcos, Sánchez Carrión fue testigo de excepción de la militarización del régimen colonial. En 1818, año en que recibió su título de abogado, el trujillano fue expulsado de San Marcos por el virrey Pezuela. Lo anterior determinó su alejamiento de la política y su retiro al pueblo de Sayán. Desde ahí aplaudió la llegada de la Expedición Libertadora, aunque mantuvo distancia frente a la transacción política que permitió el surgimiento del régimen

89 El decreto del gobierno protectoral que posibilitó la reapertura de la esfera pública limeña fue publicado en *Gaceta de Gobierno*, 17 de octubre de 1821.

90 Faustino Sánchez Carrión, 'Carta sobre la inadaptabilidad del gobierno monárquico al estado libre del Perú,' en Raúl Ferrero, *El liberalismo peruano: contribución a una historia de las ideas* (Lima, 1958), pp. 83–93. Esta carta fue una respuesta a la discusión que con la finalidad de apoyar el régimen monárquico constitucional, Bernardo Monteagudo propició en la Sociedad Patriótica de Lima. Para los términos de la discusión véase César Pacheco Velez, 'La Sociedad Patriótica de Lima de 1822. Primer capítulo en la historia de las ideas políticas en el Perú republicano,' en *Histórica* vol. XXIX (Lima, 1978).

91 Para un estudio detenido de las movilizaciones políticas del 25 y 26 de julio de 1822, que determinaron el triunfo de la opción republicana y que tuvieron como caja de resonancia la prensa limeña véase: McEvoy, 'El motín de las palabras,' pp. 32–53.

protectoral. Las críticas de Sánchez Carrión al régimen impuesto por San Martín, en alianza con sectores sobrevivientes de la nobleza, arreciaron en la medida que el trujillano percibió, junto con otros miembros de la 'intelligentzia' nativa, que la independencia no conduciría a la instauración del régimen republicano en el Perú.

Un análisis de la 'Carta sobre la inadaptabilidad del gobierno monárquico' permite aproximarnos a un republicanismo maduro el que además de reiterar los viejos temas que le precedieron — virtud, orden y ciudadanía — fue capaz de introducir nuevos argumentos y una estrategia política exitosa. Un acercamiento a la retórica republicana, post-Independencia, ayuda a que descubramos ciertos elementos que lo emparentan con el republicanismo norteamericano, del cual Thomas Paine fue precoz vocero. Cabe anotar que la influencia de Paine entre los escritores peruanos no surgió de improviso. La misma puede rastrearse, como hemos observado previamente, al último lustro del siglo XVIII. En efecto, el argumento de la distancia geográfica utilizado por Vizcardo y Guzmán en su 'Carta a los Españoles Americanos', y retomado años después por *El Sol del Perú*, guarda una enorme similitud con lo expuesto por el panfletero inglés.[92] Por otro lado en *La Abeja Republicana*,[93] periódico que se encargó de publicitar los escritos de Sánchez Carrión y de Paine, se pone en evidencia la presencia de una de las ideas fundamentales del autor del *Common Sense*: aquella que planteó que a partir de la instauración

92 'La naturaleza nos ha separado de España por medio de inmensos mares' ('Carta a los Españoles Americanos,' en Juan Pablo Vizcardo y Guzmán, *Obras completas* (Lima, 1998), T. I, p. 215. 'Ahora sí tenemos una Patria que nos pertenece, una Patria que no será subastada a cuatro mil leguas de distancia, una Patria sobre la que no especulará la codicia española' (*El Sol del Perú*, 4 de abril de 1822).

93 Entre los periódicos que optan por la defensa de la república destaca la labor de la *La Abeja Republicana*. 'Pequeño y laborioso', a decir de Alberto Tauro del Pino, como el insecto del cual obtenía su nombre, el periódico trabajó por los ideales republicanos que en los planes del Protectorado fueron, de acuerdo a Tauro, dejados de lado. El periódico apareció los días jueves y domingo de cada semana. En su año de vida (Agosto 1822–Abril 1823) *La Abeja* fomentó el quiebre de las concepciones de la aristocracia criolla y se propuso efectuar un trabajo tenaz y sistemático para demostrar la oportunidad y la viabilidad de la idea civil. El periódico declaró hallarse sujeto a un programa. Dirigir la opinión de los ciudadanos, defender los principios republicanos vinculados a la libertad, igualdad, seguridad y propiedad y convencer a los lectores mediante la alegación de los argumentos comprobados por la razón fueron algunos de los fundamentos del mismo (véase prólogo de Tauro a la edición facsimilar de *La Abeja Republicana*).

de un gobierno republicano era posible empezar el mundo de nuevo.[94] Lo anterior, unido a una característica esencial del imaginario político de Paine, su ambigüedad entre una visión lockeana de la sociedad (en busca de los derechos naturales de individuos que competían unos con otros) y la noción del bien común (lo que aludía a los valores de una sociedad corporativa), permiten entender porque su modelo resultó tan atractivo para una 'intelligentzia' que, como la peruana, estaba buscando argumentos para oponerse al monarquismo oficialista sin dejar de lado los aspectos comunitarios de la cultura política peruana.[95]

Sánchez Carrión, al igual que Paine, fue uno de los creadores del lenguaje secular de la revolución política y cultural limeña que la independencia trajo a la superficie. En dicho lenguaje, desarrollado a lo largo de tres décadas, los descontentos, las aspiraciones milenaristas y las tradiciones culturales fueron expresadas mediante un vocabulario simple y elocuente.[96] La posibilidad que tuvieron los republicanos peruanos de hegemonizar la esfera cultural estuvo estrechamente unida al declive de la nobleza peruana. La misma fue seriamente golpeada por la política económica del gobierno protectoral.[97] En su 'Carta sobre la inadaptabilidad' Sánchez Carrión sacó la discusión política a la esfera pública[98] y defendió al sistema republicano, del que Estados Unidos era el abanderado,[99] como la única salida viable para curar los males del país. Estos males no sólo eran políticos sino también culturales.[100] Lo que hace único a

94 'Estamos en el principio de los tiempos: nuestra sociedad se va a formar como si el mundo hubiese acabado de salir de las manos de su Creador' (*La Abeja Republicana*, 26 de setiembre de 1822). Para el mismo tema en Paine, *Political Writings*, p. 120.

95 Para la visión ambigua de Paine véase Foner, *Thomas Paine*, pp. 71–106. Para la ambivalencia del republicanismo peruano véase McEvoy, 'El motín de las palabras,' pp. 50–1 y 'Forjando la nación: usos y abusos del paradigma republicano,' pp. 196–203.

96 Sánchez Carrión se propuso omitir todo lo que oliera a 'erudición insípida e impertinente'. Para una aproximación a la sencillez republicana véase, por ejemplo, el artículo 'La sencillez es el sello de la verdad,' en *Los Andes Libres*, 31 de julio de 1821.

97 McEvoy, 'El motín de las palabras,' pp. 27–8.

98 'No es esta una negociación de gentes privadas, ni se ha propuesto esclarecer la sucesión de un mayorazgo' (Sánchez Carrión, 'Carta sobre la inadaptabilidad,' p. 84)

99 'Los ingleses de Norte América fueron colonos como nosotros, aspiraron a su Independencia y la consiguieron; asentaron felizmente las bases de su Constitución. Con solo trocar la cara al Norte vemos abierto el inefable libro, en que con caracteres de oro se lee Libertad, Igualdad, Seguridad y Propiedad' (*Ibid.*, p. 93).

100 'Debilitada nuestra fuerza, y avezados al sistema colonial, cuya educación debe habernos dado una segunda naturaleza, ¿qué seríamos?, ¿qué tendríamos?, ¿cómo hablaríamos ante la presencia de un monarca? … Seríamos excelentes vasallos y nunca ciudadanos … y nuestro mayor placer consistiría en que Su Majestad extendiese su real mano para que la besemos… ' (*Ibid.*, p. 88).

Sánchez Carrión, y en eso su labor es comparable con la realizada anteriormente por Paine, es su capacidad de cristalizar un nuevo lenguaje político mediante una retórica clara y concisa. El uso de frases capaces de cautivar la atención de su audiencia ('seríamos excelentes vasallos y nunca ciudadanos') y su alejamiento del lenguaje erudito, del cual sus antecesores habían empezado a tomar distancia, forjaron estrechas conexiones con la experiencia común del público lector. A través de su 'elocuencia democrática' Sánchez Carrión comunicó su visión de la nueva sociedad que debía de surgir luego de las guerras de la emancipación. En dicha visión se pusieron de manifiesto muchas de las ideas discutidas en Lima desde 1791.

La 'utopía republicana' que cruza todo el siglo XIX y parte del XX y que tiene como características la búsqueda del bien común y del orden, la solidaridad entre las clases sociales, la preocupación por el desarrollo de la virtud ciudadana y el papel que en todos los anteriores desarrollos les correspondía a los intelectuales y a la educación, aparece por primera vez y de manera elocuente en la 'Carta sobre la inadaptabilidad'. Si bien es cierto, como hemos intentado probar en este trabajo, mucho del contenido conceptual del republicanismo peruano se fue gestando desde los años de la Ilustración, fue la discusión frontal con la tesis monarquista, la que lo proveyó de sustento teórico y de las características que hoy le reconocemos. La visión utópica de la sociedad post-Independencia en la que, en palabras de Sánchez Carrión, la población se centuplicaría, las costumbres se descolonizarían, la ilustración llegaría a su máximo y las calles lucirían empedradas de oro y plata, transformando al cementerio colonial en 'patria de vivientes' muestran inocultables influencias católicas pero también ciertos rasgos del republicanismo radical y utópico de Paine.[101] La cristalización del discurso republicano mediante una praxis concreta, evidenciada en las movilizaciones del 25 y el 26 de julio de 1822, permite entrever la gran mutación por la que atravesó el republicanismo peruano. En el escenario provisto por la ciudad de Lima el intelectual nativo, cuya identidad estuvo tradicionalmente asociada al acto de escribir, se transformó en un actor político. Mientras ensayaba su audaz experimento el impotente letrado de antaño logró convocar a los 'ciudadanos lectores', aquellos miembros de la vieja 'república de las letras', instaurada en los años de la Ilustración. Las características 'multiclasistas' del motín promovido por la 'intelligentzia' republicana nos ha permitido sugerir que su visión era la de una sociedad guiada por un bien común armonioso, más que por uno dividido en clases en conflicto. La apuesta de estos letrados convertidos en

101 Para las dimensiones utópicas en Paine, véase Foner, *Tom Paine*, p. xvi.

políticos fue por el orden y por la necesidad de preservar ciertos valores tradicionales, los que como su misma posición social, eran amenazados por la revolución que, paradójicamente, ellos fomentaron con sus palabras.

Epílogo: los desafíos de la República

El 17 de agosto de 1822, a escasas semanas de la instalación del Primer Congreso Constituyente, Faustino Sánchez Carrión envió una segunda carta a *La Abeja Republicana.* En la misma el futuro secretario de la Primera Asamblea Constituyente pretendió alertar al público lector sobre los peligros de una 'república mal constituida'.[102] Cada institución civil adolecía, en palabras del escritor trujillano, de 'un secreto defecto'. Para el caso de la república éste era la anarquía, que podía conducirla 'en contra de su mismo objeto'. Para ser 'libres, grandes, prósperos y felices' no era suficiente 'desear y pedir república'. Y es que si a cambio de las esperanzas que la república había suscitado, los peruanos iban a obtener 'la túnica de Hércules teñida con la sangre del Centauro' era preferible no aceptarla. Así, en unos cuantos meses el republicanismo peruano cambió de tono. Del idealismo inicial se paso a un pragmatismo cauto y definitivamente menos optimista.

La solución al inmenso desafío planteado por la Independencia, que ya había sido percibido algunos años antes por la intelectualidad norteamericana,[103] demandó de una solución prágmatica. La misma debió de guardar distancia de la utopía igualitaria y de la efervescencia revolucionaria de la primera hora. En la etapa post-protectoral la tarea se centró en realizar la difícil transición de una comunidad retórica a una comunidad política. Para

102 'Nunca fue más tiranizada la república romana que cuando la rigieron los decenviros ... que los venecianos se lisongean de llamarse repúblicos, obedeciendo a un senado aristocrático; y que Marat y Robespierre humanados tigres, casi dejaron yerma la Francia por cimentar la República' ('Carta remitida a *La Abeja Republicana* sobre la forma de gobierno conveniente al Perú,' en Ferrero, *El liberalismo peruano*, pp. 95–6.

103 Para fines del siglo XVIII los teóricos políticos norteamericanos estaban desarrollando la idea que el conflicto social era inevitable. James Madison rechazó la idea de una sociedad 'enteramente ficticia' en la que todos poseían los mismos intereses. Ninguna sociedad podía consistir de un grupo homogéneo de ciudadanos. Era por ello necesario construir un gobierno capaz de balancear los grupos de interés, evitando que las facciones se atacaran entre sí. Para Madison un gobierno representativo más que ser un experimento utópico era un instrumento institucional capaz de evitar que los faccionalismos destruyeran al Estado. La democracia podía crear anarquía y por ello una buena constitución requería que un gobierno 'mixto' chequeara las pasiones de la gente y de los grupos de interés. Para este punto véase Richard Hofardster, *The Idea of the Party System* (Berkeley, 1969).

Sánchez Carrión la clave para mantener la armonía política era la separación de los poderes. El símil que utilizó para explicar su visión era la del sol alrededor del cual todos los planetas giraban 'sostenidos por dos fuerzas opuestas'. Lo anterior evitaba que los componentes de este peculiar sistema solar se saliesen de 'sus órbitas' posibilitando, así en esa 'admirable máquina' un orden que no se perturbaría 'sino con el fin de los tiempos'. En sus palabras era 'la oposición de la naturaleza' la que mantenía a 'toda la naturaleza en paz'. La meta era desconcentrar el poder político que la agudización de la Guerra de la Independencia había llevado hasta límites insoportables. Sánchez Carrión propuso la construcción de un sistema político que, a la manera norteamericana, fuera capaz de crear un balance entre los diferentes grupos de interés. No era por ello una coincidencia que el epígrafe de su segunda carta celebrara, una vez más, al sistema político de los Estados Unidos.[104] Lo que no quedaba claro en la carta era la base social de aquellos grupos sobre los que descansaría el edificio republicano. ¿Existían aquellos grupos en el Perú post-guerra o eran parte de la estrategia retórica que el escritor político introducía en una discusión que, debido a la presencia de los españoles en la sierra peruana, resultaba secundaria?

La comunidad política imaginada por Sánchez Carrión además de estar asociada a un elemento tan concreto como la propiedad, estableció, como lo hicieron sus predecesores, estrechos vínculos con el honor y con la virtud. El ciudadano propietario, honorable y virtuoso fue el puntal principal del republicanismo peruano post-Independencia. Los elementos que daban realce a la ciudadanía, propios del humanismo cívico del que bebió la 'intelligentzia' peruana a lo largo de tres décadas, provenían de una formación estrictamente retórica. Si bien es cierto, como hemos observado anteriormente, detrás de la propuesta del republicanismo post-Independencia subyace una teoría del Estado, con claras reminiscencias del federalismo norteamericano, el discurso político limeño siguió reposando en la retórica. Lo anterior muestra lo dificultoso que fue para la intelectualidad nativa transformar 'la república de las letras' y de 'los ciudadanos lectores' en un sistema político eficaz con individuos de carne y hueso, capaces de controlar sus pasiones para habitar ese mundo previsible y ordenado que aquellos ilustrados tardíos tanto añoraron.

104 El epígrafe de la carta reproducía una cita textual del tercer artículo de los Artículos de Confederación firmados en 1781 por los trece estados originales de los Estados Unidos: 'By these articles, the thirteen United States severally entered into a firm league of friendship with each other, for their common defence, the security of their liberties, and their mutual and general welfare' (Jedidiah Morse, *The American Universal Geography*, Boston, 1796).

CHAPTER 3

Church and Liberal State Strategies on the Dissemination of Print in Nineteenth-Century Chile

Sol Serrano and Iván Jaksić

In contrast to Europe, where literacy and schooling followed distinct paths, in Chile — as in the rest of Latin America — the expansion of reading and writing was due to the formation of the public educational system after independence from Spain. In the early republic literacy was restricted to the upper strata of urban society, a very small segment of a predominantly rural (80 per cent) population.[1] Between 1810 and 1840 public funding for education was allocated to this group, in a clear effort to educate a male republican elite. It was only in the 1840s that the Chilean state pursued a systematic policy for the expansion of literacy through primary schooling. Perhaps the most visible sign was the creation of the Normal School for the training of teachers in 1842, whose direction was entrusted to the Argentine exile Domingo Faustino Sarmiento. That was also the year that saw the foundation of the University of Chile, an institution designed to supervise the emerging national educational system. This strong state emphasis, and its early results, can be determined by glancing at some telling statistics: by 1853, there were 318 private schools teaching 8,300 students and 272 public schools teaching 13,465 students. Five years later, in 1858, the number of private schools had shrunk to 244, with practically the same number of students (8,564), while public schools had nearly doubled (to 450), teaching 21,349 students. According to the census of 1854, 13.5 per cent of the population was literate.[2]

State policy on primary education — foundation of schools, training of teachers, development of teaching methods, in addition to the selection, printing and distribution of school texts — was difficult to implement due not just to the poverty of state resources, but principally because of the unequal social and regional demand for education. Indeed, the state confronted the rural realities of a country with a highly dispersed population.

1 Simon Collier, *Ideas and Politics of Chilean Independence, 1808–1833* (Cambridge, 1967).

2 *Anuario Estadístico de la República de Chile*, vol. 1 (1916), p. 4, and *Censo Jeneral de la República de Chile, 1854* (Santiago, 1854).

In addition, even where modest concentrations of population existed in villages and towns, parents expected their children to perform rural work.[3]

The egalitarian promises of the liberal state, that is, of individuals who are equal before the law, assumed a society that had already assimilated the practice of literacy and understood its value. Political citizenship required it, and was thus written into the Constitution of 1833.[4] This was only an indication of the importance assigned to literacy, for the expectations went far beyond it to define the border, as the Venezuelan intellectual Andrés Bello put it in 1848, between 'barbarism and the emergence of civilisation'.[5] The political and educational statements of the period provide abundant evidence of the identification between civilisation and written culture, in opposition to barbarism and orality.

The first important efforts made by Spanish Americans to promote literacy took place when the region was still fighting for independence. It was Andrés Bello, in collaboration with the Colombian Juan García del Río, who from England launched a series of orthographic reform proposals intended to facilitate the acquisition of written language. The essay 'Indicaciones sobre la conveniencia de simplificar i uniformar la ortografía en América,' published in the journal *Biblioteca Americana* in 1823, proposed a break with the Spanish Royal Academy's rules for orthography, which were based on etymology.[6] The authors argued that it made no sense to continue to use mute letters, such as the 'u' in *que* or 'h' in *hora.* Even less, to use different letters, or combinations of letters, to represent the same sound, as was the case with the letters 'c', 'k', 'q' and 'ch', (as in the case of *christiano*). The authors' proposals for simplification extended to the substitution of the letter 'y' by 'i', and 'g' by 'j', in such cases as *general* and *genio*, where the sound of 'g' was so clearly distinct from that in *gusto* or *guerra.*

3 Sol Serrano, '¿Quién quiere la educación? Estado y familia en Chile a mediados del siglo XIX,' in Pilar Gonzalbo (ed.), *Familia y educación en Iberoamérica* (Mexico, 1999), p. 153.

4 Article 8 of the Constitution declared 'active citizens' those who knew how to read and write. See Luis Valencia Avaria, *Anales de la República*, 2nd ed. (Santiago, 1986), p. 174.

5 Andrés Bello, 'Memoria correspondiente al curso de la instrucción pública en el quinquenio 1844–1848,' *Obras completas*, 26 vols. (Caracas, 1982), vol. XXI, p. 33. References to other texts by Bello belong to this edition and will be cited heretofore by volume number (in Roman numerals) and page (in Arabic numbers).

6 *Biblioteca Americana*, no. 1 (1823), pp. 50–62. This article was reprinted in another Spanish-language journal published in London, *El Repertorio Americano*, no. 1 (October 1826). It is included in Bello's *Obras completas*, vol. V, pp. 699–87.

Bello and García del Río preferred a simplified alphabet that consisted of 26 letters with their respective sounds:

A	B	CH	D	E	F	G	I	J	L	LL	M	N
a	be	che	de	e	fe	gue	i	je	le	lle	me	ne

Ñ	O	P	Q	R	RR	S	T	U	V	X	Y	Z
ñe	o	pe	cu	ere	rre	se	te	u	ve	exe	ye	ze

It is important to note that Bello and García del Río differentiated between 'r' and 'rr,' considering them distinct letters on the basis of their sounds, and the same with the letters 'l' and 'll.' Their central objective was summarised as follows:

> It is necessary to change the names of the letters, as we propose, in order to facilitate reading, because it is of extreme importance, especially for those who are beginning to understand syllable constructions, that the very name of the letter conjures up the sound it must receive in syllabic combinations.[7]

Bello and García del Río advanced their reform proposals in a critical spirit. They believed that the etymological criterion for spelling used by the Spanish Royal Academy, which assumed an already literate, if not highly educated, public, represented an obstacle to literacy in a largely uneducated population such as the Spanish American. Independence required, in their view, appropriate rules to make literacy more accessible. Their objective was even more ambitious than the simple acquisition of reading skills: the spread and deepening of knowledge, which they considered 'the only means to establish rational liberty, and with it, the means for culture and public prosperity'.[8] Civilisation, in short, was associated with writing.

Once in Chile, where he arrived in 1829, Bello had an opportunity to implement these orthographic reforms. Only those pertaining to the substitution of the 'y' for 'i' and that of the 'g' by the 'j' lasted for any length of time (into the early twentieth century), in part because of resistance to them, in part because the very success of literacy made the urgency of the more radical changes less compelling. From the beginning of his life in Chile, Bello attempted to correct problems of Spanish pronunciation, and

7 *Ibid.*, p. 61. This view is already present in the Gramática by Antonio de Nebrija (1492): 'tenemos de escrivir como pronunciamos, y pronunciar como escrivimos'. There is a facsimile edition of this source, by Antonio Quilis (Madrid, 1989), p. 143.

8 *Ibid.*, p. 62.

to standardise and institutionalise the teaching of the language. For instance, in his 'Advertencias sobre el uso de la lengua castellana', which was published in several installments in the periodical *El Araucano* between 1833 and 1834, Bello criticised Chilean usage because of 'improprieties and defects', which consisted in 'giving words a meaning other than what they should have, forming and pronouncing them erroneously, or using them irregularly'.[9] His overall purpose was threefold: to promote an educated form of Castilian through the emerging public educational system, to introduce a grammar that would regulate the correct use of language and to disseminate letters through the medium of print.[10]

Bello's defence of an educated and well-structured language had a direct relationship to the construction of the national state. Without a uniform language of national scope there could be no hope of achieving the level of communication, understanding and cooperation required by the representative political system sanctioned by the Constitution. A threat to the integrity of an educated language represented, therefore, a threat to the integrity of state and nation.[11] Bello articulated this concern in his famous prologue to the *Gramática de la lengua castellana destinada al uso de los americanos* (1847):

> … the greatest evil of all, and one which, if it is not controlled, will deprive us of the precious advantages of a common language, is the torrent of grammatical neologisms which inundate and render obscure much of what is written in America, and which by altering the structure of the language tend to change it into a multitude of irregular, undisciplined and barbaric dialects; embryos of future languages which, during a long development, would reproduce in America what happened in Europe during the dark period of the corruption of Latin. Chile, Peru, Buenos Aires, Mexico, would each speak their own language, as happens

9 Obras completas, vol. V, p. 147.

10 See Alfredo Torrejón, *Andrés Bello y la lengua culta. La estandarización del Castellano en América en el siglo XIX* (Boulder, CO, 1993), and Julio Ramos, 'Saber decir: lengua y política en Andrés Bello,' in *Desencuentros de la modernidad: literatura y política en el siglo XIX* (Mexico, 1989), pp. 35–49.

11 Angel Rama argued that there was a great deal of continuity between the colonial and national periods in Spanish America. He believed that this continuity resided in the power of an educated class to assign central importance to writing and to impose norms on a popular speech that it could not quite control. From our perspective, in the national period there was rather an imperative of national organisation, facilitated by the dissemination of writing, which accounts for the effort to expand literacy. In effect, the purpose of extending literacy was to provide citizens with the instruments for participation in a representative political system. See Angel Rama, *The Lettered City*, translated by John Charles Chasteen (Durham, NC and London, 1996).

> in Spain, Italy and France, where certain provincial languages predominate but a number of others exist besides them, hampering the spread of enlightenment, the execution of laws, the administration of the State, and the national unity.[12]

With the publication of the *Gramática*, which became the most influential text of its kind in Spanish America, Bello accomplished the crystallisation of an educated Spanish that was adapted to the particular requirements of the region after Independence (separation from the Latin grammatical model; incorporation of local variants legitimised by widespread usage), and yet without departing fundamentally from the use sanctioned by the Spanish Royal Academy. Still, there was the practical challenge of how to disseminate this approach through the public educational system.

During the 1840s Chile experienced a political and cultural conjuncture that has generated enormous historiographical interest, and for good reasons. At this time, a number of South Americans, including Argentine exiles, and Chileans — the most prominent names included Bello, Sarmiento, Juan Bautista Alberdi, Vicente Fidel López and José Victorino Lastarria — converged to discuss central issues of political organisation and educational development. During a period lasting no more than a decade and a half, Chile became a political and ideological laboratory for the examination of liberal views and the construction of new republics.[13] With the inauguration of the University of Chile in 1843, these and other intellectuals had a direct impact on national education as members of the Faculty of Philosophy and Humanities, which had the responsibility for curriculum development for primary and secondary schools, as well as for the adoption of school texts.

In our view, perhaps the most notable conceptualisation of the relationship between liberal society and the expansion of literacy, and their implementation in the public educational system, was that of the brothers Miguel Luis and Gregorio Víctor Amunátegui in their award-winning *De la instrucción primaria en Chile. Lo que es, lo que debiera ser* (1856). Both were moderate liberals, and both very close to their mentor Andrés Bello. Miguel Luis,

12 This translation is by Frances M. López-Morillas, in Iván Jaksić (ed.), *Selected Writings of Andrés Bello* (New York, 1997), pp. 101–2.

13 There is a large literature on this period, but a still unsurpassed source is by Diego Barros Arana, *Un decenio de la historia de Chile, 1841–1851*, 2 vols. (Santiago, 1905– [the second volume was printed by Imprenta y Litorgrafía Barcelona] 1913). On education, and specifically on the role of the University of Chile, see Sol Serrano, *Universidad y nación: Chile en el siglo XIX* (Santiago, 1994). On the various polemics of the period, see Ana María Stuven, *La seducción de un orden: las elites y la construcción de Chile en las polémicas culturales y políticas del siglo XIX* (Santiago, 2000).

in particular, was the prototype of the nineteenth-century liberal intellectual: professor of humanities at the *Instituto Nacional* (the leading secondary school); high official in the Ministry of Foreign Relations; congressman; journalist; member of the Faculty of Philosophy and Humanities; and general secretary (the equivalent to a Provost) of the University of Chile; minister of justice and public education; presidential candidate in 1876; and, above all, one of the principal historians of the time.[14]

In their work the Amunáteguis established a relationship between sense-perception, acquisition of knowledge and the organisation of society. Chile, in their characterisation, was a deaf-mute country in the world of civilised nations, for he who did not know how to read was deaf and he who did not know how to write was mute. Orality was the equivalent of barbarism, in that it did not transcend the narrow circle defined by the senses, and relations among members were those of nature rather than of culture. Only writing permitted the accumulation, storage and dissemination of knowledge, and hence morality and progress. The nation, that is, that form of organisation based on the voluntary association of individuals equal before the law embodied in a constitution, was the civilised community that emerged from literacy.

The Amunáteguis argued that it was the duty of the state to educate the entire population in order to make each individual a member of that civilised community. Such individuals would thus become political and economic participants in both the public and the private spheres. The views of these authors, in short, shared the consensus of the period on the value of education for defining and refining customs, disciplining unruly passions, moderating thought and serving as the pillars of social order and stability. Ignorance provided easy prey for caudillos and demagogues, and manifested itself through violence. In contrast, politics in a republic was conducted through the exchange of opinion, and especially through the press. 'The day when everyone, including the humblest of workers, reads in order to learn about the policies of the government, and the platforms of political parties, that will be the day when the era of revolutions will end. Differences will then be resolved through press articles and not through bullets in battlefields. There will be floods of ink, not blood.'[15]

Literacy in general, and writing in particular, was of critical importance for two central aspects of the organisation of the state in the post-

14 Carlos Morla Vicuña (ed.), *Don Miguel Luis Amunátegui, 1828–1888* (Paris, n.d.). The biographical section is by historian Diego Barros Arana.

15 *De la instrucción primaria en Chile. Lo que es, lo que debiera ser* (Santiago, 1856), p. 69.

Independence period: the preparation of government documents and the codification of civil law. Andrés Bello was once again a crucial figure in both respects. Guillermo Feliú Cruz has shown how official documents from the *Patria Vieja* period (1810–14) until Lircay (1830) were written with a rhetorical flair derived from Roman oratory as well as moral and religious oratory.[16] After his arrival in Chile in 1829, Bello steered the writing of these documents toward a more neutral, but perhaps more authoritative tone. Diego Portales, the most powerful political figure of the 1830s, quickly recognised Bello's writing talents and asked him to prepare the annual presidential address. The Venezuelan expatriate displayed such effectiveness in this regard that he wrote for three consecutive presidents: Joaquín Prieto, Manuel Bulnes and Manuel Montt. Between 1831 and 1860 he wrote 29 texts that played a critical role in projecting a tone of authority and continuity in official communications. As a member of the Senate (from 1837), Bello also had a role in responding to the presidential address, so that he had nearly full control over the exchange between these two branches of representative government.

Such influence can also be appreciated through an examination of documents on international relations, which Bello routinely prepared during the years he occupied the position of *oficial mayor* (under secretary) at the Ministry of Foreign Relations, formally from 1830 to 1852, but in practice since 1830. In the first edition of his *Principios de Derecho de Gentes* (1832), one can read:

> The reasons and arguments that are to be used in [international] negotiations must be derived from the principles of international law which rest on the foundations of the history of modern nations, and on a profound knowledge of their interests and common goals. The style must be, as in the case of letters and other forms of communication, plain, clear, and correct. It should not preclude firmness and forcefulness, when the matter requires it. Nothing does more to debase writings of this kind than the use of a boastful or sarcastic tone. Hyperbole, apostrophe and in general the affected style of orators and poets must be expunged from the language of government and its representatives, and used only in proclamations addressed to the people, which allow, and even require, the fervour and adornments of eloquence.[17]

16 Guillermo Feliú Cruz, *Andrés Bello y la redacción de los documentos oficiales administrativos, internacionales y legislativos de Chile* (Caracas, 1957), p. 109.

17 Andrés Bello, *Principios de derecho de gentes* (Santiago, 1832), p. 254. We quote from the first edition, because the text was slightly changed in the 1844 and 1862 editions. It is included in *Obras completas*, vol. X, p. 403.

In the opinion of historian Diego Barros Arana, Bello 'elevated the tone of our diplomacy through documents which were based on careful and thoughtful study, and written in correct and dignified language'.[18] Miguel Luis Amunátegui, for his part, stated that 'the numerous official documents prepared by Bello stand out for the forcefulness of their reasoning and the appropriateness of their erudition, as well as the suitability of the style, which is always elegant and temperate, never loud or pompous'.[19] Although obviously partial to Bello, neither Barros Arana nor Amunátegui failed to identify the deliberate style of the official documents. The language was indeed sober and direct, perhaps in an effort to buttress the notion of an impersonal state subject to norms. A uniform style also projected a sense of coherence among the various offices of the government. Bello used the same approach in his preparation of civil legislation that culminated in the *Código Civil de la República de Chile* (1855). Bello devoted considerable effort to preparing, despite the complexities of the subject, a readable text. He aimed for economy, but also, and perhaps principally, for clarity because the written law was soon to be the juridical basis of the republican system, and as such it demanded accessibility. Article 20 of the *Código Civil* states that 'the words of the law are to be understood in their obvious and natural connotations, according the generalised use of those words'.[20] Article 21 further specified that 'the technical terms of an art or science are to be understood according to the meaning which is given to them by those who practice that art or science'.[21] The entire Section 5 of the preamble to the civil code is devoted to the 'definition of various words of frequent use in the laws', spelling their meaning in detail through 27 articles.[22] Just as custom was stripped of the force of law, thus did the words acquire a precise and universal meaning in Chilean civil legislation.

The scholar Jaime Concha has firmly established the relationship between the juridical and grammatical aspects of Bello's work. As this author states, 'between grammar and law there are *a limine* exchanges that, naturally, will show up in the respective treatises of Bello. A grammar is a

18 Diego Barros Arana, *Estudios biográficos*, en *Obras completas*, vol. 13 (Santiago, 1914), pp. 243–4. He extended this view to Bello's other official documents: 'Bello was in charge of writing the most important government documents, to which he brought correctness and clarity in the style as well as seriousness and discretion in the essence', *Historia jeneral de Chile*, 16 vols (Santiago, 1902), vol. XVI, p. 179.

19 Miguel Luis Amunátegui, *Vida de don Andrés Bello* (Santiago, 1882), p. 363.

20 *Obras completas*, vol. XIV, p. 42.

21 *Ibid.*, p. 43.

22 *Ibid.*, pp. 44–58.

"code" of the language, which has its "laws" and its "rules" of proper usage; for its part, a code is a series of "articles" which has a basic morphology whereby definitions contain a minimum of phrases, because "law" tends to coincide with the structure of the "sentence". Its economy is grammatical.'[23] As Concha implies, it is also possible to extend the relationship between grammar and law to the literary aspects of the language: they can both be polished for the sake of clarity and force.

Bello's experience with literary composition, be it prose or verse, can be traced back to his education at the colonial University of Caracas. Bello was a prolific writer of poetry and literary criticism. While in London, he copy-edited a translation of the New Testament, which undoubtedly helped him convey religious themes in an accessible language. In 1835, he published his well-known treatise on prosody, the *Principios de ortología y métrica.* Perhaps less known is his *Compendio de la historia de la literatura* (1850), which he prepared as a text for secondary school teaching. There one can find some revealing references to the development of oratory in Latin literature. 'Rome produced,' Bello stated, 'many notable orators, as could not but happen under a popular government, in which eloquence was a sure means to acquire a reputation and to climb to the highest positions in the republic'.[24] In reviewing the role of several of these orators, Bello did not hide his preferences for those whose work seemed to fit the same purposes of republican nation-building in Chile. In particular, he was less than enthusiastic about popular mobilisations triggered by the oratorical skills of a leader. Instead, he favoured oratory that was persuasive, derived from arguments based on reading, or at least from the sober use of oral language. He identified with Quintilian, for whom oratory was the art of speaking well, a skill that flourished among persons of high moral probity. Bello was less sympathetic to Cicero, whose contributions he acknowledged, but added that the Roman orator 'displayed a lack of political will that made him compromise his conscience in order to achieve higher positions, add fuel to his immoderate thirst for glory, a false glory … because it consisted of a search for personal influence, and the applause of a vain and corrupt public'.[25] Applied to Chile, his selection of Roman figures shows a view of citizenship that rejects demagoguery and assembly-like politics. He promoted, instead, an austere citizenry, characterised by political moderation and civic commitment. Such choices had already been articulat-

23 Jaime Concha, 'Gramáticas y códigos: Bello y su gestión superestructural en Chile,' *Revista de Humanidades y Ciencias Sociales*, no. 42, second semester (1997), pp. 17–36.

24 *Obras completas*, vol. IX, p. 125.

25 *Ibid.*, vol. IX, pp. 172—3.

ed by Bello in the 1820s, when he commented on Maillet-Lacoste's *Parallèle de Tacite et de Cicéron* (1826): 'In Cicero we often find the attitudes of a man of letters; but in Tacitus we always find the noble pride of the citizen.'[26] Tacitus, it should be noted, subordinated oratory, which in his *Dialogus* he regarded as in decline, to morality and education. Moreover, as the classical scholar Ronald H. Martin has pointed out, 'Tacitus' style is marked by a fastidious and continuous avoidance of the trite and the hackneyed.'[27]

It is not coincidental, perhaps, that the main contrast between Cicero and Tacitus is that of an orator and a writer, however much they might excel in eloquence.[28] The emphasis on *written* eloquence, as above oratory, is also that of the Scottish Enlightenment, and in particular of Hugh Blair in his *Lectures on Rhetoric and Belles Lettres* (1783). Bello knew and followed the Scottish philosophy of Common Sense, and, as we suggested in a previous article, he drew inspiration from the Scottish Enlightenment for his conceptualisation of the University of Chile.[29] To this, one must add his familiarity with the Scottish scholars of rhetoric, who included George Campbell and his *The Philosophy of Rhetoric* (1776). But it was Blair who had the greatest influence in Chile. It is well worth discussing this in some detail.

Blair's main work was translated and published in Spain by José Luis Munarriz between 1798 and 1801.[30] There is evidence that by 1826, that is, under the rectorship of Carlos Ambrosio Lozier at the *Instituto Nacional* in Santiago, there were 300 copies of Blair's text, a book that was used in

26 *Ibid.*, p. 748.

27 Simon Hornblower and Anthony Spawforth (eds.), *The Oxford Classical Dictionary*, 3rd ed. (Oxford and New York, 1996), p. 1470.

28 In the words of Kenneth Cmiel, 'Unlike Ciceronian rhetoric, the new Scottish school rarely discussed how to speak to the common people. In the very subjects emphasised, Scottish rhetoric paralleled the wider gentry withdrawal from popular culture. Ciceronian rhetoricians, with their keen interest in popular eloquence, rarely discussed the written word. The new rhetorics, however, spent much time talking about the canons of written eloquence.' See his *Democratic Eloquence: The Fight over Popular Speech in Nineteenth-Century America* (New York, 1990), p. 35. As this author shows, the Scottish school had great influence in the United States.

29 Iván Jaksić and Sol Serrano, 'In the Service of the Nation: The Establishment and Consolidation of the Universidad de Chile, 1842–1879,' *Hispanic American Historical Review*, vol. 70, no. 1 (February 1990), pp. 139–71.

30 José Luis Munarriz, *Lecciones sobre la retórica y las bellas letras, por Hugo Blair*, 4 vols. Las traduxo del inglés don Joseph Luis Munarriz (Madrid, 1798–1801). Subsequently, the book by Antonio de Capmany, *Filosofía de la elocuencia* came out in 1812 (reprinted in 1842). This last book had less influence in Chile, but Bello quoted him often. They coincided in their rejection of the increasing use of French neologisms in Spanish.

secondary schools for the rest of the nineteenth century.[31] This means that Blair's rejection of purely oral eloquence, and his emphasis on writing, was well established in Chile even before the arrival of Bello in 1829. In this respect, the Venezuelan thinker could advance his views on the basis of ideas in circulation since the earliest years of the republic. The teaching of rhetoric, moreover, had roots in the colonial period. Juan Egaña, later a patriot of note, had taught it at the University of San Felipe in Santiago since 1802, and continued to teach it after Independence at the *Instituto Nacional* from its foundation in 1813 and until his retirement in 1823. Some of the earliest examples of Chilean eloquence come from Egaña, including his 'Discurso sobre el amor a la Patria' (1807) and, after Independence, the supervision of student eulogies on Simón Bolívar, Lord Thomas Cochrane, Bernardo O'Higgins, José de San Martín and the Indian warrior Lautaro.[32] Egaña acknowledged the importance of Blair when, in 1826, he prepared a report on the *cátedra* (chair) of Eloquence and Belles Lettres at the *Instituto Nacional*: 'It is studied following the text of Hugh Blair, excellent philologist. But to this day there is little emphasis on actual composition, as well as critical analysis of good discourses. In my view, this is the most important way to acquire fluency in speech and writing.'[33] Egaña's successors in the chair of rhetoric (alternatively called Belles Lettres, or simply Literature) were Ventura Marín and Antonio García Reyes, who continued to use Blair's text. In fact, Munarriz' translation was reprinted in 1842.[34] One can conclude from this, then, that José Victorino Lastarria's statement to the effect that José Gómez Hermosilla's *Arte de hablar en prosa i verso*, supposedly a dominant text imposed by Bello, was not accurate.[35] When Diego Barros Arana prepared the principal text on rhetoric, published in 1867, he considered Blair's text to be the most important, calling

31 Domingo Amunátegui Solar, *Los primeros años del Instituto Nacional, 1813–1835* (Santiago, 1889), pp. 322–3. The author states that 'The text by the academic Munarriz had two great advantages for [Spanish] American students. First, it was translated into very good Spanish and, second, made frequent reference to Spanish literature, both mediaeval and modern, with sound judgments about its writers and using numerous quotes. Thus, for instance, it transcribed in its entirety the well-known sonnet by Lope de Vega, *Daba sustento a un pajarillo un día*, which today all [secondary school] students memorise.'

32 Juan Egaña, *Antología*, edited by Raúl Silva Castro (Santiago, 1969), pp. 145–9.

33 Amunátegui, *Los primeros años*, pp. 231–3.

34 Ramón Briseño, *Estadística bibliográfica de la literatura chilena*, 2 vols. (Santiago, 1862), vol. I, p. 68.

35 José Victorino Lastarria, *Recuerdos literarios: datos para la historia literaria de la América española i del progreso intelectual de Chile*, 2nd ed. (Santiago, 1885), p. 221.

it 'a magisterial work in which the fundamental principles of literature are amply expounded, with as much science [i.e., erudition] as good taste'.[36]

Barros Arana's book, *Elementos de retórica i poética* marks the culmination of the effort by generations of liberal scholars and educators to establish and institutionalise a culture of writing. Beginning with the arguments of Bello regarding literacy and the correct usage of language, the publication of the *Gramática* in 1847, and the concurrent expansion of national education, the new liberal generation could now promote the study of written language as a means of refining customs and advancing to higher levels of civilisation. Barros Arana's book covered the central issues of rhetoric with a wealth of detail, including reflections on style and eloquence, versification and literary analysis. He discussed the character and the rules for various forms of written oratory (sacred, deliberative, legal, academic and military), history, fiction, didactic compositions, journalism and the epistolary genre. That is, a wide spectrum of writing forms. It is relevant here to consider Barros Arana's conceptualisation of such studies, and in particular his notion of literature:

> With this name we designate the rules that observation and good taste suggest to educated persons so that they can judge literary works, and compose them. If literature, understood in this latter sense, cannot aspire to provide us with unchanging rules for the composition of literary works, at least it can teach us to guide our judgment and to avoid the defects that might vitiate our writings.[37]

Literature, in short, was an instrument of civilisation. Following Blair, Campbell and Bello, Barros Arana argued that the cultivation of language and good taste had positive effects for social, as well as personal, development. That is why it was important to promote literacy, so as to begin a process that would advance to higher degrees of civilisation. Mere study would not erase differences of talent, but Barros Arana believed that knowledge of literature, just like knowledge of the laws in civil society, could provide a means of social mobility, as well as an appreciation of the social order.

> I do not presume to affirm that rules in literature are indispensable. Men of genius did not need them for centuries, and even now they could easily disregard them. But genius is a rarity in nature. What rules can do is to help persons of more limited intelligence, guide their steps, show them the goals to which they should aspire, and keep them on track.

36 Diego Barros Arana, Elementos de retórica i poética, vol. 3 of *Obras completas* (Santiago, 1908), p. 4.

37 *Ibid.*, p. 11.

> Rules do not give artificial means to say what is appropriate to say. But when intelligence, study and practice have laid out the foundations, rules help us to discriminate between what we need and what we might discard. They, in and of themselves, are not enough to make writers out of people whom nature gave limited intelligence; but they do help those who are committed to the life of letters, and they do refine the taste of those who seek only enlightenment and relaxation in literature.[38]

Through this kind of argumentation and study, the highly literate and liberal generation of Barros Arana demonstrated its command of written culture and the techniques for its dissemination. Writing was a critical element in the construction of a liberal society, that is, a society of free individuals, and hence the emphasis on its liberating aspects: such society would transcend both the corporate arrangements of the colonial past, which stifled individual initiative, and an oral culture that kept individuals tied to the immediacy of small communities. A modern nation, therefore, was built on universal principles, allowed individuals to communicate far beyond their geographical confines and was made possible by writing. Liberals seized on the implications of writing to advance their view of society through books and, especially, through the press. Ecclesiastical circles, for the reasons we will now examine, had a slower and more ambivalent reaction to the potentialities of written culture.

The importance of the book for the emergence of Protestantism, in contrast to the centrality of liturgy for Catholicism, has long occupied scholars and is at the bases of debates on the relationship between religion and capitalism.[39] In Latin American historiography, especially its colonial strand, a central concern has been religious syncretism, as well as the ritual — rather than conceptual — encounter between Catholicism and local religions. But the role of the Church under the republic, especially its attitude with regards to the secular state and specifically its approach to written culture, has not been well covered. Here we propose some interpretive approaches.

On the basis of the Chilean case, we argue that the institution was highly literate at the top, but deeply oral at the base. This was a reflection of the larger society, and perhaps because of this, the Church did not develop a strategy to confront — or embrace — the implications of written culture. This only happened when the liberal state, now firmly in control of

38 *Ibid.*, p. 17.

39 The classic formulation is that of Max Weber in *The Protestant Ethic and the Spirit of Capitalism* (1904–05).

the public sphere, forced the Church to compete for the support of the larger society. That is, it forced it to enter into debates, in an attempt to shape public opinion.

This view may seem to be contradicted by an examination of the educational activities of the Church, but we argue that after the expulsion of the Jesuits in 1776 there was only limited attention paid to primary education.[40] In 1823, the government demanded that the regular orders maintain schools, and determined their level (primary or secondary) according to the number of convents in each city. Hence, there should have been 28 primary, six grammar and five philosophy schools. But the decree was far from fully implemented. In 1830, the recently installed conservative government returned confiscated properties to the regular orders, but it insisted that they each run a school. The inability to comply had much to do with the general situation of disorder and lack of means afflicting the Church after Independence, as well as with an early history of conflicts with the liberal policies of the state. But the consolidation of the conservative government in the 1830s did not contribute to any significant increase in parochial schools. The statistics of the period are not very reliable, but some figures provided by the Ministry of the Interior in 1834 suggest that there were 1,300 students in municipal, convent-run and archbishopric schools, plus 900 in private schools. When statistics became reliable, with the publication of the *Anuario Estadístico*, the trend was quite clear: In 1853 there were 18 convent-run schools educating 1,213 children. By 1858 the number of students had dropped to 977, although the number of schools remained the same. In 1863 convent-run schools disappeared from the statistics because they were subsumed under the category of municipal schools, which were themselves in decline compared to those funded by the national government.

The decline of parochial and convent-run schools was confirmed by Archbishop Rafael Valentín Valdivieso's thorough review of the archdiocese of Santiago between 1853 and 1863: out of 57 parishes, only one convent-run school was identified as such by the parish priest of Curimon, Los Andes, and one school for girls in Valparaíso, run by the Congregation of the Sacred Heart.[41]

40 Francisco Antonio Encina believes that by the end of the colonial period, each convent had a primary school, which would bring the number to 45. There is no hard evidence to support this claim. See his *Historia de Chile*, 20 vols. (Santiago, 1951), vol. V, p. 554.

41 Some parish priests provide numbers of schools, but without describing them. Others refer to them as municipal, private, national, hacienda-based and even household-based. *Archivo del Arzobispado de Santiago* [henceforth AAS), Libro de Visita de S.S. Monseñor Rafael Valentín Valdivieso, vols. 192, 193 and 194.

Under the leadership of the archbishop the Catholic Church hierarchy made a serious effort to reform the training of the clergy (the Seminary of Santiago had been reopened in 1837), reestablish communal life in the congregations, organise the dioceses through tightened rules for the administration of the sacraments, parish registries and rural missions. This process of internal reform was a response to both the increasing regalism of the government and the ubiquitous presence of liberal opinion. Monsignor Valdivieso, who became archbishop in 1843, led the Church in an ultramontane direction.[42]

During this process of internal reform, the circulation of printed materials was seen to be a crucial contributing element, though it was not initially understood as such. The *Revista Católica* was founded in 1843, but did not have a wide circulation. In fact, it was not listed in the inventory of any parish. In 1847 a *Catálogo eclesiástico de ambos cleros* was published, containing information about priests, their assignments and parishes. But the clergy did not always submit the information required, and thus the *Catálogo* did not appear regularly until 1855. Perhaps the most useful publication was the *Boletín eclesiástico*, which compiled all decrees, statutes, edicts and pastorals of the Diocesan Prelate. The first volume appeared in 1859, and included all ecclesiastical records housed at the archives of the Archbishopric from 1830 to 1852. It became an annual publication for the rest of the nineteenth century. In addition to these periodical publications, each parish maintained correspondence with its respective bishop on a variety of ecclesiastical matters. They also received printed circulars and pastoral edicts from the archbishop. As the parish inventories show, this was the most common printed material received during the middle years of the nineteenth century. This does not mean, however, that every parish received all that was printed: 48 of the 56 parishes visited by the archbishop had some sort of circular from the bishop, on bookkeeping, parish rights and the like, and 31 had pastorals.

Pastorals first reached the parish priests, and were then supposed to be posted for three days on the door of each church. Even towards the end of the century, pastorals closed with the statement that in order to reach 'the ears of all our beloved parishioners, we mandate that all priests and

42 Carlos Silva Cotapos, *El clero chileno durante la guerra de la Independencia* (Santiago, 1911), and *Historia eclesiástica de Chile* (Santiago, 1925); Sergio Vergara, 'Iglesia y estado en Chile, 1750–1850,' *Historia*, vol. 20 (1985), pp. 319–62; Fernando Aliaga Rojas, *La Iglesia en Chile. Contexto histórico* (Santiago, 1985), and Antonio Rehbein, 'El clero diocesano y su presencia evangelizadora en Chile durante el siglo XIX,' *Anuario de Historia de la Iglesia Chilena*, vol. 8 (1990), pp. 69–85.

rectors read this our pastoral in parts during holidays and those that follow its reception, at the parish Mass or at the time of highest attendance by the faithful'.[43] The parish priest served as an intermediary between the written and the oral worlds.

Sermons at the better endowed churches, such as those of Santiago, tended to be quite long. José Zapiola, one of the sharpest contemporary observers, recalled hearing Monsignor Manuel Vicuña preach for three hours at the Church of La Estampa in 1820.[44] It is difficult to assess to what degree, if any, such sermons held the attention of the churchgoers, but there were some highly popular speakers. Perhaps not surprisingly, such sermons tended to appeal to the emotions rather than to the theological mind. Those who addressed the latter were considered to be 'academic orators', whose sermons were directed to an educated public.[45] In the rural parishes, which constituted the great majority, priests did not always preach and the faithful rarely, if ever, read the pastorals posted on the church doors.

The inventories of the parish archives provide some insights into the importance of writing for the Catholic pastoral. First, there are the manuscript volumes of baptism, marriage and death records. Second, there are the books of ecclesiastical and civil correspondence (only 19 of the parish inventories give any account of correspondence with civil authorities). And third, there are the printed records: 38 had pastorals from bishops; seven had papal encyclicals and three had papal bulls; 15 had the *Catálogo de ambos cleros*, the publication containing information about the diocesan clergy; only two had an issue of the *Boletín eclesiástico*, and nine had a copy of the last Synod, that of Monsignor Manuel de Alday (1762), which was still in force.

This less than copious printed literature was centrally relevant to the administrative functions of the parish. Printed materials pertaining to liturgy were even more scarce. Only 13 parishes had any type of liturgical book: some had missals, manuals for the administration of the sacraments, the Toledo manual or the manual for the burial of infants. Only toward the

43 'Pastoral colectiva y encíclica de S.S. Leon XIII, en las cuales se examinan las doctrinas del liberalismo moderno,' *Boletín eclesiástico*, no. 9 (1886), p. 912 and ff.

44 *Recuerdos de treinta años, 1810–1840*, 5th ed. (Santiago, 1902), p. 126. The great parliamentary speeches of the second half of the nineteenth century lasted about two and a half hours, perhaps more, but they were published in the press the following day, and usually debated. In contrast, very few sermons were published, and they usually consisted of eulogies to the well-known dead. See Manuel Antonio Román (ed.), *Oradores sagrados chilenos* (Santiago, 1913).

45 The testimony of Benigno Cruz on the popular preaching of Manuel José Irarrázabal is particularly interesting. See Román, *Oradores*, p. 8.

end of Valdivieso's pastoral visit was the category of 'liturgical books' included in the inventory of the parish of Lampa (1863). Only three parishes had a book on spirituality, be it that of Saint Ignatius, the *Ejercicios* by Torrubia or the *Verdades eternas* by Rosignoli. In the parish of Pencahue (province of Talca), there were two novels, 'one on *ánimas*, and the other on the Immaculate Conception of the Virgin Mary'.[46] Only the parish of El Sagrario (the oldest of central Santiago) had a non-religious book, the *Anuario Estadístico.* Lastly, parishes housed the equipment needed for missions, including a portable confessional, but the inventories show no evidence of any witten materials such as prayers, invocations, or novenas.

Religious associations and *cofradías* (lay brotherhoods) provided another realm for the circulation of devout literature. The Venerable Third Order of the San Agustín Church in Santiago had copies printed, in 1813, of the Novena of the Sacred Heart of Jesus and the *novenario* of the *Señor de Mayo.* In 1824 the order printed 100 copies of the *La caida de nuestro Señor Jesús*, as well as 400 copies of indulgences granted by the Pope. Later, it used printed materials for all the administrative activities of the order, such as invitations, schedules, constitutions, prayers and also the *Manual Agustiniano*, of which as many as 2,500 copies were printed in 1872.[47] We have found among the records of the Santo Domingo Church that the Rosary Society (*Cofradía del Rosario*) printed novenas, compilations of indulgences and 400 copies of the devotional of the Blessed Virgin in 1860.[48]

The Church hierarchy looked on the expansion of printed materials with some scepticism, linking it to that of profane books and to the liberal periodical press rather than as a means for the promotion of devout practices. Before he became bishop of Santiago, Manuel Vicuña became a crusader against the diffusion of non- or anti-religious literature: he rummaged suspiciously through private libraries and even organised a group that exchanged 'improper' literature with alternative works, or money. It is in that context that one can understand the dubious statistics cited in his first pastoral as bishop:

> It is just outrageous these days to witness the tireless philosophical campaign for the corruption of the minds. It is not just the three million and more immoral and impious books that it has put into circula-

46 AAS, 'Visita Pastoral,' vol. 193, folio 109r.

47 Archivo Iglesia de San Agustín, Venerable Orden Tercera, Libros de Cuentas, 1813, 1824, 1872, n.d.

48 Archivo Iglesia Santo Domingo, Libro de Actas del Consejo de la Cofradía del Rosario, 1590–1863, folio 106, 129r; Libro de la Archicofradía del Rosario de 1848 a 1862, n.d.

> tion in the past few years. What is really astonishing is the diabolical device that allows it to accommodate the different classes of people by producing compilations, summaries, extracts and other pieces at negligible prices so that anyone can buy them. In ten years, 35 editions of Voltaire have been published in France, one with two thousand copies. That is how, as a writer says, there will be four million two hundred thousand volumes of Voltaire alone in the hands of the people.[49]

It was at Vicuña's urging that in 1832 the government named a commission to review book imports. In addition to the bishop's appointees, the government named a reluctant Andrés Bello (he was against censorship) and the somewhat more compliant Mariano Egaña and Ventura Marín (a professor at the *Instituto Nacional* who soon succumbed to mental illness). Vicuña revealed his utter contempt for books, even those that could have helped his cause, in that he made no effort to build libraries when he started the reorganisation of parishes in 1837.

It was Monsignor Valdivieso who looked more seriously into the potential of printed materials. It was during his tenure as archbishop that the *Revista Católica* was published in 1843. Its original objective was primarily internal: to inform the views of priests with regards to key religious themes as well as Church-State relations. Increasingly, it became a medium to debate the policies of the regalist state and liberal opinions in the press. The 'Prospect' stated that the objective of the *Revista* was to show the importance of religion for addressing the moral needs of society. It defined its primary readership as priests, especially those who performed their duties in isolated regions, and secondarily the faithful. It further added that 'In a country whose organisation, administrative structure and civil legislation is closely connected to that of the Church, it is advisable to disseminate those general notions that help maintain the good relations that Catholic nations must have with their religion.' The *Revista* announced that it would publish national and international religious news not covered by the liberal press. It also stated that it would publish the statements of diocesan prelates which, up to that point, were largely unknown even within ecclesiastical circles.[50]

49 Alejandro Vicuña, *Vida del ilustrísimo señor D. Manuel Vicuña Larraín* (Santiago, 1912), p. 119.

50 'Prospect,' *Revista Católica*, 9 March 1843. This periodical appeared bi-monthly and accepted subscriptions in private homes in the capital of each of the country's provinces.

In its declaration of aims, the *Revista Católica* indicated that it would not become involved in political matters. That could not be avoided, however, for its articles were commented on by the liberal press, and thus ideological as well as doctrinal positions were publicly aired. The circulation was limited outside ecclesiastical circles, and beyond the most eager liberal journalists, but Valdivieso understood that politics and the press went together and that not even the Church could escape that relationship. Thus far, Chilean politics was still determined by the conflict between the defenders of the presidential authoritarianism sanctioned by the Constitution of 1833, and those liberals who fought to change it to gain access to political participation and to a wider range of liberties. But this changed in 1857, when a seemingly minor dispute between the ecclesiastical *cabildo* and the archbishop escalated into a major dispute that altered the landscape of Chilean politics.[51] This happened because members of the *cabildo* appealed to civil courts, which ruled in their favour. Archbishop Valdivieso refused to comply on the grounds that this was an internal Church matter, and his defiance earned him a sentence of expatriation. The original accusers backed down in order to avoid a full-fledged crisis, but the so-called 'affair of the *sacristán*' revealed the potential implications of a struggle between a regalist state and an ultramontane Church. Conservatives in the government split, with those closest to the Church forming the Conservative Party and joining the opposition, while those loyal to the regalist President Manuel Montt formed their own National Party. The liberals saw an opportunity in the split, and allied themselves with the ultramontanes. Such an alliance created its own split within the liberals, some of whom formed the Radical Party, of even more drastic secularising tendencies.

It was at this critical conjuncture that religion became the centre of political conflict and produced a thorough realignment of political forces. Valdivieso now fully understood the importance of the press and displayed consummate skill in using it. His closest collaborator was his nephew, the priest Crescente Errázuriz, who described how difficult it was to advance clerical opinions in a predominantly liberal press. The Church's strategy to maintain a presence in the public sphere was to request government protection from the verdict of the Supreme Court. The hierarchy knew that the government would not grant it, but the strategy worked as the liberal press

51 See Alberto Edwards, *El gobierno de don Manuel Montt, 1851–1861* (Santiago, 1932), pp. 180–90; Simon Collier, 'Religious Freedom, Clericalism, and Anticlericalism in Chile, 1820–1920,' in Richard Helmstadter (ed.), *Freedom and Religion in the Nineteenth Century* (Stanford, 1997), pp. 302–38; and Timothy R. Scully, *Rethinking the Center: Party Politics in Nineteenth- and Twentieth-Century Chile* (Stanford, 1992), especially chapter two.

covered the issue thoroughly. 'The central point', stated Larraín Gandarillas, 'are very different from those of Catholics … For us Catholics the Church is the house of the Lord, a public place where the faithful meet to worship God, who is present in the altars. We believe in the real presence of Jesus Christ … But Protestants do not view temples as places that sanctify the presence of Christ. For them, these are merely places for prayers, reading and explanation of the Bible, activities that can take place in private dwellings.'[52] José Clemente Fabres, another great polemicist who defended the Catholic cause in the Congress, added that 'Catholic practice embraces everything from birth to death, every day; its rituals have the splendour and majesty that can capture a man's interest; it has even more, which is direct communication with God, because in every Catholic church God is there just like in heaven.'[53] Fabres's words caused laughter among his colleagues, but he insisted that Protestantism was the embodiment of everything opposed to Catholicism because it had neither sacraments nor ceremonies. Despite these efforts, the law of religious tolerance was passed in 1865.

The ecclesiastical hierarchy and the great majority of conservatives defended the exclusive practice of Catholicism not only because of the abhorrence of Protestantism, but also because of the fear of religious indifference. It was during this decade of the 1860s that Catholics and the hierarchy devoted serious attention to the press as a way to reach the various segments of the population. In addition to *El Independiente*, the *Estrella de Chile* was published in 1865 as the organ of the Sociedad de Amigos del País, founded that year by Abdón Cifuentes, the most active and militant conservative of the period, who participated in the creation of other Catholic organisations and periodicals. Papers addressed to workers were also founded, such as *El Obrero Católico* in Talca in 1867, *El Talquino* in the same city in 1868, *El Mensajero del Pueblo* in Santiago in 1870 and *El Verdadero Liberal* in San Felipe.[54]

The following decade was crucial for the progress of liberal reforms restricting the powers of the president and advancing the secularisation of the state. President Federico Errázuriz took office in 1871 with the support of conservatives and some liberals, but the alliance fell apart in 1873 as the result of educational policies that upset the conservatives. Liberals

52 *Sesiones del Congreso Legislativo* [SCL], Diputados, 5 June 1865, p. 15.

53 SCL, Diputados, 9 September 1974, p. 56. Fabres made these statements during the discussion on reform of Article 5 of the Constitution.

54 Sergio Grez, *De la 'regeneración del pueblo' a la huelga general. Génesis y evolución histórica del movimiento popular en Chile (1810–1890)* (Santiago, 1997), p. 536.

and radicals formed a governing coalition whose principal agenda was secularisation. At this critical moment, the hierarchy understood more than ever the need for their own newspaper, and helped found the *El Estandarte Católico* in 1874.[55] The first issue of this paper defined its mission by pointing out the limitations of books for defending Catholicism: 'A newspaper is essentially a weapon of war, perhaps the most powerful for the times in which we live. Good books are, without a doubt, enormously helpful, but they are far from meeting the needs of the present generation. They cannot do that because they are not available to all, because they are not current and because the number of people who look for healthy nourishment in them is too small … It is a hopeless task to try to stop the flood of impiety with books that contain fundamental truths which the enemies of religion routinely dismiss …'[56]

The conflict between Church and State was exacerbated by the series of laws adopted in 1883–84 that secularised birth, marriage and death. The response by the Church was to strengthen Catholic associations and, especially, educational institutions and the press. This was in line with Vatican policy, as proclaimed by Pope Leo XIII in several encyclicals disseminated by Chilean pastoral letters. 'One of the most urgent priorities of our time is the support and diffusion of the Catholic press,' proclaimed an episcopal pastoral in reaction to the promulgation of secular laws. A clear expression of this Church policy was the foundation of the *Unión Católica* in 1883 which, following European precedent, served as an umbrella for all lay Catholic associations. The Unión played an important role in the dissemination of the press in the provinces — it founded the immensely popular *El Chileno*, also known as the cook's paper, in Santiago, *La Unión* in Valparaíso and *El Llanquihue* in the southern city of Puerto Montt — and the promotion of Catholic workers' societies. In education, perhaps the greatest example was the creation of the Catholic University in 1888.[57]

55 On the foundation of this paper, and the differences with El Independiente, see Crescente Errázuriz, *Algo de lo que he visto* (Santiago, 1934), p. 33.

56 'Nuestra Obra,' *El Estandarte Católico*, 29 July 1874. Some scholars believe that this editorial was written by Crescente Errázuriz, which is highly possible, given that he was the paper's founder and principal writer. Carlos Fernández Freite, *Biografía de D. Crescente Errázuriz* (Santiago, 1935), p. 54.

57 See Abdón Cifuentes, *Memorias*, 2 vols. (Santiago, 1936), especially volume II for a detailed account of these activities. See also Ricardo Krebs et al., *Catolicismo y laicismo: seis estudios* (Santiago, 1981). We believe that Catholic education was also strengthened by the arrival of various religious congregations during the second half of the nineteenth century, and which concentrated on teaching (14 out 19 of those teaching women in 1893).

The founder of the Unión Católica, Abdón Cifuentes, called on Catholics to strengthen the thusfar feeble Catholic press. Citing de Tocqueville, he proclaimed that after the people, the press was the most important power in society. 'Some call it the leprosy of modern society', he stated, 'while others consider it the protector of public liberties. But the fact remains that without a paper to defend it, any political association is powerless.' Echoing the words of the liberal Amunátegui, Cifuentes, who was a conservative but staunch republican, considered the press as a public space for the confrontation of ideas: 'To the bloody struggles of the past, the columns of a paper; to the lances, quills.'[58]

The shaping of public opinion, the dissemination of printed materials especially by means of the press and the struggle for the loyalty of not just the elites, but of the larger society, prompted the Church to try to understand, and ultimately embrace, the power of the written word. This was quite a shift for an institution so lettered at the top, and so oral in its pastoral and in its popular base. But in the meantime, liberals dominated both, the medium and the message.

58 'Discurso relativo a las asociaciones católicas leido en el Círculo Católico de Santiago en Octubre de 1883,' in Abdón Cifuentes, *Colección de discursos de Abdón Cifuentes*, 3 vols. (Santiago, 1916), vol. III, p. 290.

CHAPTER 4

The Power of the Pulpit in Nineteenth-Century Guatemala

Douglass Sullivan-González

The mestizo caudillo Rafael Carrera and his allies forged a certain political stability in Guatemala from 1839–71, especially from the early 1850s until the death of the caudillo in 1865. In these latter years Guatemala's political chaos subsided and the economy rebounded, aided by the cochineal boom and the introduction of coffee. The Catholic Church regained a certain prominence during the conservative years as clerics and faithful, especially Spanish-speaking mestizos (*ladinos*) from eastern Guatemala followed prominent rural clerics to support the Carrera regime from internal and external threats. Strong evidence suggests that a theological discourse emanated from churches in the capital and countryside that affirmed that God had chosen Guatemala as His own. Like Israel, if the people of Guatemala obeyed and protected the Church, then God would continue to grant them peace and prosperity. If they disobeyed, God would certainly punish. Catholic discourse during the conservative years coalesced in and through these events to create a sense of nation, especially among the inhabitants of the capital and *ladinos* in eastern Guatemala.[1]

Carrera's triumph signalled a break with white Creole dominance of Guatemala's government and commenced the fragmentation of the Central American state. As part of their insurrectionary desiderata Carrera and his troops demanded a restoration of the customs and traditions that had been eclipsed by the 'enlighted' liberal Central American state. Carrera issued a call for the return of the exiled archbishop and persuaded the regular orders to reconstruct their convents and ministries among Guatemala's heterogeneous population.[2] Evidence indicates that Carrera worked with a groundswell of support. For example, New Year's Day festivities in 1840 shattered class and racial barriers momentarily as people

1 I express my thanks to the University of Pittsburgh Press for allowing me to use material drawn from my book *Piety, Power, and Politics. Religion and Nation Formation in Guatemala, 1821–1871* (Pittsburgh, 1998) and to *The Americas* for material from my article published in the July 1997 issue of the journal.

2 Agustín Estrada Monroy, *Datos para la historia de la Iglesia en Guatemala*, vol. 2 (Guatemala, 1974), pp. 545–82.

filled the church to celebrate the potential of the new direction of Guatemala and an end to the internecine wars. A restored Church, a hopeful administration and an empowered mestizo caudillo gathered in the cathedral to demonstrate the unshakeable alliance of the new Guatemala. The US diplomat John Stephens witnessed the religious mass commemorating the New Year and reported:

> The shops were shut as on a Sunday; there was no market in the plaza. Gentlemen well dressed, and ladies in black mantas, were crossing it to attend grand mass in the Cathedral. Mozart's music swelled through the aisles. A priest in a strange tongue proclaimed morality, religion, and love of country. The floor of the church was thronged with whites, Mestizoes, and Indians. On a high bench opposite the pulpit sat the chief of the state, and by his side Carrera, again dressed in his rich uniform. I leaned against a pillar opposite and watched his face; and if I read him right, he had forgotten war and the stains of blood upon his hands, and his very soul was filled with fanatic enthusiasm; exactly as the priests would have him. I did verily believe that he was honest in his impulses, and would do right if he knew how. They who undertake to guide him have a fearful responsibility. The service ended, a way was cleared through the crowd. Carrera, accompanied by the priests and the chief of the state, awkward in his movements, with his eyes fixed on the ground, or with furtive glances, as if ill at ease in being an object of so much attention, walked down the aisle. A thousand ferocious-looking soldiers were drawn up before the door. A wild burst of music greeted him, and the faces of the men glowed with devotion to their chief. A broad banner was unfurled, with stripes, black and red, a device of death's head and legs in the centre, and on one side the words, 'Viva la religión!' and on the other, 'Paz o muerte a los Liberales!' Carrera placed himself at their head, and with Rivera Paz by his side, and the fearful banner floating in the air, and wild and thrilling music, and the stillness of death around, they escorted the chief of the state to his house. How different from Newyear's Day at home![3]

Religious discourse during the Carrera years explicitly evolved an understanding of nation. Indeed, piety, popular power and caudillo politics merged to construct a multi-ethnic and multi-class alliance that underpinned the emergence of the Guatemalan nation-state. During this 30-year

3 John Lloyd Stephens, *Incidents of Travel in Central America, Chiapas, and the Yucatán*, vol. 1 (New York, 1969 [1841]), pp. 307–8.

period clerical sermons systematically developed a theological understanding of Guatemalan social events. The clergy used biblical and philosophical criteria to affirm the good in society, prophetically denouncing the evils they believed would destroy the fabric of the social order. Their messages attempted to demonstrate a history of salvation belonging to those peoples and nations that obeyed divine law, and to characterise the bloody revolutions that engulfed nations in horrible conflict as divine punishment for deviating from that law. If it were to be different from the nations engulfed in civil wars and to live in peace, Guatemala would have to protect its Church and hold dear its sacraments. Guatemala was to become like Israel, a chosen nation called to fulfill the law of God.

15 September, the Anniversary of Independence from the Spanish crown in 1821, proved to be the crucial ritual celebration where religious and political interpreters reassessed the past in order to fashion the future. Anniversary celebrations of Independence were established by the National Constituent Assembly in 1823 (with the first one held in 1824), while Guatemala still formed part of the newly-constituted Central American federation. Records show anniversary celebrations were consistently held on 15 September throughout the nineteenth century.[4] Even when the Catholic Church was under pressure by Morazán and his allies, religious leaders followed government orders to hold mass.[5] Only in 1857 was no civic or religious function held due to the cholera epidemic.[6] By

4 The earliest mention of celebration comes from Asamblea Nacional Constituyente, 'Decreto de 26 Agosto que dispone la festividad el día 15,' Guatemala [1823], AGCA B 78.25, Exp. 16934, Leg. 727. Numerous references to the 15 September celebration can be found in the Guatemalan Archivo General de Centro América (AGCA), Archivo Histórico Arquidiocesano 'Francisco de Paula García Peláez' (AHAG) and the Biblioteca César Brañas (CB) archives. Annual governmental requests to the Catholic leadership for religious services commemorating Independence preceded the celebrations by two to four weeks. For example, see Pedro N. Ariagga to Francisco García Peláez, Guatemala, 12 August 1850, AHAG 1850.121, Box T2 100. Thanks to the hard work and professional interest of Carmen Valenzuela de Garay, archivist of the César Brañas library, an updated list of 15 September sermons and speeches is available for the researcher. See Arturo Taracena Flores, 'Oradores Oficiales en las Celebraciones de la Independencia desde el año de 1831,' photocopy, CB 41052, for a listing dating from 1831 to 1934.

5 J.A. Alcayaga to Secretario General, Guatemala, 13 September 1829, AGCA B 94.1 Exp 32417 Leg. 1396.

6 Arturo Taracena Flores, 'Oradores Oficiales'.

1829 departmental heads celebrated the 15th with a thanksgiving mass and street celebrations.[7]

During most Independence celebrations religious and political leaders convened for a mass and a sermon reflecting on Independence. In the capital and at departmental administrative centres local officials, dignitaries and military leaders were the invited guests. For example, in 1845 leaders of the principal corporations, public officials, foreign consuls and other prominent authorities made up the audience in the cathedral. Artillery salutes, tolling of church bells and military bugle calls filled the air as elite capital residents cleaned house fronts and sidewalks and lit streets in celebration. After his military and political triumph Rafael Carrera was a frequent participant and honoured guest at these celebrations.[8]

During the 1830s liberal administration in Guatemala secular political leaders delivered the majority of the published anniversary speeches. Thereafter, however, religious leaders' prayers and sermons dominated printed discourse until the successful liberal insurrection in 1871. From the late 1830s to the late 1840s, religious sermons in the cathedral paralleled political speeches in the palace. By the mid-1850s and throughout the 1860s religious leaders maintained exclusive right over the interpretative significance of the anniversary celebration. The cleric Juan José Aycinena preached at least 12 of the 28 sermons commemorating Independence from 1837 through 1864, wielding enormous influence in the yearly ritual. In addition, many copies of these imprints circulated outside Guatemala's capital.[9]

7 Gobierno de Guatemala, 'Circular,' Guatemala [1829], AGCA B 87.1 Exp 28851 Leg. 1189. Records indicate that celebrations took place sporadically in most departments during the 1830s. However, it is not possible to determine which departments celebrated and which ones did not. In 1835, Chiquimula and San Marcos responded affirmatively, and in 1836, Escuintla officials called for similar demonstrations. See Circular a los Gefes Departamentales, Guatemala, 28 August 1835, AGCA B 87.1, Exp. 28997, Leg. 1191, and Carranza a las Municipalidades, Guatemala, 10 September 1836, AGCA B 119.3 Exp. 58617, Leg. 2541.

8 'Quince de Setiembre,' *Gaceta Oficial* 2 (25 Sept 1845),p. 67; and '15 de Setiembre de 1842' *Gaceta Oficial* (17 Sept. 1842). P. 267. On Carrera, see Pedro de Aycinena to Francisco García Peláez, Guatemala, 13 September 1854, AHAG 1854.214, Box T2 112; Manuel Echeverría to Francisco García Peláez, 13 Sept. 1855, Guatemala, AHAG 1855.267, Box T2 116. See also Miguel Arrazola, 'Discurso,' in *Relación de las fiestas con que se celebró en la Antigua Guatemala el XXX Aniversario de la Independencia y la inauguración del Palacio Municipal en la parte reedificada en el presente año* (Guatemala, 1851).

9 Chiquimula's *corregidor*, Esteban Lanquin, advised governmental authorities that he had received 12 copies of the 1841 anniversary speech and had circulated these. See Esteban Lanquin to Ministro General del Supremo Gobierno del Estado, Chiquimula, 10 October 1841, AGCA B 119.2, Exp. 57696, Leg. 2529. Copies of Aycinena's 1862 sermon were also circulated to all Church clerics in 1862. See Francisco García Peláez to Church clerics, Guatemala, 27 October 1862, AHAG 1862.365, Box T3 77.

Today, three-quarters of the speeches delivered from 1831 to 1871 survive in private and public archives.[10]

During the Anniversary celebrations of the 1830s, liberal political discourse severely criticised Spanish conquest and its aggression against native peoples.[11] Liberal ideologues attempted to become the vicarious spokespersons of the fallen indigenous people as they denounced the monarchy and the Catholic Church while preaching liberty and progress.[12] The *Patria* for these speakers was all of Central America, not just the state territory known as Guatemala. Citizens would be guaranteed equality, but equality would come to mean the transformation of the Indian into a Spanish-speaking Creole. The implementation of liberal policies — secularisation of the state, colonisation projects, unbridled faith in reason and progress — alienated the masses and ultimately translated into an attack on indigenous communities and lifestyles. In summary, as Lowell Gudmundson concluded, 'Liberals' inability to develop a series of images, an identity, a discourse capable of galvanising mass support was a basic problem.'[13]

10 Arturo Taracena Flores, 'Oradores Oficiales'. The Taracena Flores Collection, located at the UT–BLAC, contains the greatest number of these speeches. Guatemala's University of San Carlos' César Brañas collection has the second largest collection.

11 José Matías Quiñones, *Al soldado ilustre de la patria … en el Aniversario de Nuestra Gloriosa Independencia* (Guatemala, 1835); Simón Vasconcelos, *Boletín Oficial* (15 Sept. 1835), p. 876; José Francisco Barrundia, *Discurso pronunciado el día 15 de septiembre de 1836* (Guatemala, 1836), p. 1; and Pedro Molina, *Discurso acerca de la utilidad de la Independencia de Centro-América* (Guatemala, 1837), p. 1 (hereafter *Discurso 1837*); and Un Militar, *Observaciones sobre el discurso pronunciado por el Bachiller José D. Milla, en el Aniversario de la Independencia de Centro-América* (Guatemala, 1846), p. 3 (hereafter cited as *Observaciones*). For other Independence speeches delivered during the 1830s, see José Barrundia, 'Al nacimiento de la Patria en el 15 de septiembre,' in *El Centro-Americano Extraordinario* (15 setiembre 1833), pp. 199–206; and Mariano Gálvez, 'Discurso,' *Boletín extraordinario. Segunda parte* (30 Sept. 1832).

12 Quiñones preached in Los Altos, the general area surrounding Guatemala's Quezaltenango, Totonicapan and Sololá, which temporarily split from Guatemala to join the Central American Federation in the late 1830s and 1840s. Quiñones claimed to represent the Quiché Indians who were 'humiliated' in the 16th century by Spanish conquest but now had become a sovereign state of the Central American Union. See José Matías Quiñones, *Sermón predicado en la parroquia de Totonicapan el dia 25 de diciembre de 1838, con motivo de la instalación de la Asemblea Constituyente del Nuevo Estado de los Altos, de la Unión Centroamericana* (Los Altos, 1838), p. 1, CB 3091. See also Pedro C. Bustamante, *Boletín Extraordinario*, segunda parte (30 Sept. 1832), CB 1505.

13 Pedro José Valenzuela, 'Discurso sobre la igualdad de clases y diferencias de aptitudes,' *Boletín Oficial* (1 Sept. 1831), pp. 127–40. See also Pedro Molina, *Discurso 1837*, pp. 3–5; and Lowell Gudmundson and Héctor Lindo-Fuentes, *Central America, 1821–1871. Liberalism before Liberal Reform* (Tuscaloosa, 1995), pp. 108.

Catholic clerics responded to the religious dimension of the Carrera revolt, evolving a religious discourse that accounted for Carrera's indigenous support and the Church's need to reconstitute a religious institution dismantled by liberals. In 1840 the Catholic cleric Aycinena called for the restoration of the peoples' traditions, an appeal which would simultaneously affirm the autonomy of indigenous communities and restore Catholicism to its previous rank. Those 'traditions,' he said, 'were the authentic expression of the will of the people', and they had revolted in order to recover them. General Rafael Carrera was to be praised as the 'Restorer of the people's custom'.[14] Just three years earlier Aycinena had not been so confident of the rebels' intentions and had expressed an elite fear of the religious fanaticism of Carrera's 'savages' as he appealed to the role of reason in moulding traditions to the principles of eternal justice. He had commented in his 1837 anniversary homily that the majority indigenous peoples were 'swallowed up in the most crass ignorance and didn't even understand our language'. He wrote off their religious devotion as nothing but 'idolatrous acts'.[15] By 1840 Aycinena had changed his tune: not 'savages' but 'the people'; not 'religious fanatics' but 'protectors of our custom'. Aycinena's reversal probably represented the effort of a white elite to come to terms with a successful insurrection of mestizos and Indians. By accepting this explosive political reality, he adroitly sought to formulate a tradition which included both Indians and the religious institution in the make-up of a new Guatemala.[16]

14 Juan José de Aycinena, *Discurso pronunciado en la casa del Supremo Gobierno del Estado de Guatemala. El Quince de Setiembre Aniversario XIX. de su Independencia del Gobierno Español* (Guatemala, 1840, hereafter cited as *Discurso de 1840*).

15 Juan José de Aycinena, *Discurso que en la fiesta de acción de gracias celebrada en la catedral de Guatemala el 15 de setiembre de 1837* (Guatemala, 1837), pp. 5–10 (hereafter cited as *Discurso 1837*). This disgust with the popular religiosity of the non-white Guatemalans ran deep and for a long time within elite discourse. Vicente Molina retorted in 1842 that 'fanaticism had made the people more addicted to religious ceremonies than to moral principles'. See Victor Molina, *Discurso pronunciado el 15 de septiembre de 1845 vigésimo cuarto Aniversario de la Independencia de Guatemala* ... (Guatemala, 1845), p. 6. See also Andrés Andreu, *Discurso pronunciado el 15 de septiembre de 1839* (Guatemala, 1839), p. 5.

16 Aycinena, *Discurso de 1840*, p. 10. See also Manuel Echeverría, *Discurso que el 15 de setiembre de 1844, Aniversario XXIII de la Independencia de Centro-America* ... (Guatemala, 1844), p. 4. Aycinena's reversal earned him the scorn of his liberal colleagues. Much liberal historiography views this switch as a conservative scheme to co-opt the ignorant and pliable Carrera. The Church made a strategic and at times, fearful, alliance with Carrera.

Thus, the fear of social chaos became a dominant theme in religious discourse. Triumphant liberalism had led to institutional repression of the Catholic Church, and now, a victorious mass of Indians and mestizos threatened. What could rein in the passions which had led to these unsettling times? Achieving order and peace depended on the restoration of religion. The clerics grew to believe that Guatemalans must commit themselves to God in order to calm the troubled sea of revolution continually threatening Guatemala.

The calls for a restored tranquility would be based on the primacy of the Church. José Nicolás Arellano and Basilio Zeceña joined Aycinena in claiming historical confirmation for the principle that without religion neither society nor liberty would endure.[17] Aycinena proclaimed that 'a people without religion cannot have morals, and a people without morals are incapable of governing themselves. For this reason, governments, whatever their form may be, ought to protect religion as a base of public morality, as fundamental to good traditions. Without these elements, Republics cannot survive.' Bloody revolutions indicated that a given nation was founded on human interests, not divine. As in the biblical period of the judges, nations were destroyed for departing from the path of God.[18] Francisco García Peláez drove home this point in his 1843 Anniversary sermon: like the Hebrews who spent 40 years wandering in the desert because of their rebellion, so too Guatemala had spent 22 years aimlessly roving since Independence.[19]

17 Juan José de Aycinena, *Discurso pronunciado el 15 de setiembre de 1850, XXIX Aniversario de la Independencia de Guatemala* (Guatemala, 1850), p. 12 (hereafter cited *as Discurso 1850*); José Nicolás Arellano, *Sermón predicado el 15 de setiembre de 1845, vigésimo cuarto Aniversario de nuestra Independencia del Gobierno Español en la Santa Iglesia Catedral de Guatemala* (Guatemala, 1845), pp. 6–7 (hereafter cited as *Sermón 1845*); and Basilio Zeceña, *Sermón que en la función de gracias celebrada el día 1 de enero de 1844 en la Sta. Iglesia Catedral antes las Supremas Autoridades del Estado Guatemalteco* (Guatemala, 1844), pp. 4 and 11 (hereafter cited as *Sermón 1844*).

18 Aycinena, *Discurso 1840*, p. 4. See also Juan José Aycinena, *Discurso pronunciado el 15 de setiembre de 1848, XXVII Aniversario de la Independencia de Guatemala* (Guatemala, 1848), p. 11; Bernardo Piñol, *Discurso que en el solemne acción de gracias que mandó celebrar el supremo gobierno de la República de Guatemala por el restablecimiento de la paz el día 11 de febrero de 1849* (Guatemala, 1849), p. 5; and José Antonio Urrutia, *Exhortación dirigida al pueblo de Guatemala en el llano del inciènso en la fusilación de Feliciano Masariego el dia 3 de mayo de 1849* (Guatemala, 1849), p. 5. Even the Civil War in the United States was interpreted as divine punishment for straying from Divine Law. See Juan José Aycinena, *Sermón predicado en la festividad del primer aniversario de la dedicación solemne del Templo Catedral de la Archdiócesis de Santiago de Guatemala* (Guatemala, 1861).

19 This 1843 Anniversary sermon by Francisco García Peláez was quoted by Lorenzo Montúfar in his *Reseña histórica de Centro América* (Guatemala, 1888), vol. 4, p. 177. No copy of this sermon has been located in any of the researched archives.

Despair did not overcome these ecclesiastical authorities even as they warned of societal doom. Recourse from the horrible epidemic of war lay in religion, the 'cement of the social edifice'.[20] France, stated Aycinena, was capable of transforming itself into an ordered country out of the carnage of revolutionary war only by re-establishing Catholicism. With the restoration of Catholicism by Bourbon forces in France, religion, the solid rock of society, had produced peace among the French. No institution or political theory, claimed Aycinena, could match the Christian principle of brotherly love that kept people united and assured true liberty.[21]

The central theological motif which emerged in these anniversary sermons was the divine pact, or covenant, between God and his people realised first with the chosen people of Israel through their leader Moses, and then for all believing people through Jesus of Nazareth, the Christ. This theology can be traced back to what could be called the first anniversary sermon of Independence, preached by Guatemala's vicar general, José María Castilla, in 1821: 'We must be virtuous if we desire heaven to protect our liberty.' Quoting scripture, Castilla called all to 'be faithful to our religion, and we will be blessed; if not, God will turn us over to ourselves, and we will become prisoners of our enemies'.[22] The religious historian, Agustín Estrada Monroy credits Castilla with turning the tide of debate in favour of Independence that very day as Castilla publicly broke with the Guatemalan Archbishop Casáus y Torres, who had vigorously opposed Independence from Spain. Doubtless due to Castilla's continued educa-

20 Aycinena, *Discurso 1850*, p. 9.

21 Aycinena, *Discurso 1840*, p. 3. See also: Arellano, *Sermón 1845*, p. 8; Aycinena, *Discurso 1850*, pp. 4, 9, 12; Juan José de Aycinena, *Discurso pronunciado el 15 de setiembre de 1853, XXXII Aniversario de la Independencia de Guatemala* (Guatemala, 1853), p. 4 (hereafter cited as *Discurso 1853*); and Juan José Aycinena, *Aniversario XXXVIII de la Independencia de Guatemala. Discurso religioso pronunciado en la Santa Iglesia Catedral el 16 de septiembre de 1859* (Guatemala, 1859), p. 14; and Manuel Francisco Velez, *Discurso político-religioso pronunciado en la S.I. Catedral el 15 de setiembre de 1869. XLVIII Aniversario de nuestra Independencia de la Monarquía Española* (Guatemala, 1869), pp. 15–16 (hereafter cited as *Discurso 1869*). France's 'fall from grace' and ensuing social chaos was illustrative of a society's straying from the straight and narrow. In the first Independence sermon, Castilla remarked that France, once made up of pious people, now found itself divided into parties and bathed in blood. See José María Castilla, *Al heroico pueblo de Guatemala* (Guatemala, 1821), p. 8; and José Mariano Domínguez, *Sermón pronunciado en esta Santa Iglesia Catedral el 24 de junio, con motivo de la augusta ceremonia de la instalación del Soberano Congreso de estas provincias* (Guatemala, 1823), p. 5.

22 Castilla, *Al heroico pueblo*, p. 6.

tional and administrative leadership roles, his theological insight was reflected over the coming decades in the sermons of many fellow clerics.[23]

Prior to Independence most clerics understood the covenant community to comprise the Spanish monarchy and its bountiful lands in the Americas. In a sermon celebrating Spain's supposed liberation from Napoleon in 1808, the Dominican Luis Escoto proclaimed that God had placed Spanish Europe and America under the protective embrace of Holy Mary, the Divine Mother.[24] The archdeacon of Guatemala's Catholic Church, Dr Sicilia y Montoya, compared the Spanish monarchs Charles IV and his son, Ferdinand VII, to Abraham and Isaac respectively during the same festive occasion. Ferdinand's ascension to the throne in 1808 was nothing less than the intervention of the angel of the Lord in favour of the monarchy.[25] Sermons prior to Independence thus reflected a covenant between the Spanish monarchy and God.

Some clerics identified Central America as the 'nation' due to their experience with the Central American Federation in the 1830s. In late 1839 the exiled archbishop, writing from Havana, mourned the continued wars in Guatemala and the inability 'to consolidate a new order, a permanent peace and the union of the states'.[26] Manuel Zacarías Velásquez reflected during his 1844 sermon that the compassionate God had spared 'Central America' from the Wars of Independence.[27] But the chief political ideologue and elite clergyman, Aycinena, challenged the organic unity of the

23 Agustín Estrada Monroy, *Datos para la historia de la iglesia en Guatemala*, vol. 2, pp. 277–8. Within the numerous sermons printed during the first half of the nineteenth century, none could be found attributed to Castilla save the 1821 sermon. Recently arrived in the country in 1838, John Stephens encountered the reverend Castilla and confirmed the cleric's prominence and his elite education. Castilla was on his way to Havana to negotiate for the archbishop's return from exile in Cuba. See Stephens, *Incidents of Travel*, vol. 1, p. 49.

24 Friar Luis Escoto, *Sermón que en la acción de gracias que el comercio de la ciudad de Guatemala tributó a María Santísima por haber libertado ambas Españas Europea y Americana de las asechanzas y tiranía de Napoleon* (Guatemala, 1808), p. 7.

25 Sicilia y Montoya, 'Oración eucarística que pronunció … el martes 13 de diciembre de 1808 en la solemne acción de gracias que celebrar la M.N.Y.M.L. ciudad de Guatemala por la exaltación del Sr Rey D. Fernando VII al trono de las Españas,' in *Guatemala por Fernando Séptimo el día 12 de diciembre de 1808* (Guatemala, 1808), p. 13.

26 Francisco Ramón Casaus y Torres to Antonio Larrazábal, Havana, Cuba, 8 Nov. 1839, AHAG no. 41, Box T3 56.

27 Manuel Zacarías Velásquez, *Discurso político-religioso pronunciado en la Santa Iglesia Catedral de Guatemala el día 15 de septiembre de 1844* … (Guatemala, 1844), p. 1 (hereafter cited as *Discurso 1844*).

federation and propagated the theological vision of God's covenant with the Guatemalan nation alone.

While writing from exile in the United States in the 1830s Aycinena ridiculed the federation's birth as a political idea forced upon its people in a 'top-down' fashion. As a representative to the Convention of Central American States in 1839, he authored congressional decrees permitting Central American states to reconstitute themselves, thus formally weakening the federal alliance.[28] With Morazán's execution in 1842 (on 15 September no less!), the fragile federation entirely crumbled. In March 1847 Guatemala was declared to be an independent republic. Now political events forced a recasting of the covenant to fit the emerging nation-state. The consequences of such a shift would lead to a fateful alliance with Carrera, and implicitly, to a recognition of the loss of Catholic hegemony in an increasingly secularised world.[29]

As Guatemala's civil war drew to a close, Aycinena demanded Guatemalans to see how the law of Moses represented God's covenant with Israel: 'God himself called it his Covenant'. Therefore, Guatemalans ought to conform to God's law, as did the children of Israel in the time of Moses. Aycinena rejoiced that Guatemalan authorities recognised that the Mosaic law would be the foundation of Guatemala's peace and prosperity. Archbishop García Peláez agreed in 1856 that Guatemala, like Israel, recorded its promises with God in its own covenant of Independence. In 1858, Aycinena prodded his listeners to 'persist in our covenant' (*persistais en vuestro pacto*) and uphold it continually and keep its commandments forever.[30]

No wonder Juan José Aycinena became the prime interpreter for this novel theology during the Carrera years.[31] In 1858 and in other sermons

28 Juan José Aycinena, *El toro amarillo*, Biblioteca de Cultura Popular '20 de Octubre', vol. 54 (Guatemala, 1980); and Juan José Aycinena, *Respuesta* (Guatemala, 1839), pp. 1–4.

29 Lorenzo Montúfar asserts that Juan José Aycinena authored the October 1842 statement of Guatemala's president, Mariano Rivera Paz, that God's continued blessing of Guatemala was evident in the 15 September 1842 execution of Morazán. Though there is cause for suspicion in much of Montúfar's criticism of Aycinena (due to Montúfar's unyielding obsession with this elite leader), I am inclined to agree, since the theological assumptions of Rivera Paz's statement closely mirror Aycinena's views. See Montúfar, *Reseña histórica*, vol. 4, p.16.

30 Aycinena, *Discurso 1850*, p. 6; *XXXVII de la Independencia de Guatemala*, p. 5; *XLII Aniversario de la Independencia de Guatemala*, pp. 6, 10; Francisco de Paula García Peláez, *Discurso pronunciado en el 15 de septiembre de 1856 XXXV Aniversario de la Independencia de Guatemala* (hereafter cited as *Discurso 1856*), p. 2.

31 For a descriptive biography of Juan José Aycinena, see David Lee Chandler, *Juan José de Aycinena, idealista conservador de la Guatemala del siglo XIX* (Antigua, Guatemala, 1988).

he elaborately traced the story of salvation from the fall in the Garden of Eden through the Mosaic covenant. When humanity broke the law in the garden, God castigated and banned humans from its pleasures. The same principle applied to Abraham, Isaac and the chosen people of Israel: 'Blessings if you obey the commandments of our Lord our God; and damnation if you do not obey them.'[32] The tablets of the law delivered to Moses formed the basis of the Pentateuch, which Aycinena called Israel's 'Magna Carta'. If Israel obeyed, God would protect them from calamity, from other vile nations and heal their land.[33] Aycinena rhetorically asked:

> What more could a nation desire than what this magnificent promise offers? … Behold the reason why our Republic, being a Catholic congregation, has the right to appropriate the divine promise, and if we fulfill the divine condition — and time will tell — God will not change the rules: He will reward the good and punish the evildoers.[34]

The famous archbishop, Francisco de Paula García Peláez, followed suit: this 'holy alliance' was ratified in all the towns and villages, and when alien constitutions provoked revolt, the masses, he said, burst forth to present their own constitution. García Peláez saw Carrera's final triumph over Morazán, on 19 March 1840, as the triumph of a people who wanted to hold religion sacred and to rid the country of those constitutions which had not.[35] Zeceña

32 Juan José Aycinena, *Aniversario XXXVII de la Independencia de Guatemala. Discurso religioso pronunciado en la Santa Iglesia Catedral el 16 de septiembre de 1858* (Guatemala, 1858, hereafter cited as *Discurso 1858*), p. 12 Additionally, consult Aycinena, *Discurso 1837*, p. 6; Aycinena, *Discurso 1850*, p. 7; and Juan José de Aycinena, *Sermón que en la fiesta anual que celebra el I. Colegio de Abogados el día 18 de octubre de 1857* (Guatemala, 1857), p. 6.

33 Aycinena, *Discurso 1858*, p. 7; and Juan José Aycinena, *Aniversario XLII de la Independencia de Guatemala. Discurso religioso pronunciado en la Santa Iglesia Catedral el 16 de setiembre de 1864* (Guatemala, 1864), pp. 9–10 (hereafter, *Discurso 1864*). Additionally, consult Juan José de Aycinena, *Sermón predicado el 24 de Agosto de 1862. Trecentésimo Aniversario de la Reforma de Carmelitas Descalzas en la Iglesia de Santa Teresa de esta ciudad conventual de la misma orden* (Guatemala, 1862), p. 5. See also Bernardo Piñol, *Sermón que el día 29 de mayo de 1839 en la acción de gracias por la solemne instalación de la asamblea constituyente del Estado de Guatemala* (Guatemala, 1839), pp. 3–4 and 7; and Tomás Suaso, *Sermón predicado el quince de setiembre de mil ochocientos cuarenta y uno, Aniversario XX de nuestra Independencia del Gobierno Español, en la Santa Iglesia Catedral de Guatemala* (Guatemala, 1841), p. 1.

34 Juan José Aycinena y Piñol, *Aniversario XL de la Independencia de Guatemala. Discurso religioso pronunciado en la Santa Iglesia Catedral el 16 de septiembre de 1861* (Guatemala, 1861), pp. 9–10, (hereafter cited as *Discurso 1861*).

35 García Peláez, *Discurso 1856*, p. 4.

and Piñol reaffirmed García Peláez's proclamation: divine obligations fulfilled meant prosperity; obligations ignored resulted in adversity.[36]

The contractual relationship between God and Israel, which reflects a distinctive characteristic of the Israelite religion, has been understood to signify the conscious formation of Israel as a tribal confederacy. In his *Sociology of Religion*, Max Weber commented that, historically, the formation of political associations entailed subjugation to a tribal god. In Israel's case, the mutual promise, or covenant, with Yahweh distinguished the Israelite from other ancient religions. Not only was Israel ethically responsible to Yahweh, but Yahweh was also obligated to respond and fulfill his part of the bargain.[37] With the destruction of feudal Europe and the emergence of the modern nation-state, communities continued this conscious process of reformulating their relationship to the divine. In Geneva, the reformer John Calvin spirited the rule of the righteous and influenced a similar tradition developed by the Puritans in revolutionary England.[38]

In the United States and South Africa, the notion of a covenant community emerged within the reformed heritage, especially linked to the problematic notion of predestination. Puritans in the colonial United States regarded New England as a New Israel, a covenant community. Governor Winthrop preached that 'we are entered into Covenant with [God] for this work' and, if there is any breach of this Covenant, 'the Lord will surely break out in wrath against us'.[39] In South Africa, the victory at Blood River of a small contingent of Afrikaners over a vast Zulu army in December 1838 became the celebrated 'Day of the Covenant', known today as 'Day of the Vow'. Paul Kruger, the 1881 president of Transvaal, preached that this 1838 victory at Blood River proved that God had selected the Afrikaners as his chosen people; the loss of Natal in 1843 and Transvaal in 1877 to British annexation represented God's punishment for

36 Zeceña, *Sermón 1844*, p. 11; Garcia Peláez, *Discurso 1856*, p. 2; Piñol, *Sermón 1839*, p. 9. Guatemalan clerics held to this one theological assumption more than most. Friar Juan de Jesús Zepeda surpassed most of his colleagues by treating this theological affirmation with great agility: 'God allows ephemeral triumphs of evil in order to punish those who offend him and to test His chosen ones in the crucible of adversity', *Descripción del Templo de San Francisco de Guatemala, concluido el 22 de febrero de 1851, conteniendo una oración …* (Guatemala, 1851), p. 11.

37 Weber, *The Sociology of Religion* (Boston, 1922), p. 16.

38 Sydney E. Ahlstrom (ed.), *Theology in America. The Major Protestant Voices from Puritanism to Neo-Orthodoxy* (Indianapolis, 1967), pp. 24–33.

39 Alan Simpson, 'The Covenant Community,' in John M. Mulder and John F. Wilson (eds.), *Religion in American History: Interpretive Essays* (New Jersey, 1978), pp. 19–20.

the Afrikaner's failure to honour their vows.[40] In both New England and South Africa, covenant theology formed a national community over and against an indigenous people. Theology created a new history, endowing a nation-building people continuity with ancient Israel, while demarcating community boundaries to exclude those they wished to dominate.

Guatemalan clerics went to great lengths to draw out the analogy between Guatemala and Israel. No other nation enjoyed such privilege as did Guatemala. As a chosen nation, Guatemala was called to fulfil its moral obligations.[41] García Peláez testified to Guatemala's covenant with God: as the children of Israel had committed themselves to the ten commandments presented to Moses on Mount Sinai, so too Guatemala should remember its emancipation from the government of Spain with the articles of Independence. Article 10 of this new Tablet, the 'religious alliance contracted with God our Lord',[42] the *Scripsit in tabulis verba fœderis*, stated:

> The Roman Catholic religion which we have professed in the past centuries and which we will profess in the future, will be preserved pure and unaltered, keeping alive the religious spirit which has always distinguished Guatemala, respecting the ecclesiastical ministers, secular and regular, protecting their persons and property.[43]

Reiterating one of José María Castilla's affirmations in his 1821 sermon, Aycinena testified that God providentially ordered the events surrounding the declaration of Independence on 15 September 1821. God had chosen Guatemala since 'emancipation cost not one extraordinary effort, nor any painful sacrifice'.[44] Guatemala could count itself as blessed and chosen.

To what extent had Independence not cost 'one extraordinary effort?' No other single affirmation kindles more passionate debate in contemporary Guatemala each 15 September.[45] Aycinena preserved and transmitted this

40 Leonard Thompson, *The Political Mythology of Apartheid* (New Haven, 1985), p. 170.

41 Aycinena, *Discurso 1858*, p. 14.

42 García Peláez, *Discurso 1856*, p. 2. Additionally, consult Aycinena, *Discurso 1853*, pp. 5–6; and Aycinena, *Discurso 1858*, pp. 4 and 7.

43 *Facsimile del Acta de Independencia de Centro América. Firmada en la ciudad de Guatemala el 15 de septiembre de 1821* (Guatemala, 1934).

44 Juan José Aycinena, *Discurso religioso pronunciado en la S.M.I. de Santiago de Guatemala, el 15 de septiembre de 1855. Aniversario XXXIV de Independencia* (Guatemala), pp. 3–4.

45 'En el día de la patria,' *Siglo Veintiuno* (15 September 1991), p. 10. *Siglo Veintiuno*'s editorial page challenged head-on the lingering notion that Independence cost nothing by highlighting the resistance and sacrifice of many Indians and Creoles who either died in armed resistance (Manuel Tot in Verapaz) or were jailed. This troubling assertion must have originated in the stark contrast with neighbouring Mexico's bloody insurrection that stimulated a caste war led by Miguel Hidalgo.

interpretative tradition initiated with Castilla's 1821 Independence sermon. Castilla had proclaimed that 'Guatemala had witnessed the birth of its liberty without its cradle being stained by a single drop of blood'.[46] By the late 1830s, the clerics Aycinena, Zeceña and Herrarte, and the politician, Pedro Molina, had reaffirmed Castilla's assertion.[47] By 1844, though, precisely when Carrera briefly distanced himself from the Catholic prelates, other clerical interpretations surfaced, challenging this bloodless rendering of Independence. Friar Manuel Zacarías Velásquez lambasted the Spanish conquerors, venerating Bartolomé de las Casas and lauding indigenous resistance. Zacarías Velásquez confronted the notion of a gratuitous Independence by saying: 'I will never forget that in my own cloister some fathers of Central America's liberty were made prisoners!'[48] He was referring to the 'Conspiracy of Belén', when, in December 1813, these Dominican friars were captured for planning armed insurrection to liberate Central America from Spanish control.[49] Nevertheless, Zacarías Velásquez's statements were more the exception than the rule. By the 1850s, with the consolidation of Carrera's conservative regime, Guatemala's singularity, its choseness, was reaffirmed: Guatemala had become a 'rare comet' before many nations.[50]

Many of the clerics purposefully underscored the importance of the peaceful transition from colony to independent state, which contrasted so sharply with events in Mexico. When thousands of peasants had rallied to Father Miguel Hidalgo's cry for independence in Mexico, Creoles in general refused to support him and were consequently identified with, and slaughtered alongside, Spanish officials in the battle of Guanajuato. The painful memory of the Creoles' predicament during the 1810 Mexican

46 Castilla, *Al heroico pueblo*, p. 6.

47 Aycinena, *Discurso 1837*, p. 5; Zeceña *Discurso el día 15 de setiembre de 1839, Aniversario 18 de la Independencia* (Guatemala, 1839), p. 15; Molina, *Discurso 1837*, p. 2; and José Mariano Herrarte, *Sermón predicado el quince de setiembre de mil ochocientos cuarenta, Aniversario XIX de nuestra Independencia del Gobierno Español* (Guatemala, 1840), p. 3. See also Aycinena, *Discurso 1850*, p. 3.

48 Zacarías Velásquez, *Discurso 1844*, p. 8. His printed text referred to the clerics Ruiz, Miguelena and Soto.

49 The friars were held in jail until 1819, when Fernando VII issued a general pardon. For further information on the conspiracy of Belén, see J. E. Arellano, 'Nicaragua,' in *América Central*, vol. 6 of Enrique Dussel's *Historia general de la iglesia en América Latina* (Salmanca, 1985), p. 225.

50 Miguel Muñoz to Francisco García Peláez, Guatemala, 15 December 1858, AHAG 1858.360, Box T2 124.

insurrections weighed heavily on the minds of Guatemalan Creoles who faced daily the whims of a caudillo supported by a giddy, non-white multitude. The Mexican revolutionary experience sent chills down the spines of the Guatemalan Creole elite.[51] In contrast, political transformations like that in Guatemala, which assured continued order and elite control, were deemed wise and prudent. Aycinena praised the people of Guatemala for their 'patience' in not provoking senseless revolutionary fervour in order to gain independence from Spain. He then extended his argument by demonstrating through the bloodless events of Independence that God had chosen Guatemala, not the reverse. Just as Israel had responded to its election by preserving the Pentateuch, so Guatemala must now respond to its election and forever hold to the promises made on 15 September 1821.[52]

With decisive military victories in the 1850s and with Carrera's regime firmly entrenched, history now confirmed the clerics' theological assertions. Now that Guatemala was fulfilling its obligations, God had blessed and protected it from adversity. The liberal governments of El Salvador and Honduras, having agreed in 1851 to re-establish the Federal Republic of Central America, waged war on conservative Guatemala in an attempt to make it join the enterprise. Carrera's troops crushed the invaders and thus maintained Guatemala's independence. This victory was all the proof necessary to confirm the clerics' theological insight. Antonio Larrazábal expressed his gratitude for the

51 According to Estrada Monroy, Guatemala's Archbishop Casaus y Torres was hand-picked to respond to Hidalgo's *Grito de Dolores*. Casaus y Torres wrote the *Cartilla de párrocos*, which was printed and circulated in Mexico and Central America. See Estrada Monroy, *Datos*, vol. 2, pp. 223–37. Also, Alejandro Marure published a perceptive tract in 1838 reminding his compatriots of what happened to European colonists in Santo Domingo (Haiti), who were killed indiscriminately by the former slaves in their revolt. Marure's words reflected a constant fear among white Guatemalans as he warned of a possible caste war, which could end 'in our complete destruction'. See Alejandro Marure, *Memoria sobre la insurrección de Sta. Rosa y Mataquescuintla en Centro-América* (Guatemala, 1893), pp. 21–2.

52 Juan José de Aycinena, *Discurso 1864*, pp. 5–11. Additionally, consult Juan José de Aycinena, *Aniversario XL (sic) de la Independencia de Guatemala. Discurso religioso pronunciado en la Santa Iglesia Catedral el 16 de Septiembre de 1862* (Guatemala, 1862), p. 4; Aycinena, *Discurso 1850*, p. 3; Aycinena, *Discurso 1858*, pp. 7 and 11; and Juan José de Aycinena, *Aniversario XXXIX de la Independencia de Guatemala. Discurso religioso pronunciado en la Santa Iglesia Catedral el 16 de Setiembre de 1860* (Guatemala, 1860), p. 9.

divine shielding of Guatemala, noting that the country's religious piety had made this possible. Even the caudillo Carrera affirmed that Providence had continued to protect those who truly believed.[53]

In 1857 two Guatemalan generals and other military men died from cholera while fighting William Walker's troops in Nicaragua. This North American filibusterer had threatened to invite Protestants to the region. In a funeral speech, Aycinena eulogised the Guatemalans for fighting the 'intrusive, cruel and bloodthirsty foreigners who desired to abolish our worship'. Aycinena relied on God's 'strong arm' since these Guatemalans, like the Maccabees, died in the strict observance of Divine law and in their fervour to protect Guatemala's religion.[54]

The 1857 cholera epidemic proved to be a setback to the Church's view that God favoured Guatemala as long as its people protected its religion. One Jesuit tried to put a positive twist on the epidemic proclaiming that the pestilence must be God's way of cultivating their happiness. Another member of the regular clergy attempted to hold fast to the notion that the Guatemalans must have broken the covenant by pointing out their continued state of sinfulness. Ignacio Cambrils integrated the lessons learned from the historic 1773 earthquake that had levelled the old city in Antigua with the concurrent 1857 cholera epidemic that was ravaging the countryside. He argued that 'your sins led you to these tragedies, your brutal passions, your dishonesty, your drunkeness, and other horrible sins provoked the wrath of God to send the earthquake or to send the cholera'. Cambrils begged them to call on God to forgive them and release them from the grip of cholera.[55] It was, however,

53 Antonio Larrazábal, 'Funerales celebrados en la Santa Iglesia Catedral,' *Gaceta de Guatemala* (21 March 1851), p. 3; Rafael Carrera to the People of Guatemala, Chiquimula, 5 February 1851, AHAG Box 61 T6; and Francisco García Peláez, *Nos el Doctor D. Francisco de Paula García Peláez ...* (Guatemala, 4 January 1851). In the archbishop's call for prayer, he reiterated that the spirit of rebellion and discord were God's way of making the people atone for their sins. See also García Peláez, *Discurso 1856*, p. 8. In Aycinena, *Discurso 1853*, p. 8, Aycinena affirmed God's watchful care over Guatemala at the very moment invaders tried to conquer Guatemala.

54 Juan José de Aycinena, *Oración fúnebre que pronunció en la S.I.M. de Guatemala el día 14 de enero de 1857, en las exequias solemnes por el descanso de los SS. Generales D. Mariano Paredes y D. Joaquín Solares, y demas gefes, oficiales y soldados muertos en la campaña de Nicaragua* (Guatemala, 1857), p. 3.

55 Padre Rafael Pérez, *La Compania de Jesus en Colombia y Centro-América despues de su restauración* (Valladolid, 1896-98), p. 30; and Ignacio de Cambrils, *Cronicón*, p. 2.

the successful Capuchin missions to eastern Guatemala that 'redeemed' the people from their sins, and in the Church's understanding, finally released them from the plague. As Archbishop García Peláez thanked the Capuchins for their work noting that 'the hand of the Omnipotent has touched us, sending the cholera epidemic, in order for us to recognise how divine justice weighs in against our straying'.[56]

It was Carrera's imperialistic defeat of El Salvador, the holdout of liberals, in 1863 that evidenced God's definitive favour. Carrera had challenged the leader of El Salvador's government that had taken strong measures against its clergy, and through a difficult war, had overthrown the tyrant of the Catholic Church. The abbess of the Capuchin Convent, Sister María Clara, wrote to Carrera praising his triumph over the enemies 'of our religion', while Aycinena declared that all Guatemalans must honour him with the title, 'the Father of our Country'. García Peláez also wrote to Carrera, congratulating him on his victory, stating 'Providence had favoured our holy cause'.[57]

The Guatemalan clerics' successful transmission of their unique covenant theology can in part be measured by the response of their vociferous critics. In their elite opponents' jibes one senses their utter disgust with the clerics' theological rendition of Guatemalan history. These elite adversaries held the clerics in contempt for creating a historical narrative that closely linked Guatemala's past struggles with a sacred tradition, while unctuously anointing its present administration with divine approval. One anonymous pen unleashed a series of attacks on the famed Guatemalan novelist, José Milla, who had preached on Independence Day in 1846. Calling Milla the 'apostle of backwardness', the undisclosed critic attacked Milla for not denouncing the horrors of the conquest and for revising the history of the Independence movement to make it appear that the aristocratic families 'spontaneously' favoured Independence. Angered by Milla's comparison of Guatemala to Israel's captivity in Egypt, the author countered Milla's history by

56 Ignacio de Cambrils, *Cronicón*, p. 78.

57 Sor María Clara to Rafael Carrera, Capuchin Convent in Guatemala, 3 Dec. 1863, AGCA B 118.6, Exp. 53312, Leg. 2443, Fol. 4; Juan José Aycinena to Rafael Carrera, Guatemala, 17 November 1863, AGCA B 118.6, Exp. 53278, Leg. 2443, Fol. 15; and Francisco García Peláez to Rafael Carrera, 16 Nov. 1863, AGCA B 118.6, Exp. 53278, Leg. 2443, Fol. 14.

exclaiming that Independence was liberation from the slavery of clerical abuses and the colonial inheritance of privilege.[58]

The cleric Prudencio Puertas went so far as to proclaim that Carrera was the Moses who had led his people out of captivity.[59] In a terse, published response to his speech, a group of Salvadorans expressed their surprised disgust that the 'guerrilla' Carrera had been compared to Moses. In their attempt to humiliate Puertas, they scornfully asked:

> Did Carrera divide the sea with his staff so that his army could pass through, and then bury his enemies in its wake? Did he quench the thirst of his army by making water come out of rocks? Did he make manna rain from the skies to feed his hungry people? Has anything similar to this occurred in Guatemala? No; consequentially, Father Puertas has played with the Holy Scripture like a child, like a fool, like a wicked man.[60]

In spite of their critics' skilful attacks, Guatemalan clerics continued preaching their theological vision of Guatemala's past, present and future. Far from a reformed heritage yet theologically close to the spirit of the covenant communities of the United States and South Africa, the Guatemalan clerics broke definitively from the spiritual and political boundaries associated with the Spanish Crown. New theological and political boundaries created a national consciousness circumscribing the covenant community of God. Strangely enough, a kind of Protestant posi-

58 Un Militar, *Observaciones*, p. 1. Like Milla, clerical and non-clerical discourse often focused on the Spanish Conquest. In 1841, Basilio Porras minimised the historical blame falling on Spanish descendants of the conquistadors in nineteenth-century Guatemala. On the contrary, these descendants, exclaimed Porras, deserved credit for Independence from Spain. By the late 1860s, Christopher Columbus was described as a messenger of God. See Basilio Porras, *Discurso de ley pronunciado en el Salón de sesiones de la Asamblea Constituyente el 15 de setiembre de 1841* (Guatemala, 1841), p. 2; and José Antonio Urrutia, *Aniversario XLVII de la Independencia de Guatemala. Discurso religioso pronunciado en la Santa Iglesia Catedral el 15 de setiembre de 1868* (Guatemala, 1868), pp. 6–7. Milla did respond to the charges in, *Esplicación de algunos de los conceptos contenidos en el discurso pronunciado en el salon del Supremo Gobierno del Estado de Guatemala, el dia 15 de septiembre de 1846, aniversario XXV de la Independencia Nacional* (Guatemala, 1846).

59 Prudencio Puertas, *Discurso 1854*, pp. 9–10.

60 Unos Salvadoreños, *Observaciones al discurso pronunciado por el presbítero don Prudencio Puertas en la catedral de Guatemala, el 15 de setiembre de 1854* (San Vicente, 1855), p. 4. Challenges to the Guatemalan and Salvadoran Catholic Church intermittently emanated from critics in El Salvador. See Manuel Suárez, *Aniversario XL de la Independencia de Centro-América. Discurso pronunciado en el salón del Supremo Poder Ejecutivo de la Republica del Salvador el 15 de setiembre de 1861* (San Salvador, 1861).

tion on nationhood developed in response to the distinctive challenge faced by the Guatemalan clerics. As the bishop of Chiapas congratulated the Guatemalan archbishop on his 1857 anniversary sermon and his pastoral letter on the war in Nicaragua, he noted particularly that García Peláez had 'bonded patriotic feelings and earthly successes with the eternal and holy ideals of our Divine Religion that we profess'.[61]

Two foreigners commented on how well established and popular the Catholic Church had become once again. The US diplomat, Henry Savage, commenting on the increased presence of the Jesuits in the country, penned a vicious anti-Catholic message to his superiors in 1853. In his objections one can almost sense the profound religiosity that was beginning to sweep Guatemala:

> A revival of old superstitious ceremonies which had fallen into disuse has been effected, and it is asserted that the processions of idols and large dolls decorated with an awful display of jewelry and tussel, during the last Holy Week have never been surpassed in pomp and solemnity, while the female part of the community neglect their domestic concerns to satisfy spiritual cravings, have sunk into a heathenishlike superstition and expect the attainment of their salvation from mere ceremonial observances. The perversion of a religious sentiment that characterises the principles of the rigidly Catholic party, and which causes the bigot to view with kindred hatred any intellectual advancement, seems here to be on the ascendency.[62]

In any study of discourse and ritual, especially one concerned with an emerging nationalism, the historian cannot fail to examine, no matter how difficult it may be, the degree to which elite discourse was or was not appropriated by the community. But complicating this unavoidable query is the question of method: how can one measure popular appropriation or rejection of these invented and adopted traditions if the majority of the populace was illiterate? It will always be nearly impossible to know their heart and minds. What becomes crucial is to study the action, the conflicts produced within these communities during the nation-building moment and examine how the dominant group responded to the challenge.

61 Carlos María Obispo de Chiapas to Francisco de Paula García Peláez, San Cristobal de las Casas, Mexico, 13 June 1857, AHAG 1857.191, Box T2 122.

62 Henry Savage to L. Marchy (Secretary of State), 31 May 1853, Guatemala. US Department of State, *Despatches from United States Ministers to Central America, 1824–1906* (microfilm).

Victor Turner, who viewed conflict as the essence of the human social drama, pointed out the potential of religious ritual to redress and reintegrate groups who threaten social breach, and at the same time the potential of ritual to escalate crisis moments, giving birth to irreparable schism among social groups.[63] For example, when an explosion at an artillery unit assigned to salute Guatemala City's celebration of the 1837 Anniversary of Independence left one dead and one badly burned, an investigation was immediately ordered to see if the detonation was purposeful or accidental.[64] Participants clearly recognised that this had been a crisis moment in a ritual with potential significance for the life of a political community. Disturbances in the ritual posed a threat to the government's legitimacy. Remember that in 1837 popular revolts were surfacing in Guatemala's eastern mountains and in key Indian villages in the western highlands. Though the investigation claimed that sparks from the third round of artillery fire ignited the ammunition box, popular perception might not have easily concurred with the official conclusion, thus further eroding the government's credibility. Civil disturbances thus provide a lens to measure the strength and weakness of state hegemony.

Religious and political celebrations became critical opportunities to show popular disgust with the clerics and their message. 'Unfortunate incidents' were reported in Zacapa during the 1840 Independence festivities. In Santa Lucía Cotzumalguapa, near Escuintla, the priest complained that various drunken individuals disrespected him during the anniversary celebration in 1855 and Archbishop García Peláez called on authorities to punish the irreverent men.[65] When one priest did not celebrate Independence in Chiquimula in 1865, he was immediately thrown in jail by the chief magistrate.[66] Father Cayetano Serra caused a public uproar when he challenged García Peláez's theological justification for Guatemala's involvement in the filibuster war of 1856. Evidently Serra had preached that the war was not

63 Victor Turner, *Dramas, Fields and Metaphors: Symbolic Action in Human Society* (Ithaca, New York, 1974), pp. 38–42.

64 Juan Arévalo, Juicio Criminal, 19 Sept. 1837, Guatemala, AGCA B 90.1, Exp. 30894 Leg. 1269.

65 Yndalecio Perdomo to General Minister of Supreme Government, Chiquimula, 26 September 1840, AGCA B 119.2, Exp. 57365 Leg. 2526; José María Mondragón to Corregidor del Departamento de Escuintla, Escuintla, Sept. 1855, AGCA B, Leg. 28567, Exp. 183, Fol. 4; and Francisco García Peláez to Manuel Echeverría, Guatemala, 24 Sept. 1855, AGCA B, Leg. 28567, Exp. 183, Fol. 3.

66 Yanuario Xiron to Francisco García Peláez, Chiquimula, 15 Sept. 1865, AHAG 1865.353, Box T4 71.

fought to sustain the Catholic faith nor to conserve the Independence of Central America, nor to defend the Republic of Guatemala. The theological powerhouses — José María Barrutia, Juan José Aycinena, Prudencio Puertas and Bernardo Piñol — complained to the archbishop that Serra's sermon threatened schism and chaos.[67] In 1869, Juan La Canal wrote that military officials scandalised the people of Escuintla during the 15 September festivities. Not only had they dissolved the military band but were conspicuously absent from the event. He reported that 'they have been severely punished by the general rebuke of the people!'[68]

One of the most humorous scandals to rock religious and political boats took place in Rabinal in Baja Verapaz in 1862. Salamá's parish priest, Juan Valdez, notified the archbishop that the municipality leader of Rabinal had organised a celebration honouring Independence and picked a local leader, Nicolás Blanco, to give the honorary speech. Blanco, however, literally read, word for word, a copy of a 1835 sermon written by Matías Quiñones, a priest who wholeheartedly had supported the Independence of Los Altos in its brief breakaway from Guatemala and who had additionally used the occasion in 1835 to attack conservative renditions of Guatemala's history. Blanco's speech thus attacked the Spanish conquerors for utilising Christianity to cover up their ambitions and praised the Mexican hero, Hidalgo, for initiating the Mexican independence movement. The 1835 speech also concluded with praise for the past federal system heralded by Morazán's ideological descendants. Both Rabinal's mayor and Nicolás Blanco received verbal reprimands: they were 'ignorant' and 'incapable' of putting together such a speech.[69] Consequentially, copies of Bishop Juan José Aycinena's 1862 Independence sermon were circulated to all parish priests in Guatemala in order to avoid future 'mistakes'.[70]

Historians and Guatemalan enthusiasts must be pondering why no mention of the renowned Crucified Christ of Esquipulas exists in this

67 José María Barrutia, Juan José Aycinena, Bernardo Piñol, Julián Alfaro and Prudencio Puertas to Francisco García Peláez, Guatemala, 1857, AHAG 1857.100 T2 121.

68 Juan La Canal to Ministro de Gobernación de Justicia y Negocios Eclesiásticos, Escuintla, 17 Sept. 1869, AGCA B, Leg. 28618, Exp. 141, Fol. 2.

69 Juan E. Valdez to J. M. Barrutia, Salamá, 11 Oct. 1862, AHAG 1862.376, T3 77.

70 Cordillera '15 Septiembre,' 27 Oct. 1862, AHAG 1862.365, Box T3 77. One cannot help but wonder if the *alcalde* and community friends feigned ignorance as a resistance strategy or if indeed they could not fathom the larger community in question in the elite political struggles.

analysis of religion in nineteenth-century Guatemala. Evidence suggests that the shrine's importance transcended the narrow political boundaries and appealed to a broad Meso-American population. Located in the eastern corner of Guatemala, the town of Esquipulas serves as a principal border town to both Honduras and El Salvador. Whereas the Virgin of Guadalupe resided within the colonial and national confines of Mexico City, the patron saint of Esquipulas transcended the immediate nineteenth-century borders of the Central American nations and did not lend itself to the creation of a religiously-inspired national identity.

By the beginning of the twentieth century the Crucified Christ of Esquipulas began to feature prominently in the religious identity of the Guatemalan Catholic Church. With the natural death of Carrera in 1865 and the collapse of the conservative regime to the Winchesters and Remingtons of its liberal opponents, the Catholic Church suffered a new round of public pressure and harassment. The growth attained during the Carrera years quickly dwindled as the Barrios regime systematically enforced classic Latin American liberal measures against the religious institution and its representatives. General Barrios pursued a secularising policy against the Church, exiled the archbishop and closed down most of the regular orders. Church officials adjusted to an even harsher reality than experienced during the years of the Central American Federation.[71]

During the last two decades of the nineteenth century, parish priests began to record an increasing number of miracles attributed to the shrine at Esquipulas. With publications in 1904 and 1914, the parish priest Juan Paz Solórzano charted the history and attraction of the 'Crucified Lord of Esquipulas'. According to his written records, soon after its sculpting, witnesses gave credit to the holy shrine for ten miracles in the 1600s and seven in the 1700s. Records from 1800 through to the end of the conservative era, the 1870s, indicate only four miracles. From the 1880s a marked change took place. From 1880 through 1911, parish priests recorded 28 different miracles attributed to the Crucified Christ of Esquipulas.[72]

Given the increased notoriety of the shrine, Paz Solórzano and other parish priests petitioned the archbishop to consecrate and declare that the Holy Christ of Esquipulas would be the Principal Patron of the

71 H. J. Miller, *La iglesia católica y el estado en Guatemala, 1871–1885* (Guatemala, 1976), pp. 117–83.

72 Juan Paz Solórzano, *Historia del Señor Crucificado de Esquipulas de su santuario; romerías; antigua provincia eclesiástica de Chiquimula de la Sierra y actual vicaría foránea; como también de otras muchas cosas dignas de saberse* (Guatemala, 1914), pp. 21–39.

Ecclesiastical Province of Guatemala (*Patrón Principal de la Provincia Eclesiástica de Guatemala*). In 1916, Archbishop Riveiro accompanied by Juan Paz Solórzano and a host of other priests, anointed the shrine and consecrated it.[73] Within four decades of that consecration, Esquipulas would contribute one of its sons to lead the Guatemalan Catholic Church: Monseñor Mariano Rossell y Arellano. The shrine featured prominently in Archbishop Rossell's challenge to the democratically elected government of Jacobo Arbenz and his political goals. Archbishop Rossell initiated a national campaign in 1953 to confront 'atheistic communism', and carried the Crucified Lord of Esquipulas from town to town to spread his theological and political message. In addition to his very prominent role, Rossell also energised the decaying Catholic institution, and under him the number of clerics and lay leaders more than tripled within Guatemala.[74]

Thus the shrine of Esquipulas, given pressure from the secularising state apparatus, increased devotion and praise for the miracles performed and the intentional hierarchical support at the local and national level, assumed a greater part of the Guatemalan religious identity. Additionally, the hostile Protestant presence now significant in voice and number in some way enhanced the prestige and identity of Guatemala's Catholicism. Beginning in 1889 and throughout the twentieth century, any historic analysis of the shrine from the apologetic perspective of the Catholic officials necessarily included a conceptual and theological defence of Catholic shrines and subsequent theological challenges to Protestant views.[75] In sum, by the twentieth century the shrine of Esquipulas equalled the heart and soul of Guatemalan Catholicism, a reality born of political and theological pressure.

During the Carrera years the Guatemalan clerics attempted to rebuild a devastated institution within a new geopolitical entity. They had fashioned a nationalist discourse during the caudillo's rule. Grounding their theological understanding of salvation history in the Biblical notion of the covenant community, clerics adapted to the changing geopolitical boundaries and prompted loyalty to the emerging nation of Guatemala. Religious discourse

73 Juan Paz Solórzano, *Segunda parte de la historia del Señor Crucificado del Santuario de Esquipulas* (Guatemala, 1916), pp. 8–11. See also Agustín Estrada Monroy, *Datos para la historia de la iglesia de Guatemala*, tomo III (Guatemala, 1979), p. 364.

74 R. Bendaña, 'Guatemala,' *América Central: Tomo VI*, in Enrique Dussel's *Historia General*, pp. 365–72. See also José Luis Chea, *Guatemala: la cruz fragmentada* (San José, Costa Rica, 1988), pp. 71–87.

75 See Muñoz, *Doctrina cristiana sobre el culto de las imágenes*, pp. 5–25; and Paz Solórzano, *Historia del Señor Crucificado de Esquipulas*, pp. 104–29.

dominated anniversary celebrations of Independence and reflected a sense of Divine election. History did not sustain the Catholic clergy's covenant theology. Shortly after Carrera's death in 1865, the Catholic Church endured another season of institutional repression with the liberal triumph of 1871. By the end of the century Catholic clerics looked to the religious shrine of Esquipulas to find meaning in a hostile political world. Despite the setbacks the Church endured, Catholic clerics bequeathed a legacy of the nation to a land fragmented by language and by powerful elites.

CHAPTER 5

Emilio Castelar en Hispanoamérica: república, liberalismo y el poder de la oratoria*

Eduardo Posada-Carbó

I

'Venir a España', escribió Rubén Darío, 'y no conocer la Alhambra, y el Museo de Pinturas … y a Castelar, es no venir a España.'[1] Quienes hoy vienen a España siguen visitando la Alhambra y los museos de pinturas; pero muy pocos saben quizá de la existencia de Emilio Castelar (1832–99), mucho menos de su importancia. En 1893, sin embargo, cuando el poeta nicaragüense recordaba su almuerzo con Castelar en Serrano 40,[2] la fama de Castelar tenía escasos paralelos. Hombre de letras, publicista, político y, por encima de todo, orador, Castelar lideró el movimiento liberal y republicano en España durante la segunda mitad del siglo diecinueve. 'Monarca intelectual', le llamó entonces Darío – un calificativo desafortunado para quien llegó a presidir la Primera República española entre setiembre de 1873 y enero de 1874. Pero según Darío, 'muerto Víctor Hugo', no había 'testa coronada que el mundo admire más'. Ciertamente su renombre tuvo alcance internacional, aunque fue en Hispanoamérica, y así mismo en Francia, donde tuvo quizá más resonancia. Como lo expresara uno de sus biógrafos, tras su muerte 'cundió rápidamente la noticia por España y América y puede decirse que el duelo, no fue ya nacional, sino que en él vistió de luto toda la raza latina'.[3]

* Una primera versión de este ensayo fue presentada en el seminario 'La influencia española y británica en las ideas y en la política latinoamericana, siglos XIX y XX', organizado por el Institute of Latin American Studies y el Instituto Universitario Ortega y Gasset en Madrid, en 1997. Una versión de este artículo aparecerá en le revista *Hispania.* Agradezco las estimulantes observaciones y valiosas sugerencias de Charles Hale, Malcolm Deas, Carlos Malamud, Alastair Hennessy, Carlos Dardé, Víctor Peralta, Florentino Portero, Charles Powell e Iván Jaksíc.

1 Rubén Darío, 'Un almuerzo con Castelar,' *La Literatura de El Heraldo*, Bogotá, 1893, p. 189.

2 Aunque de acuerdo con uno de sus secretarios, Castelar vivía en Serrano 28, esquina a la de Hermosilla, R. Alberola, *Emilio Castelar. Memorias de un secretario* (Madrid, 1950), p. 27.

3 E. Barriobero y Herrán, *Don Emilio Castelar* (Madrid, 1930), pp. 56–7.

¿Cómo definir la influencia de Emilio Castelar en las ideas y en la política de Hispanoamérica? ¿Cuál fue su real dimensión? ¿Qué razones explicarían el enorme atractivo que parece haber ejercido entre intelectuales y políticos hispanoamericanos? Tales son algunos de los interrogantes que me propongo explorar en este ensayo. Y digo explorar porque el propósito se tropieza con dificultades. Ante todo, intentar delinear con mediana exactitud el influjo de Castelar exigiría un conocimiento más profundo de la historia del pensamiento en Hispanoamérica y España. El historiador, en cualquier caso, no tardaría en identificar el eclecticismo tal vez dominante — lo que siempre vuelve arriesgada cualquier empresa de trazar influencias intelectuales. Por lo demás, la misma obra de Castelar volvería trabajoso todo empeño: por su volumen y por el tedio que inevitablemente produce la lectura de una retórica ya en desuso.[4]

Lo preferible de Castelar, según Benjamín Jarnés, eran sus cartas;[5] pero con la excepción de su correspondencia editada por Adolfo Calzado y de algunos legajos en el Archivo Histórico Nacional de Madrid, no parece existir una fuente sólida que permita estudiar sistemáticamente sus comunicaciones epistolares.[6] Abundan, en cambio, sus trabajos publicados. Aunque existen muy pocas re-ediciones de sus libros — novelas, biografías, ensayos literarios, relatos de viaje, monografías históricas y, por supuesto, discursos políticos.[7] La biblioteca de Pablo Turiel, una de las colecciones privadas más completas de libros de Castelar que se conoció a comienzos de este siglo, contaba con 48 títulos en 101 volúmenes — donde se excluía de todas formas su vasta labor periodística.[8] 'No se le leyó

4 'Es difícil evaluar hoy la fama de Castelar,' ha escrito Charles Hale en *The Transformation of Liberalism in Late Nineteenth-Century Mexico* (Princeton y New Jersey, 1989), p. 41. Tras señalar que el oyente contemporáneo se recreaba frente al 'vistoso ropaje retórico' de los discursos de Castelar, María Cruz Seoane anotó: 'Hoy, el lector se pone un poco nervioso y hasta se irrita'. Véase su *Oratoria y periodismo en la España del siglo XIX* (Madrid, 1977).

5 Benjamín Jarnés, *Castelar, hombre del Sinaí* (Madrid, 1935), p. 12.

6 Adolfo Calzado (ed.), *Correspondencia de Emilio Castelar, 1868–1898* (Madrid, 1908). Las cartas de Castelar en el Archivo Histórico Nacional de Madrid se encuentran en la sección Diversos títulos y familias. Debo a Carlos Dardé esta útil referencia. En conversaciones con Ezequiel Gallo, supe que parte de la biblioteca de Castelar pasó a ser propiedad del Jockey Club de Buenos Aires.

7 Los recorridos por las librerías de Madrid en busca de libros de Castelar o sobre Castelar han sido para mí frustrantes. Sin embargo, es posible encontrar algunos títulos en las ferias o en los mercados de libros viejos, a subidos precios – ¿indicio de un mayor interés reciente por la vida y obra del tribuno?

8 Bernardo Herrera Ochoa, *Castelar, su infancia y su último año de vida* (Madrid, 1914), p. 170. Un rápido inventario de su obra aparece en Barriobero, *Don Emilio Castelar*, pp. 59–61.

y no se le lee,' expresó Jarnés, 'porque su obra gigantesca aturde, exige enormes sacrificios de tiempo.'[9] Aturdimiento y sacrificios: también presentes cuando apenas se han leído, como en mi caso, lo confieso, fragmentos de su obra.

El propósito de este ensayo es analizar la influencia de la figura y obra de Emilio Castelar fuera de España, en particular su repercusión en el mundo intelectual y político de Hispanoamérica, aunque también, pero en menor medida, en otras fronteras. A continuación, describo la fama internacional de Castelar y los diversos medios a través de los cuales se le conoció y admiró. En la sección III examino algunas de las razones que permiten explicar el enorme atractivo de su obra en Hispanoamérica. Finalmente analizo el poder de su oratoria y la paradoja de su influencia entre quienes casi nunca le escucharon. Importa aclarar de antemano que este ensayo no es un estudio del pensamiento de Castelar. Su objetivo es mostrar la dimensión internacional de quien fuera quizá la figura española de la segunda mitad del siglo diecinueve más conocida fuera de España.

II

Emilio Castelar nació en Cádiz en 1832.[10] Su salto a la vida pública se produjo tras un discurso que pronunció en un mitin del partido progresista, en la Plaza de Oriente de Madrid, el 25 de setiembre de 1854. Un cronista de *La Epoca*, allí presente, describió 'la fácil palabra de un joven … que cautivó la atención de los oyentes'.[11] Cautivó también la atención de la pren-

9 Jarnés, *Castelar, hombre del Sinaí*, p. 13.

10 No son muchos los trabajos modernos sobre Castelar; pero al momento de revisar este ensayo, se publicó el libro de Jorge Wilches García, *Emilio Castelar. La patria y la república* (Madrid, 2001). Véase también Carmen Llorca, *Emilio Castelar. Precursor de la Democracia Cristiana* (Madrid, 1966). Se han publicado, sin embargo, varios trabajos sobre diversos aspectos de su vida y obra, algunos ya citados en este ensayo en notas anteriores, que aportan datos de interés. Véase también Emilio Oliver Sanz de Bremond, *Castelar y el período revolucionario español, 1868–1874* (Madrid, 1971); Nancy A. Rosenblatt, 'Emilio Castelar, teórico, publicista y político republicano,' *Revista de Estudios Políticos*, vol. 186 (Madrid, 1972); y Luis Esteve Ibañez, 'El posibilismo. La política de Castelar,' *Canelobre*, vol. 22 (Alicante, 1991), pp. 29–38. Una visión anglo-sajona contemporánea se encuentra en David Hannay, *Don Emilio Castelar* (Londres, 1896). Los trabajos de Carlos Dardé sobre el republicanismo español durante el siglo XIX sirven para ubicar a Castelar en el contexto político de la época. Véanse, en particular, sus ensayos: 'La larga noche de la Restauración, 1875–1900,' en N. Townson (ed.), *El republicanismo en España, 1830–1977* (Madrid, 1994), pp. 113–38; y 'Los republicanos,' *Historia General de España y América* (Madrid, 1982), tomo XVI-2, pp. 130–56. Véase también el libro ya clásico de Alastair Hennessy, *La república federal en España* (Madrid, 1966).

11 Llorca, *Emilio Castelar*, p. 29; y Bariobero y Herrán, *Don Emilio Castelar*, pp. 21–5.

sa progresista, *El Tribuno del Pueblo* y *La Soberanía*, donde comenzaron a aparecer artículos del joven Castelar contra la monarquía. Sus primeros fallidos intentos de llegar a las Cortes se vieron compensados por sus conferencias en El Ateneo, donde pronto ganó 'reputación de orador elocuentísimo', y en la Cátedra de Historia de España en la Universidad Central.

La temprana incursión de Castelar en la vida pública española tuvo eco casi inmediato en Hispanoamérica. En 1858, un escritor peruano, José Silva Santisteban dedicaba ya 'lisongeras e inmerecidas palabras' a Castelar en su libro *Derecho Constitucional*.[12] Aunque fue en las siguientes dos décadas cuando su fama alcanzó dimensiones extraordinarias. En 1869, el colombiano Rafael Núñez — entonces cónsul en Le Havre y corresponsal de periódicos hispanoamericanos, y pronto presidente de su país — consideraba que Castelar se encontraba 'a la altura del apostolado de las ideas'.[13] Núñez había conocido personalmente a Castelar. Otros estadistas y hombres de letras hispanoamericanos también recordaban especialmente sus encuentros con el 'apóstol' español. El chileno Luis Orrego Luco tuvo la oportunidad de tratarlo en las veladas de la Condesa de Pardo Bazán, donde 'Castelar charlaba en su maravilloso lenguaje que parecía un largo monólogo, brillántisimo, con bordados de viejas casullas y penchos de pedrería dibujados por orfebres'.[14] En efecto, visitar a Castelar, como lo describió Darío, se convirtió en una especie de peregrinaje para los hispanoamericanos cultos. También como Darío, el colombiano José María Quijano Wallis pensaba que a España debía irse principalmente por tres cosas, aunque no coincidiesen en todos los tres motivos: 'visitar la Alhambra, asistir a una corrida de toros y oír a Castelar'.[15] Quijano Wallis le había conocido en Madrid en 1879, cuando tuvo la oportunidad 'de verlo, oírlo y admirarlo en la tribuna'.[16] Otros, como el argentino Domingo Faustino Sarmiento — con quien Castelar brindó por el futuro de la democracia y por la unión entre España y América en 1867 — le conocerían en París.[17]

12 Emilio Castelar, 'La universalidad de la democracia,' en *Ensayos literarios* (Madrid, 1880), p. 69.

13 Las corresponsalías de Núñez se publicaban en varios periódicos colombianos, así como en *El Nacional* de Lima y *El Continental* de Nueva York. Estas fueron reproducidas en sus *Ensayos de Crítica Social* (Rouen, 1874), ver p. 126.

14 Luis Orrego Luco, *Memorias del tiempo viejo* (Santiago, 1984), p. 106; ver también pp. xxiv y 105.

15 J.M. Quijano Wallis, *Estudios, discursos y escritos varios* (París, 1908), p. 101.

16 Quijano Wallis describió a Castelar como 'un hombre fornido, de mediana estatura, ancho pecho, grandes ojos negros, tez morena, espesos mostachos que cubrían los gruesos labios, cabeza redonda y muy calva', *idem.*, p. 99.

17 Charles Hale, 'Political and social ideas,' en L. Bethell (ed.), *Latin America. Economy and Society, 1870–1930* (Cambridge, 1989), p. 229.

La admiración por Castelar en hispanoamérica se reflejaba en otras comunicaciones menos directas. Desde El Salvador, recibía sacos de café que le enviaba el presidente de este país, don Rafael Saldívar.[18] En la mesa de Pedro Balmaceda, hijo del presidente chileno, podían verse 'libros con autógrafos de Castelar'.[19] En 1875, el Ministro de Honduras en Londres le consultaba sobre 'un asunto muy delicado' entre su embajada y los tribunales británicos ya que se le consideraba 'el Hombre Público contemporáneo más respetado y querido de todas las Repúblicas Hispanoamericanas'.[20] Pero quizá los mejores ejemplos de la apreciación que se tuvo por Castelar los dieron los periódicos que acogían regularmente sus corresponsalías y reproducían sus escritos sobre los más variados temas: en *La Nación* de Buenos Aires, *La Tribuna* y *El Siglo* de Montevideo, *El Nacional* de Lima, *El Siglo* de la Habana, *El Mercurio* de Valparaíso, o en *El Monitor Republicano* de México. Sus colaboraciones en estos periódicos le proporcionaban recursos económicos significativos.[21]

Los vínculos de Castelar con el mundo intelectual latinoamericano pueden también seguirse a través de los prólogos que escribió en sus libros. En 1868, Castelar prologaba los *Ensayos biográficos* de J.M. Torres Caicedo.[22] En 1875, un texto de H.F. Varela sobre la revolución que acompaño a la elección de Manuel Pardo como presidente del Perú incluía un comentario de Castelar — 'La estabilidad social en América'. Un año más tarde, el estudio del abogado y constituyente argentino Luis V. Varela sobre sistemas electorales era precedido por un 'juicio crítico' de Emilio Castelar. Y en 1880, Castelar prologaba las memorias del periodista español Ramón

18 Alberola, *Emilio Castelar*, p. 61.

19 Enrique Campos Menéndez, 'Rubén Darío en Chile. La lágrima y el vino,' *El Mercurio*, 11 de abril de 1993.

20 Cartas de Carlos Gutiérrez y de Ramón de Silva Ferro, Londres, 9 de octubre de 1875 y París, 9 de octubre de 1875 a Emilio Castelar; Archivo Histórico Nacional, Madrid (AHN). Diversos Títulos y Familias, Legajo 2410.

21 Jarnés, *Castelar. Hombre del Sinaí*, p. 113; y Hale, *The Transformation of Liberalism*, p. 47. Muchos otros periódicos simplemente reproducían escritos y discursos suyos, con los cuales es frecuente toparse en cualquier lectura de prensa de la época. Para el caso colombiano, por ejemplo, sin estar dedicado sistemáticamente a éllo, he descubierto por lo menos reproducciones de artículos de Castelar en *El Zipa* (Bogotá), 8 de mayo de 1879; *El Empresario* (Tunja), 1 de julio de 1880, *Papel Periódico Ilustrado* (Bogotá), 28 de noviembre de 1882 (Edición facsimilar, Cali, 1976), p. 83; y *Literatura de El Heraldo* (Bogotá, 1893), pp. 3-5.

22 J.M. Torres Caicedo, *Ensayos biográficos y de crítica literaria sobre los principales publicistas, historiadores, poetas y literatos de la América Latina* (París, 1868), pp. i–xxiv.

Elices Montes en México.[23] Adicionalmente, algunas de las obras de Castelar se imprimían por casas editoriales hispanoamericanas.[24]

La influencia de Castelar en México fue particularmente significativa, tal como lo ha mostrado Charles Hale. Desde 1869 y por espacio de 30 años sus colaboraciones aparecieron quincenalmente en *El Monitor Republicano*, donde ocupaban casi siempre la primera página.[25] El 'interés y la circulación' de este periódico, según Montes, se beneficiaban 'poderosamente' con las correspondencias de Castelar.[26] Existieron afinidades especiales que estimularon el acercamiento de los intelectuales y políticos mexicanos hacia Castelar. Ante todo, sus ataques contra los intentos europeos de reimponer un régimen monárquico en México, mientras alababa 'la grandeza de Juárez',[27] fueron, por supuesto, de buen recibo en círculos liberales. Posteriormente, la experiencia republicana española y las preocupaciones de Castelar sobre el orden como base del liberalismo inspiraron a ese grupo de intelectuales que se reunieron alrededor de *La Libertad* — Justo Sierra, Francisco Cosme y Telésforo García.[28] Este último, además, fue amigo personal y mecenas de Castelar.[29]

La fama internacional de Castelar, es oportuno advertir, no estuvo limitada a Hispanoamérica. Se le admiraba en Francia, en Inglaterra y, más aún, en los Estados Unidos, donde su defensa de la causa republicana era naturalmente vista con enorme simpatía. Muchos de sus ensayos fueron traducidos al inglés y al francés y publicados en prestigiosas revistas. En 1887, por ejemplo, un artículo suyo sobre Savonarola era publicado en Londres por *The Contemporary Review*, una revista londinense que ese año contó entre sus colaboradores a James Bryce, William Gladstone y Alfred Marshall.[30] *The Review of Reviews*, el *Nouvelle Revue Internationale* y *The Century*

23 E. Castelar, 'La estabilidad social en América,' en H.F. Varela, *La revolución de 1875* (Lima, 1875), pp. 74–87; 'Juicio crítico', en Luis Varela, *La democracia práctica. Estudio sobre los sistemas electorales propuestos para dar representación proporcional a las mayorías y minorías* (París y Méjico, 1876), pp. vi–ix; 'Prólogo,' en R. Elices Montes, *Cuatro años en México. Memorias íntimas de un periodista español* (Madrid, 1885), pp. vii–xxiv.

24 Por ejemplo, *El testamento político de Luis Adolfo Thiers* fue publicado en Montevideo en 1877. Sus *Semblanzas contemporáneas* fueron publicadas en la Habana entre 1871–73.

25 Hale, *The Transformation of Liberalism*, pp 37–38. Véase también su ensayo 'Emilio Castelar en Mexico', publicado en este volumen.

26 Montes, *Cuatro años en Méjico*, pp. 228–9.

27 Castelar, 'La estabilidad social en América', p. 83.

28 Sobre éste punto y, en general, sobre la influencia de Castelar en México, véase el agudo análisis de Hale, *The Transformation of Liberalism*, pp. 41–8.

29 García le había obsequiado el mobiliario de su casa; Alberola, *Emilio Castelar*, p. 29; Hale, *The Transformation of Liberalism*, p. 47.

30 Emilio Castelar, 'The call of Savonarola,' *The Contemporary Review, abril de 1887*, pp. 457–71.

Illustrated Monthly Magazine publicaban o comentaban sus trabajos.[31] Desde diversas fronteras pedían colaboraciones suyas: de la *Revue d'Histoire Contemporaine* de París, del *Fortnightly Revue* de Londres, o del *Harper's Magazine* de los Estados Unidos.[32]

Una admiradora de Nueva York, Mrs W.A. Dulton, le confesaba en sus cartas a Castelar que, desde que leyó su *Old Rome and New Italy*, 'leía y releía todos sus escritos con gran interés', al tiempo que le suplicaba: 'me escribirá usted, no una carta dictada, sino de su propia pluma, para que me cuente sobre su hogar, sobre su hermana, sobre su vida'.[33] 'Le venero como a un segundo Washington', expresaba un tal Cornelise Townsend, también desde Nueva York. En Washington, T.A. Palmer bautizaba a su hijo en su honor: Morelio Castelar Palmer.[34] Desde la monárquica Gran Bretaña también hubo muestras de gran admiración. Sus discursos despertaban entusiasmo en los más variados círculos. En 1886, el presidente de la *Association Patriotique Armenienne* le pedía copia de su intervención en al Café Riche de París, ya que lo pensaba imprimir y distribuir 'chez nos compatriotes, comme la parole de consolation, la parole de l'espérance'.[35] Quienes se aventuraban con la poesía, como J.B. Peacock de Kansas, le enviaban sus poemas para consultar 'la opinión de quien cuenta con tanta merecida reputación y fama'.[36]

III

Peregrinaciones a su residencia en Serrano, consultas, publicaciones de sus escritos y discursos en la prensa periódica, prólogos de libros, autógrafos, remesas de café y hasta pagos por sus colaboraciones: hasta aquí la evidencia parece concluyente. A Castelar no sólo se le conocía sino que se le admiraba profundamente en Hispanoamérica, así como en otras partes del mundo. ¿Pero cuáles sectores específicamente, y dónde, seguían de cerca

31 Véanse: E. Castelar, 'A defence of universal suffrage by señor Castelar,' *The Review of Reviews*, marzo 1890, p. 201; y 'Christopher Columbus,' *The Century Illustrated Monthly Magazine*, volúmenes de mayo, junio, agosto, septiembre y octubre, 1892.

32 Diversas cartas de los respectivos editores de estas revistas en AHN: DTF/2410. Véase también E. Castelar, 'The papacy and the temporal power,' *Fortnightly Review*, noviembre de 1887, pp. 676–95.

33 Carta de W.A. Dulton a Castelar, Nueva York, 25 de enero de 1888, ANH: DTF/2410.

34 Townsend a Castelar, sin fecha; hay otra carta de Townsend fechana el 14 de mayo de 1869; T.A. Palmer a Castelar, Washington, 4 de agosto de 1892; AHN/DTF: 2410.

35 Del Presidente de L'Association Patriotique Armenienne, Paris, 4 de diciembre de 1886, AHN: DTF/2410.

36 J.B. Peacock a Castelar, Kansas, 20 de noviembre de 1876, AHN:DTF/2410.

su obra? ¿Qué se leía entre sus voluminosos trabajos? ¿Qué aspectos de su obra eran más atractivos? ¿Cómo, en últimas, influía Castelar?

Es posible identificar reconocimientos explícitos a la lectura de sus escritos. Justo Sierra, uno de los líderes de los 'científicos' en México, recordaría que a la edad de veinte años ya conocía 'sus novelas, poemas líricos y sentimentales en prosa'.[37] En particular, Sierra hacía referencia a *Emilio,* su novela autobiográfica, y a su libro sobre Lord Byron. Y, sin dudas, a sus discursos. El conservador colombiano Miguel Antonio Caro — presidente encargado de la república a fines de siglo — citaba partes de sus *Lecciones sobre la civilización.*[38] En sus defensas del sufragio universal en Perú, el parlamentario Mariano H. Cornejo acudía a citas de Castelar.[39] Personas de menor prestigio intelectual y político que los de Sierra, Caro y Cornejo también dejaron testimonio de su familiaridad con la obra del 'apóstol'. En 1923, Santiago Rozo, un político conservador colombiano intrigaba ante el Presidente Ospina para que le nombrasen en un cargo diplomático en Centro América, y daba fuerza a su requerimiento aduciendo que había revisado, entre otros tantos papeles, 'alegatos de Castelar'.[40] Que éstos 'alegatos' fuesen relevantes o no a los problemas diplomáticos colombianos poco interesa en el momento. Interesa en cambio notar cómo, entre los de la clase de Rozo, se creía que citar a Castelar confería autoridad.

Una lectura más detallada de los intelectuales, políticos y estadistas hispanoamericanos de la segunda parte del siglo diecinueve permitiría trazar con mayor precisión las dimensiones de la influencia de Castelar. Adicionalmente, algunos de los temas de su obra se sugieren, en sí mismos, como naturalmente atractivos para sus seguidores en las Américas. Tales son la causa republicana y la aceptación de la independencia. Esta última es particularmente significativa, sobre todo cuando se tiene en cuenta el tardío reconocimiento de la independencia hispanoamericana por parte de España, y sus nuevas incursiones en México y en las costas del Perú y Chile en la década de 1860.

Por eso para Justo Sierra, Castelar 'era americano, era mexicano; ya su voz había resonado, bendiciendo la independencia de la América españo-

37 Justo Sierra, 'Panegírico de Emilio Castelar,' *Obras completas. Discursos* (México, 1977), vol. V, p. 260.

38 M.A. Caro, *Obras. Filosofía, religión, pedagogía* (Bogotá, 1962), vol 1, p. 554.

39 Víctor Peralta, 'Un científico en la política peruana: Mariano H. Cornejo y la república aristocrática, 1895–1920,' mimeo.

40 Carta de Santiago Rozo al Presidente Ospina, Barranquilla, 5 de febrero de 1923; Archivo del General Pedro Nel Ospina, Correspondencia recibida, 1923; en Fundación Antioqueña para los Estudios Sociales, FAES, Medellín.

la'.[41] En 1869, Castelar repetía que la independencia era 'el hecho capital de nuestro siglo', 'una de las ideas ... con que se inauguraba nuestro tiempo'.[42] Años más tarde, en 1881, recordaría cómo siempre había trabajado por 'la estrecha inteligencia entre América y España', cómo había combatido la guerra de España contra Chile y Perú, y cómo se opuso 'a la criminal intervención Europea en América' mientras conjuró 'al General Prim el día de su viaje para que no se asociase al parricida proyecto'.[43] La aceptación de la independencia no significaba rechazar la experiencia colonial que para Castelar fue, de todas formas, una acción civilizadora de la cual España no debía avergonzarse: 'los virreyes españoles pasaban por un modelo de prudencia. Nuestras leyes de Indias son uno de los monumentos más grandes'.[44] Más que aceptar la independencia, Castelar abogó por un mayor acercamiento entre España y sus viejas colonias. De acuerdo con Joseph Brandt, ésta fue una de sus grandes contribuciones: Castelar fue 'el primer iberoamericano que intentó reemplazar la influencia de los Estados Unidos en Latinoamérica'.[45]

La aceptación de la independencia de las antiguas colonias en el continente y la defensa de un mayor acercamiento entre ambos mundos no le impidieron apoyar la continuidad de la soberanía de España en Cuba y en Puerto Rico. Algunos de sus más sonados discursos, en efecto, trataron sobre 'los asuntos de ultramar'. 'La minoría republicana' – se vio obligado a aclarar en Asamblea Constituyente de 1869 – 'ni renuncia, ni ha renunciado, ni puede renunciar nunca a sus ideas capitales sobre el gobierno y la organización de los poderes de ultramar'.[46] Castelar estuvo sí en favor de

41 Sierra, 'Panegírico de Emilio Castelar,' p. 261.

42 E. Castelar, 'Iturbide,' en *Ensayos literarios*, p. 83; y *Discursos parlamentarios de don Emilio Castelar en la Asamblea Constituyente* (Madrid, 1873), vol II, p. 5.

43 Castelar, 'Prólogo,' en Elices Montes, *Cuatro años en Méjico*, pp. xxi–xxii.

44 *Discursos parlamentarios de Emilio Castelar en la Asamblea Constituyente*, p. 80. En 1869, Castelar les recordaba a los americanos: 'que nuestros soldados destruyeron aquellos imperios donde se reunían los abusos y refinamientos del despotismo con la barbarie de las tribus salvajes; que nuestros sacerdotes llenaron aquellas selvas, donde humeaban los sacrificios cruentos, con las palabras del Evangelio; que nuestros arquitectos levantaron y hermosearon sus ciudades; que ... les donamos una civilización que nos había costado quince siglos de martirio'; *Ensayos literarios*, p. 84.

45 J. Brandt, *Toward the New Spain* (Chicago, 1933), p. 52.

46 *Discursos parlamentarios*, p. 78. En 1871, volvería a expresar: '... la minoría republicana se quemaría mil veces las manos antes que hacer de la cuestión de Cuba, una cuestión de integridad nacional, una miserable cuestión de partido', *Discursos políticos de Emilio Castelar, dentro y fuera del parlamento* (Madrid, 1873), p. 188. Claro que la causa de la independencia cubana no podía ser recibida con mayores simpatías en momentos en que la misma política interna española pasaba por tormentosos momentos; Sanz de Bremond, *Castelar y el período revolucionario español*, pp. 123–28.

la autonomía de Cuba y Puerto Rico, de propiciar una relación similar a la de Canadá con la Gran Bretaña.

Su posición hacia Cuba y Puerto Rico causaba cierta frustración entre quienes, desde otros ángulos, le admiraban. 'Siento tener que rejistrar aquí' — escribió el colombiano Rafael Núñez en una de sus corresponsalías — 'que Castelar, el más apostólico de los republicanos ... se abstuvo hablar de Cuba "por razones de patriotismo".'[47] La desilusión también era compartida entre sus admiradores mexicanos.[48] Y el resentimiento era fuerte entre patriotas como José Martí o Eugenio María de Hostos.[49] Pero para Castelar, la presencia de España en las Antillas era la garantía de la continuidad de unas relaciones fortalecidas con los pueblos de América. Una y otra vez Castelar insistía, en forma siempre grandilocuente, que su tema favorito era aquel de la 'unión estrecha entre nuestra España y los pueblos americanos'; la idea de propender por una gran Confederación Hispanoamericana era, en efecto, recurrente en sus escritos y discursos.[50]

Aceptar el 'hecho necesario' de la emancipación del continente era, hasta cierto punto, un modo de defender la causa republicana: en esencia la forma americana, según Castelar, es republicana. '¡Una monarquía en América!', observaba con signos de exclamación en *La Discusión*, en 1862, al oponerse a la aventura de Maximiliano en México.[51] A comienzos de la década de 1870, tras los triunfos de Juárez, las conquistas de la estabilidad chilena, los adelantos de Mitre y Sarmiento en la Argentina, y hasta la elección de Pardo en el Perú, motivaron el optimismo de Castelar: 'América es la tierra de lo porvenir', donde los progresos de la democracia se confundían con los de la república.[52] El movimiento republicano tendía así puentes entre España e Hispanoamérica. Como lo ha mostrado Charles Hale para el caso mexicano, y como también puede observarse en las correponsalías del colombiano Rafael Núnez, los hispanoamericanos siguieron de cerca los desarrollos del republicanismo español.[53] A fines de

47 Núñez, *Ensayos de crítica social*, p. 161.

48 Antonia Pi-Suñer, *México y España durante la república restaurada* (México, 1985), pp. 73 y 75.

49 José A. Balseiro, *The Americas Look at Each Other. Essays on the Culture and Life of the Americas* (Coral Gables, 1969), pp. 107–8.

50 Ver, por ejemplo, los *Discursos políticos de Emilio Castelar*, p. 480. Su posición pan-hispanista le colocó, en efecto, en contradicción con los intelectuales latinoamericanos que, como el chileno Bilbao, habían sugerido 'desespañolizar' a América. Ver Hale, 'Political and Social Ideas,' p. 229.

51 Citado en Llorca, *Emilio Castelar*, p. 349, nota 49.

52 Véanse, en particular, su 'Juicio crítico' al libro de Varela, y su nota 'La estabilidad social en América', ambos ya citados.

53 Hale, *The Transformation of Liberalism*, p. 43.

siglo, sin embargo, la confianza de Castelar en la forma republicana se había debilitado. Sobre todo en relación con las experiencias española e hispanoamericana. 'No hable usted de República', le contestó al colombiano Quijano Wallis, quien le visitó en 1892: '… (para) ustedes los suramericanos … decir monarquía es decir despotismo, y decir república, es decir libertad. ¿Y en dónde hay más libertad efectiva y práctica que en la monarquía inglesa y en la monarquía española, y en dónde hay más despotismo que en sus repúblicas de ustedes?'. Y concluyó: 'yo soy algo más grande que ser republicano, soy demócrata'.[54] Como demócrata, su expresión más genuina fue tal vez su lucha por la expansión del sufragio, aunque consideraba que el sufragio universal era 'un gran instrumento en las repúblicas y un gran instrumento de opresión en las monarquías'.

Su postura democrática se confundía por lo demás con su defensa por las libertades y el individualismo. En aquel discurso que le ganó reputación por primera vez, en 1854, ya había hablado de la abolición de la esclavitud. Castelar fue uno de los miembros fundadores de la Sociedad Abolicionista Española, creada el 2 de abril de 1865, con el fin de propender por la liberación de esclavos en las antillas. Varios de sus discursos más difundidos tuvieron que ver con la abolición de la esclavitud en Cuba y Puerto Rico.[55] Para los latinoamericanos como Darío, Castelar 'encarnaba la libertad'. Las libertades civiles y políticas estuvieron ciertamente en el centro de sus preocupaciones. Entre la libertad y la igualdad, Castelar tomaba partido por la primera, distanciándose así de las tendencias socialistas del republicanismo que representaba, por ejemplo, Pí y Margall.[56] El mexicano Justo Sierra describió ese 'desconcierto' de Castelar 'por el carácter cada vez más socialista, es decir, más hostil a la libertad, que tomaba la democracia europea'.[57]

En efecto, los entusiasmos de Castelar por la democracia y las libertades estuvieron matizados por sus preocupaciones con los valores de la estabilidad y el orden. 'La democracia es libertad,' decía en 1872, 'pero también es autoridad; movimiento, pero también estabilidad; acción, pero freno de esta acción; derechos individuales, pero también disciplina y

54 Quijano Wallis, 'Emilio Castelar,' p. 102. 'Somos libres con todo y existir la monarquía', le dijo también a Darío; Darío, 'Un almuerzo con Castelar,' p. 190.

55 Arthur F. Corvin, *Spain and the Abolition of Slavery in Cuba, 1817–1886* (Austin y Londres) pp. 154 y 249; Castelar, *Discursos políticos dentro y fuera del parlamento*, pp. 470–94 y 513–41.

56 Para una breve discusión de estas diferencias, véase Demetrio Castro Alfín, 'Unidos en la adversidad, unidos en la discordia: el Partido Demócrata, 1849–1868,' en Townson, *El republicanismo en España*, pp. 59–85. Véase también los trabajos de Hennessy, Llorca y Sanz de Bremond, ya citados.

57 Sierra, 'Panegírico de Emilio Castelar,' p. 266.

autoridad social.'[58] Su participación en la revolución de 1868 y, particularmente, su experiencia en el poder durante los tormentosos años de la primera república le convencerían de la necesidad de un ejército fuerte.[59] Castelar rechazó el recurso republicano a la violencia. También abandonaría el federalismo en defensa del gobierno unitario.[60]

Precisamente, su optimismo sobre Hispanoamérica en la década de 1870 estuvo de alguna manera motivado por cierta percepción de estabilidad recién conquistada en el continente. El triunfo de Pardo en el Perú lo interpretó ingenuamente como una señal de que habían 'concluído en América las revoluciones anárquicas, las dictaduras sangrientas, el régimen vulgar del sable, la invasión de los pretorianos en las Asambleas y de los generales en el poder'.[61] Para Castelar el orden era prioritario; la tiranían de las mayorías, una posibilidad que debía evitarse. En su 'juicio crítico' al libro del argentino Luis Varela observaba: 'es necesario el orden antes que todo, y para fundar el orden, es necesario que las mayorías tengan un poder inspeccionado siempre y siempre discutido en la esfera legal por las minorías'.[62] El liberalismo de Castelar, ajeno a los extremos y cercano a los valores del orden, tuvo gran eco entre una generación de hispanoamericanos preocupada con la inestabilidad revolucionaria del continente — los intelectuales que, como Sierra, rodearon a Porfirio Díaz, o los liberales que, como Núnez, decidieron llegar a acuerdos con los conservadores.[63] Pero incluso conservadores dogmáticos – anti-individualistas como Miguel Antonio Caro — encontraban en Castelar herramientas de apoyo a sus argumentos. En su 'Informe sobre la ideología de Tracy', Caro citaba a Castelar para atacar al 'sensualismo' y 'al principio de utilidad', que 'han corrompido tantas conciencias'. Caro no dejaba de advertirle a los colombianos que 'la España de Cánovas, y aún la de Sagasta y Castelar, no es la España del Conde de Aranda y de los alumnos de la Francia revolucionaria'.[64]

IV

Sus convicciones políticas se modificaron tal vez con el curso de los años. Y el impacto de sus ideas varió entre los distintos países, mientras se recibían con diferentes niveles de entusiasmo en el espectro intelectual. Pero el

58 Castelar, *Discursos políticos dentro y fuera del parlamento*, p. 480.

59 Melchor Fernández de Almagro, *Historia política de la España contemporánea* (Madrid, 1972), p. 198. Sobre estos años, véase Oliver Sanz de Bremond, *Castelar y el período revolucionario español.*

60 Dardé, 'Los republicanos,' p. 141.

61 Castelar, 'La estabilidad social en América,' p. 86.

62 Castelar, 'Juicio crítico,' p. xi.

63 Hale, 'Political and Social Ideas,' pp. 228–9.

64 Caro, *Obras*, pp. 554 y 1079–80.

reconocimiento a su elocuencia fue universal, en una época — la época también de Gladstone — donde la oratoria era el arma política por excelencia, o, en palabras de María Cruz Seoane, 'el género decimonónico por antonomasia'.[65] 'Por el poder de la elocuencia', se leía en un manual londinense sobre la oratoria en 1875, 'las naciones se han elevado de la esclavitud y el barbarismo a la libertad y la civilización'.[66] Dos décadas más tarde, en 1896, Henry Hardwicke expresaba que era 'un deber de las naciones libres el promocionar la oratoria'.[67] Sin dudas, Castelar fue en el siglo diecinueve 'el orador famoso de España',[68] y su fama como orador estuvo atada a esos discursos que lo identificaban como el adalid de las libertades y la civilización.

'Pico de oro', le apodaron a Castelar en España, donde ganó su inicial reputación en la tribuna.[69] 'Votre parole magique a dissipé déja les ténebres', le escribían desde París solicitándole uno de sus discursos. Desde New Jersey uno de sus admiradores se quejaba de que 'su electrificante discurso sobre la libertad de cultos' no hubiese aparecido en el *New York Herald.* Y, desde Coventry, un tal George Bainton, quien preparaba una conferencia sobre el arte de componer discursos, le solicitaba a Castelar *'whether you gave yourself to any special training with a view to the formation of style, and also whether you can give us any information of your own methods that would aid us realise, in some degree at least, the secret of your marvellous mastery of the use of words'.*[70] No se conoce si hubo respuesta por parte de Castelar, ni si le comunicó que parte del 'secreto' estaba en escribir 'minuciosamente' los discursos de antemano. Castelar, de acuerdo con Jarnés, 'no conoció la espontaneidad ... Era un escritor que conocía sus cuartillas ... Magnífico actor que declama su papel.' Así lo observó también Quijano Wallis: era, por eso, 'inepto para la réplica'.[71]

65 Seoane, *Oratoria y periodismo en la España del siglo XIX*, p. 8.

66 T.W. Brown, *The Art of the Slver Tongue or a Key to Oratory* (Londres, 1875), p. 12.

67 Hardwicke, *History of the Oratory and Orators* (Nueva York y Londres, 1896), p. v.

68 Así lo llamó el editor de la revista *The Century Illustrated Magazine*, mayo de 1892, p. 122.

69 Arthur F. Corwin, *Spain and the Abolition of Slavery in Cuba, 1817-1886* (Austin, 1967), p. 249. Su discurso más famoso parece haber sido su 'duelo oratorio' con Manterola, el que inició con una frase que se identificaría con su estilo: 'Grande es Dios en el Sinaí ...,' Sanz de Bremond, *Castelar y el período revolucionario español*, pp. 86–7.

70 Cartas de George Bainton, Patrick Williams y del Presidente de la Association Patriotique Armenienne a Castelar, Coventry, 12 de octubre de 1887, New Jersey, 4 de julio de 1876, y Paris, 4 de diciembre de 1886, respectivamente, en AHN: DTF/2410.

71 Jarnés, *Castelar. Hombre del Sinaí*, p. 11; Quijano Wallis, 'Emilio Castelar,' p. 100. 'Castelar, por confesión de él mismo, no improvisó ninguno de los grandes discursos que causaron la admiración del mundo', *idem.* La descripción de Quijano Wallis sobre la ineptitud para la réplica de Castelar contrasta, sin embargo, con la de Antonio López Muñoz, quien en sus conferencias sobre oratoria en El Ateneo de Madrid en 1897–98 narraba una ocasión en la que, interrumpido en las Cortes, Castelar 'contestó con la celeridad del rayo'. López Muñoz, *Principios y reglas de la elocuencia en la oratoria, la declamación y la lectura* (Madrid, sin fecha, tal vez 1899), p. 114.

La magia de sus palabras había encantado también a los hispanoamericanos. ¿'Qué era' Castelar?, se preguntaba Justo Sierra. Y respondía, 'era el orador, el orador puro ... Jamás la tribuna política ha sido convertida en urna de mármol más vasta y más artística a un tiempo'.[72] Quienes se destacaban por su elocuencia, como el chileno Isidoro Errázuriz, eran 'comparables al mismo Castelar'.[73] Excepcionalmente la comparación podía tener alusiones sarcásticas y peyorativas. A fines de siglo, a la tienda de Feliciano en Bogotá, concurrían oradores como José María Rojas Garrido, 'el Castelar colombiano': 'y empezaban las ardientes conferencias ... Como en un discurso de Castelar' — recordaría Luis María Mora — 'desfilaban en tropel, delante de los ojos asombrados, sátrapas de Oriente, arcontes griegos y patricios romanos ... y no quedaba ciencia ninguna en que no penetrara la aguda crítica de los famosos innovadores ... de toda humana sabiduría'.[74] Más frecuentes, sin embargo, parecen ser las referencias de admiración, como modelo. En 1880, *El Empresario*, periódico de Tunja, Colombia, reproducía un fragmento de Castelar — 'El labrador' — con el fin de que los maestros de las escuelas, en las clases de declamación, hiciesen recitar a los niños esa 'obra maestra de la literatura española ... fruto del genio sin igual de Castelar'.[75]

Curiosamente, su fama es, sobre todo, la de un orador que se lee. '... No se le ha de oír tan sólo, se le ha de ver ...', se advertía en el prólogo a una de las ediciones de sus discursos.[76] Algunos hispanoamericanos, quienes visitaban España, tuvieron la oportunidad de verle y escucharle. Quijano Wallis retrató al orador en 1879: 'antes de empezar a hablar, tomaba posesión de la tribuna con apostura de amo, paseaba mirada relampagueante sobre el auditorio, sacaba de entre las mangas del frac los blan-

72 Sierra, 'Panegírico de Emilio Castelar,' p. 263.

73 Orrego Luco, *Memorias del tiempo viejo*, p. 54.

74 Luis María Mora, *Croniquillas de mi ciudad* (Bogotá, 1936), pp. 31–2.

75 E. Castelar, 'El labrador,' *El Empresario*, 1 de julio de 1880.

76 E. Castelar, *Discursos íntegros pronunciados en las Cortes, 1873–74* (Barcelona, 1874), p. xxx. Los mejores discursos, según David McKie, son aquellos frutos de la espontaneidad que, por consiguiente, quedan sin 'records' para la historia: 'para cada generación hay una edad de oro de oratoria política que nunca podrá ser recreada'. Véase su interesante aunque breve ensayo 'Unaccustomed as we are to hearing great speeches...', *The Observer*, 23 de marzo de 1997. El auditorio, la atmósfera, los gestos teátricos del orador son parte esencial de todo discurso. 'The words of a masterpiece of oratorial genius may be caught by the quick ear of the reporter...; but the attitude and look, the voice and gesture, are lost for ever': en William Matthews, *Oratory and Orators* (Londres, 1880), pp. 25–6. La admiración por la oratoria de Castelar entre quienes no le vieron es por ello extraordinaria.

cos puños de la camisa, asumía actitud de gladiador que se apresta a la lid … Al principio de la oración se voz era algo apagada y aguda, casi chillona pero a medida que el calor subía de punto en el discurso, el orador se erguía y crecía hasta tomar dimensiones de coloso en la imaginación electrizada de los oyentes'.[77] Para uno de sus biógrafos, se trataba de una voz 'seductora', que 'sabía empezar acariciando la piel y acabar estremeciendo las entrañas. Pasar del roce de una rosa al cardenal de un látigo.'

La mayoría de sus admiradores en Hispanoamérica, sin embargo, no tuvieron oportunidades para estas seducciones del orador, cuando no era siquiera 'preciso saber qué dice, no es preciso entenderlo'.[78] Pero sus discursos, 'apenas pronunciados, transmitíanse por telégrafo, íntegros' a Hispanoamérica, como lo recordaría Alberola, su secretario.[79]

De alguna forma, las publicaciones en los periódicos alcanzaron a tener los efectos seductores de su voz en las Cortes.[80]

Tal vez habría que hacer un esfuerzo para apreciar cómo la 'frase castelarina', escrita para ser escuchada, alcanzó a tener un gran impacto también entre quienes la leían. En su discurso sobre la forma republicana, pronunciado el 20 de mayo de 1869, decía Castelar:

> Los antiguos profetas en la forma de revelación que todas las ideas tomaban en Oriente, eran los más humildes, los más ignorantes, los más pobres de los reveladores; y sin embargo, anunciaron que Nínive sería destruída, y Nínive fue destruída; anunciaron que Babilonia sería quemada, y Babilonia fue quemada; anunciaron que un Mesías vendría, y un Mesías vino. ¿Por qué? Porque el ruido de sus cadenas les había inspirado el poema de sus esperanzas; porque desde el fondo de sus calabozos, en oscura noche, miraban siempre hacia el Oriente y columbraron la luz del nuevo día antes de que amaneciese, como columbra la alondra desde su nido de barro la alborada antes que aparezca; porque odiaban a los conquistadores y a los reyes; porque sobre la tiranía de los Baltasares, sobre el sensualismo de los Sardanápalos, sobre los ídolos, sobre los monstruosos templos, veían levantarse una grande idea, la idea de Dios unida a la idea de la Providencia; como nosotros sobre los césares, sobre los cortesanos, sobre los tronos vacilantes, vemos levantarse otra grande idea, la idea de la humanidad unida con la idea de su derecho …

77 Quijano Wallis, 'Emilio Castelar,' p. 99.

78 Jarnés, *Castelar. Hombre del Sinaí*, pp. 15, 18.

79 Alberola, *Emilio Castelar. Memorias de un secretario*, p. 72.

80 Sin la prensa, 'la elocuencia política se pierde como voz en el desierto, y los parlamentos serían instituciones casi muertas como las antiguas Cortes de nuestros reinos': en Eugenio Sellé, *Discurso de recepción ante la Real Academica Española* (Madrid, 1895), citado en Seoane, *Oratoria y periodismo en la España del siglo XIX*, p. 13.

Y añadía más adelante:

> Cuando se examina la historia, lo primero que nos admira es la rica cantidad de los hechos y la corta cantidad de las ideas. Con una idea sola vive todo un siglo: con la unidad política del mundo el siglo primero; con la idea estoica el segundo; con la idea alejandrina, el tercero; con las definiciones del dogma, el cuarto; con el advenimiento de la individualidad germánica, el quinto; … con la infusión del espíritu oriental por medio de las cimitarras de los árabes el sétimo; …con la lucha de los enciclopedistas contra todas las antiguas preocupaciones, y la lucha de la revolucion americana y francesa contra todos los antiguos poderes, el decimoctavo; con la unión entre la democracia traida por todas las revoluciones y la libertad traida por todas las ciencias, el décimonono, que ha de fundar los Estados Unidos de Europa, fórmula luminosa del porvenir y cúspide gloriosísima de la civilización universal.[81]

Esta retórica hoy nos parece arcaica. Algunos contemporáneos anglosajones criticaban su estilo por ser algo colorido. En 1890, un comentarista de la prosa de Castelar en *The Review of Reviews* anotaba que 'it is Spanish eloquence reading like scarlet flowers'.[82] A fines de siglo, la oratoria había experimentado cambios en países como la Gran Bretaña. Allí la 'elocuencia moderna' se describía en 1896 como 'más fría y sobria… confinada casi por completo a lo racional y argumentativo'.[83] Por eso quizá el historiador inglés David Hannay, también consideraban que frente al 'chorro de elocuencia' de Castelar, cualquier auditorio en Inglaterra 'se echaría a dormir o saldría volando'.[84]

No todos pensaban así; ni en Inglaterra, ni mucho menos en Hispanoamérica. El mismo Hannay concedió al final que Castelar no fue un gran estadista pero sí un gran orador. En 1869, el colombiano Rafael Núñez reportaba en sus artículos de prensa cómo en Castelar 'su talento es grande, su erudición inmensa, sus facultades oratorias admirables'.[85] Castelar, quien no parecía sufrir de modestia, ciertamente creía que su oratoria había sido su principal arma para sus conquistas políticas en España. Como le observaría a Quijano Wallis en 1892: 'con un discurso hice la libertad religiosa; con otro discurso la libertad del sufragio; y con el tercer discurso la libertad de esclavos. Con mil palabras hice libres un millón de hombres'.[86]

81 *Discursos parlamentarios de don Emilio Castelar a la Asamblea Constituyente*, pp. 6–7 y 29.

82 *The Review of Reviews*, marzo de 1890, p. 201.

83 Hardwicke, *History of Oratory and Orators*, p. 84.

84 Hannay, *Don Emilio Castelar*, p. 67.

85 Núñez, *Ensayos de crítica social*, p. 126.

86 Quijano Wallis, 'Emilio Castelar', p. 102.

V

'En nuestra época' — ha sugerido Charles Hale — Castelar 'es sólo una reliquia'.[87] Una reliquia que, sin embargo, merecería ser revalorada, sobre todo al examinarse las influencias de España en la vida intelectual y política de Hispanoamérica durante el siglo diecinueve. Podría decirse que, con Castelar, se tendieron puentes entre dos mundos que se habían distanciado tras las guerras de independencia.[88] Aunque las comunicaciones intelectuales entre España y América no sufrieron el drástico rompimiento que se supone con frecuencia, Castelar logró establecer vínculos más sólidos. Su defensa del principio republicano en momentos en que Europa intentaba reimponer su dominio en América fue, sin duda, la base del acercamiento. Su defensa de la libertad sin contradecir los valores del orden le ganó simpatías entre liberales y conservadores. Su oratoria conquistaba la imaginación de los políticos.

No conquistó a todos, es cierto. Algunos periódicos de Guatemala le acusaron de 'demagogo furioso'. En Montevideo decían que gritaba para 'ver si podía alcanzar empleo'.[89] En Colombia, *El Zipa* reproducía ataques de la prensa española contra Castelar. Y en Buenos Aires, la colonia española respondía furiosa ante las sugerencias de La Tribuna, según las cuales todos los inmigrantes españoles eran 'admiradores entusiastas de Castelar y partidarios de sus ideas'.[90] Pero la falta de unanimidad no le restó significado a la influencia que ejerció entre quienes le admiraban en Hispanoamérica. Admiradores que, como Justo Sierra, expresaron sus sentimientos también en verso:

Ave, sublime decidor, adoro
tu verbo, mundo que en las almas creas
y donde en ígneos tropos las ideas
vuelan al ritmo de tu voz de oro

87 Hale, *The Transformation of Liberalism*, p. 41.

88 Jeane DeLaney reconoce la influencia de Castelar como un antecedente al pan-hispanismo que se desarrolló desde comienzos del siglo XX en Hispanoamérica, en su ensayo 'Rediscovering Spain: the Hispanismo of Manuel Gálvez,' en Marina Pérez de Mendiola (ed.), *Bridging the Atlantic. Toward a Reassessment of Iberian and Latin American Cultural Ties* (Albany, 1996), p. 73. Creo, sin embargo, que su significado como 'puente' entre ambos mundos fue mayor que el que se reconoce en esta marginal referencia.

89 Llorca, *Emilio Castelar*, p. 76.

90 G. G. (Gil Gelpe), *La España. D. Emilio Castelar y los redactores de* La Tribuna *de Buenos Aires* (Buenos Aires, 1862), p. 4.

Las razas y los pueblos te hacen coro,
y las magnetizadas asambleas
conmueven con sus férvidas marcas
el bronce de tu trípode sonoro.

Ah! te odia la demagogia oscura,
porque el derecho salvas de la escoria,
de tu tribuna en la inviolada altura.

No logrará descoronar tu gloria:
de la calumnia la saliva impura
te unge rey ante Dios y ante la historia.[91]

91 Sierra, 'Panegírico de Emilio Castelar,' p. 265.

CHAPTER 6

Emilio Castelar and Mexico

Charles A. Hale

Gregorio Marañón, the Spanish medical scientist and man of letters, once asked a Latin American writer, a fellow boat passenger en route to Buenos Aires, which Spanish name 'resonates most forcefully in the heart of America'. The answer, 'without the least hesitation: Castelar!'[1] Though for our age he is only a relic, whose verbose and elegant style has been devoured by time, Emilio Castelar was the great Spanish parliamentary orator in an age of eloquence. His rotund phrases extolling optimistically the general progress of democracy and republicanism had a mesmerising effect throughout the Hispanic world, in America as much as in Spain itself. It was an oratory to be read as well as to be heard; in fact, Castelar's friend, Adolfo Calzado, regarded him as 'above all a great journalist'.[2] Except for the few Hispanic Americans who travelled to Spain, it was mainly through his periodic *correspondencias* to at least four Western Hemisphere newspapers that the power of Castelar's words had their political impact abroad. Despite many invitations, Castelar never went to America; despite his sympathy for American republicanism, he was basically European in sentiment, to be sure the most cosmopolitan Spaniard of his era. Castelar himself was acutely aware of the power of his words, and he freely proclaimed his oratorical triumphs and his anxieties. In November 1876, to his horror, he lost his voice in the middle of a speech, but then finally regained it to finish amidst great applause: 'the effect has been immense,' he wrote. Two years later, he confided to Calzado that he was in a quandary over a forthcoming visit to France: if he spoke in Spanish, no one would understand him; if he spoke in French, everyone would laugh. 'He whom they call Spain's premier orator would be speaking worse than the lowest of Frenchmen.'[3]

1 Marañón, 'Efemérides y comentarios' (1952), *Obras completas*, 2nd ed., 10 vols. (Madrid, 1968–77), vol. 9, p. 587. This chapter has been drawn in part from my *The Transformation of Liberalism in Late Nineteenth-Century Mexico* (Princeton, 1989).

2 *Correspondencia de Emilio Castelar, 1868–1899*, edited by A. Calzado (Madrid, 1908), p. vii.

3 *Ibid.*, Castelar to Calzado (from Madrid), 22 November 1876, p. 62; also 27 June 1878, p. 93.

Much has been written about Castelar's oratory, his key role in Spanish politics and his general importance in Latin America, including a paper by my friend Eduardo Posada-Carbó, informally titled: 'De la gloria a la glorieta'.[4] In this chapter I would like to focus on a less known aspect of the power of Castelar, the impact of his political ideas and actions on Mexico following the restoration of the republic in 1867. The continuing importance of Castelar in Mexico is symbolised by the testimony of Justo Sierra, who in an elaborate eulogy in the Mexican Congress following Castelar's death in 1899, could refer to and quote from his own youthful appreciation of the Spaniard 30 years earlier.[5]

Though born in Cadiz (quite by chance) in 1832, Emilio Castelar was fundamentally a man of the Mediterranean, and he ultimately returned to his ancestral home in Alicante in his later years. Educated in Madrid, he gained fame and notoriety in the 1850s for his eloquent lectures as occupant of the Chair of Spanish History at the Central University, and for his vigorous and combative journalism. He became a spokesman for the emerging democrats, who drew their inspiration from the radical tradition of 1812 and who attacked the moderate Liberal Union under General Leopoldo O'Donnell. From his newspaper *La Democracia*, Castelar advocated laissez-faire economics, representative government and a thinly-veiled republicanism, presented as part of an inevitable evolutionary scheme. He had no sympathy for socialism of any sort, and the issue precipitated a long-standing rivalry with his fellow democrat, Francisco Pi y Margall. In his famous tract of 1858 Castelar wrote that progress in each age has its formula; the formula of the nineteenth century is democracy. He extolled equality — not the 'absolute sovereignty of the people' or the 'absurd principle of the communist school' — but rather the principle of the 'democratic school', which recognised the 'law of diversity' by which individuals can fulfill their individual destinies. Though he defended the mediaeval tradition of the free municipality, he also saw the need for strong government, the incarnation of justice.[6] Since it was prohibited to attack the principle of monarchy, Castelar instead criticised

4 Eduardo Posada-Carbó, 'Emilio Castelar: República, liberalismo y el poder de la oratoria,' unpublished MS, June 1997. The informal title is attributed to Malcolm Deas.

5 Sierra, 'Panegírico de Emilio Castelar' (17 June 1899) in *Obras completas*, 14 vols. (Mexico, 1948–49), vol. 5, pp. 259–68; 'Emilio Castelar,' *El Renacimiento* (21 Aug. 1869), pp. 481–2 (*Obras*, vol. 3, pp. 51–3).

6 Castelar, *Ideas democráticas. La fórmula del progreso* (Madrid, 1858), pp. 51, 60, 112. The standard biography of Castelar is Carmen Llorca, *Emilio Castelar. Precursor de la democracia cristiana* (Madrid, 1966).

the 'false' liberals who made their peace with Isabel II. Becoming bolder by 1865, he scorned *el razgo*, Isabel's 'gallant gesture', alienating a portion of the royal patrimony to the nation. According to the Constitution of 1812, said Castelar, the royal patrimony already belonged to the nation.[7] By the time of the Revolution of 1868, which led to the abdication of Isabel II and ultimately to the short-lived Republic of 1873, Castelar was established as a major Democrat politician, as well as the nation's great political orator.

Castelar was first drawn to Mexico by the liberal struggle of the 1860s against foreign monarchy, supported by French troops of the Second Empire. It is a great mistake, wrote Castelar in 1864, to think that because Europe is monarchical, monarchy can be restored in America. He saw Napoleon III's adventure as destined to failure and the heroic struggle of Benito Juárez against Maximilian of Austria as comparable to the freeing of the slaves by Abraham Lincoln. Both leaders were in tune with the progress of the century.[8] Castelar had aroused the hispanophobe Ignacio Ramírez when he called for a 'union of Spain and America', but even Ramírez acknowledged that while in Spain Castelar was 'only the bastard of public opinion', in Mexico 'he has been for some time one of our brothers.'[9] Ramírez essentially excused Castelar's pan-hispanism because of his strong liberal and republican credentials. The demise of Maximilian's regime was a memorable event for Castelar, which he celebrated for many years, to the delight of Mexican readers:

> *Aun recuerdo, como si la viera hoy mismo, la célebre fiesta … donde acababa de llegar la nueva del desastre del Maximiliano a los oidos de su protector, un gran teatro adornado con todos los esplendores del babilónico lujo imperial … que aparecía el Emperador como un frío cadáver, y el Imperio como una fugaz sombra. ¡Cuán bello y extraordinario espectáculo aquel!*

[I still remember, he recalled in 1883, as if I had seen it this very day, the famous gathering … where the news of Maximilian's downfall had

7 *La Democracia* (Madrid), 21, 25 February 1865.

8 Castelar, 'El maquiavelismo de Bonaparte en América' (29 January 1864) and 'Juárez y Lincoln' (15 April 1864), in *Cuestiones políticas* y *sociales*, 2 vols. (Madrid, 1870), vol. 1, pp. 51–9 and vol. 3, pp. 49–58.

9 On Hispanic solidarity see Castelar, 'La unión de España y América' (March 1858) and 'Méjico y el gobierno español' (1859?), *Recuerdos* y *esperanzas*, 2 vols. (Madrid, n.d.), vol. 1, pp. 55–61, 87–104. Ignacio Ramírez, 'La desespañolización' (1865), *Obras*, 2 vols. (Mexico, 1889), vol. 1, p. 322. See also Romana Falcón, *Las rasgaduras de la descolonización. Españoles* y *mexicanos* a *mediados del siglo XIX* (Mexico, 1996), p. 25 and *passim*.

> just reached the ears of his protector. It was a great theatre adorned in all the splendour of Babylonian imperial luxury ... the Emperor [Napoleon III] seemed a cold cadaver and the empire a fleeting shadow. What a beautiful and extraordinary spectacle that was!]

The pretense of monarchy in Mexico, he added, had been 'crushed by the simple magistracy of a humble Indian'.[10] Shortly after the restoration of the republic in Mexico, the first of Castelar's fortnightly *correspondencias* appeared in *El Monitor Republicano*, allowing Mexicans to follow European events (and particularly the progress of republicanism) through his eyes.[11] The bond between Castelar and liberal Mexico was solidified for the remainder of the century.

It is difficult to exaggerate the volume of Spanish news that filled the Mexico City press from 1868 to 1875, covering the kaleidoscopic series of events from the abdication of Isabel II to the short-lived imported monarchy of Amadeo of Savoy, to the first Republic of 1873, to the restoration of monarchy under Alfonso XII. Castelar's 'letters' formed the heart of this avalanche of information, but it also included commentary by Mexicans, speeches by Castelar and by fellow republican presidents, Estanislao Figueras, Francisco Pi y Margall and Nicolás Salmerón, and poems by Justo Sierra. Castelar's dispatches were always given the 'place of honour', that is the entire front page (of four); and soon after they began *El Monitor* announced that their popularity prompted it to print a much larger edition than usual on the days they appeared.[12] Despite Castelar's increasing political responsibilities during these years, his commentaries were interrupted only during the months of 1873 when he was minister of state and then president of the republic.[13]

10 Castelar, 'prólogo' to Salvador Quevedo y Zubieta, *México. Recuerdos de un emigrado* (Madrid, 1883), pp. ix, xx.

11 Castelar's first *correspondencia* (dated 15 Oct. 1867), appeared in El *Monitor* on 17 Nov. 1867. The final one appeared on 9–10 Dec. 1896.

12 See the editorial comment in *El Monitor*, 17 Jan. 1868. Although news from Europe was expedited by the transatlantic cable, laid in 1866, it often took three to four weeks to arrive in Mexico City, because it traveled by cable to New York, and then by telegraph via Matamoros or Vera Cruz: Antonia Pi-Suñer Llorens, *El sexenio revolucionario español* (*1868–1874*) *ante el gobierno* y *la prensa mexicana durante la república restaurada* (Mexico, 1984), p. 74.

13 Castelar's correspondencias ceased with the one of 28 Feb. 1873 (*El Monitor*, 1 April 1873) and resumed again with the one of 29 June 1873 (*El Monitor*, 13 Aug. 1873). The second interruption came after his letter dated 7 Sept. 1873 (*El Monitor*, 18 Oct. 1873), resuming 26 Feb. 1874 (*El Monitor*, 31 March 1874). Castelar assumed the presidency on 6 Sept.

The early Mexican response to the Spanish republic was one of solidarity, captured by the final lines of Justo Sierra's poem of February 1873, 'España Libre. A Emilio Castelar'.

Para besar en el cielo,/ Tu enseña republicana
Manda el alma americana/ Sus himnos de libertad
Grita la voz de la sangre/ En nuestra jóvenes venas:
'Viva España sin cadenas,/ Salud al León Español;
Formemos un solo pueblo/ Por la libertad bendito,
En cuyo cielo Infinito/ No haya ocaso para el sol.'

[The soul of America sends up its hymns of liberty
High in heavens to kiss your republican standard.
The voice of the blood in our young veins cries out:
'Long live Spain freed of her chains; good health to the Spanish Lion.
By liberty blessed we form a single people
Whose limitless universe never sees the end of day.'][14]

Only gradually did Mexicans move beyond general excitement over the republican experiment, to ponder the insurmountable problems faced by Castelar and his colleagues, and to sort out their implications for Mexico. The liberal establishment was still basically united following the death of Benito Juárez in 1872, and the opposition to his successor, Sebastián Lerdo de Tejada, did not break into open conflict until 1876. The problems of the Spanish republic were signaled in Castelar's speeches of 1873, some of which appeared in the Mexican press, but they engendered little reflection until he resigned in January 1874.

Castelar became president in September 1873 at a time of political crisis. The unsettled years since the 1868 revolution had encouraged a revival of Carlism, the traditionalist movement to restore absolute monarchy and to preserve Spain from the ravages of atheism and liberalism. By June 1873 the republican government was battling the advancing troops of the Bourbon pretender, Don Carlos María. Even more threatening were the revolts in Andalusia to establish 'cantonalist' republics, an extreme version of federalism. Though federalism was the basic doctrine of the republican movement, championed particularly by Pi y Margall, Castelar was ambivalent toward federalism from the outset, and had no sympathy for cantonalism. As he put it, our federation 'distributes autonomy among individuals, municipalities, provinces, and states', while 'securing with force and

14 The poem was dated 14 Feb. 1873 and appeared in *El Monitor*, 30 March 1873 (not reprinted in *Obras*).

vigour the highest political conception of modern times, the unity of the *patria*, the unity of the nation'.[15] The basic problem for Madrid was to restore discipline in the army, which was riddled with sympathy for the cantonalists, as well as being weakened in the south by the need for troops to fight the Carlists in the north. The burden of restoring order fell principally on Castelar, who came into office vowing to enforce the military *ordenanza*, the death penalty for disobedience. Faced with militant Carlism and the continuing defiance of the cantonalist republic at Cartagena, Castelar suspended constitutional guarantees, closed the Cortes on 21 September and ruled by decree for three months. Refusing in late December to join formally with the conservatives under General Francisco Serrano in perpetuating the republican dictatorship, Castelar reinstated the Cortes according to his earlier pledge and was promptly voted out of office. The way was cleared for the restoration of the monarchy within a year.[16]

Castelar's political ideas were articulated during his months in office and then became a full-scale defence of his regime in the months following his resignation. They were ideas that were to have great impact in Mexico by 1878. He announced soon after taking power that his objective was to 'to create a republic of laws, of order, of authority, of government', as opposed to a republic that is a 'seedbed of disorder and anarchy'. Democracy, he proclaimed, is a historical synthesis of opposing ideas: 'progress and stability … movement and restraint … liberty and authority'. The dissident movements of right and left were for him essentially demagoguery, fomenting absolutism and socialism; and in a phrase that was later to have particular resonance in Mexico, he said he was attempting to 'convert the Republican Party into a party of government'.[17] Castelar's *correspondencias* to *El Monitor* resumed in February 1874, within six weeks of his resignation, and continued throughout the coming years. His ideas were also put forth in several speeches, especially the one at Granada on 24 May 1874, and in his private correspondence.

15 Castelar, speech of 8 Sept. 1873, in *Diario de las sesiones de las cortes constituyentes de la república española*, 4 vols. (Madrid, 1874), vol. 4, p. 2150.

16 The best account of Castelar's presidency is C.A.M. Hennessy, *The Federal Republic in Spain* (Oxford, 1962), pp. 220–43, though it is somewhat less sympathetic to Castelar than Joseph A. Brandt, *Toward the New Spain* (Chicago, 1933), pp. 285–326 and Llorca, *Emilio Castelar*, pp. 178–209.

17 See speeches of 8 and 11 Sept. 1873, in *Diario de las sesiones*, vol. 4, pp. 2150–51, 2215–16.

Although defence of his political role was obviously his major obsession, he was also preoccupied with his personal finances. As a cosmopolitan publicist and a renowned, but unemployed, republican politician, Emilio Castelar depended for his livelihood on the receipts from his American *correspondencias*, as well as on the patronage of wealthy friends. In his travels through Europe in late 1874 he was often unable to enjoy his status as a celebrity because of the pressure to send off his fortnightly correspondence. He complained to Calzado from Nice that he was confined to his hotel, doing himself the copy work three assistants had done in Madrid. 'Only from my window', he lamented, 'do I get a glimpse of this incomparable Mediterranean Sea, on whose shores I would like to live and die.' He was at the time sending off his commentaries to *El Nacional* of Lima, *La Nueva América* of Buenos Aires and the *Herald* of New York, in addition to *El Monitor*. He received 250 francs per installment from Mexico, or 500 francs a month, so there was strong incentive to keep up the pace. Since payments were sporadic, he had a persistent cash flow problem, and he relied on Calzado, his banker as well as his friend, to establish an account in Paris to make him regular advances against intermittent receipts. I'll always trust you, he wrote to Calzado, to manage the accounts 'with the precision of a banker', since I would manage them 'with the imprecision of an artist'.[18]

Castelar's defence of his regime made frequent reference to the success of the contemporary Third French Republic, which he, like the Mexicans, later saw as a political model. He pointed out that former supporters of monarchy (such as Adolphe Thiers) could become republicans and yet also repudiate the radicalism of the Commune of 1871. In fact, he frequently compared the Commune with the Spanish cantons. The French know, as we should have known, that 'all the permanent interests can find security' within the republic. But he saw Spain's problem as more extreme than that of France. When Spain was faced with complete chaos in September 1873, he argued that 'temporary despotism' to meet 'combat with combat' was necessary. Under such circumstances, it was impossible to consider reforms. By restoring the *ordenanza*, 'I saved the army and with the army I saved my patria'. A 'conservative republic' was essential to combat the two utopias — absolute monarchy and the radical canton. 'All societies must have order', he said at Granada; but order 'is particularly essential in republican societies'.[19]

18 See Castelar, *Correspondencia*, pp. 15–17 (letter from Nice), 12 Oct. 1874 and p. 29 (letter from Florence), 29 June 1875, and *passim*.

19 See speech at Granada, 24 May 1874, *Obras escogidas*, 7 vols. (Madrid, 1922–23), vol. 3, pp. 40, 13; '*Correspondencia*' of 26 Feb. 1874 (*El Monitor*, 31 March 1874).

As he turned more conservative, Castelar repudiated the radical republican, Manuel Ruiz Zorrilla, reiterating that his programme involved 'complete separation from socialists and federalists of all shades'; and he presented once again his conception of a strong presidency within a conservative republic. At the same time, he could admit to Calzado that the restoration of the monarchy 'has wounded me to the depths of my heart'.[20]

Castelar's actions and his vigorous defence of them met a generally sympathetic response in Mexico, though on the eve of Castelar's fall, Justo Sierra was mildly critical of him for his apparent reliance on conservative generals and his persistent hard line in the face of insurgency in Cuba. Its Cuba policy, he said, reveals the old Spain 'that killed our [José María] Morelos and sent us [Félix María] Calleja', not the Spain 'that was rejuvenated by liberty'.[21] Sierra took solace in the fact that unlike Spain, liberalism in America could proceed unobstructed, free from the threat of absolutism or of socialism (which he identified with the cantonalist uprisings). His bland optimism of early 1874 was to change sharply within three years, as Mexico faced political crisis with the rise of Porfirio Díaz and the triangular conflict of 1876.

It was in 1878–80, with the founding of the newspaper *La Libertad* by a self-styled 'new generation' of Mexican liberals, that the ideas and experience of Emilio Castelar had their most profound impact on Mexican political life. Within ten days of its founding, there appeared in the paper a key editorial entitled 'El Sr. Castelar y el programa de *La Libertad*'.[22] The newspaper brought together a 25 to 30-year-old cohort of intellectuals who saw in the fledgling regime of Porfirio Díaz the opportunity for Mexico to move beyond the recent factional conflicts within the Liberal Party toward a new political stability and a new base for national progress. The future leaders of the *La Libertad* group, Justo Sierra, Francisco Cosmes and Telésforo García, had supported the claims to the presidency by the president of the Supreme Court, José María Iglesias, in the face of the 'illegal' re-election of Sebastián Lerdo in 1876. The dispute between the claimants led to armed conflict, but was soon eclipsed by the rebellion of a third claimant, Porfirio Díaz, whose 'popular' forces swept the field. In the course of 1877 the future *La Libertad* cohort came to accept the victory of Díaz, and by January 1878 had launched their 'regenerating' programme. This programme was articulated as 'scientific politics' or its corollary 'conservative-liberalism'.

20 Castelar to Ruiz Zorilla (from Garrucha), 11 Sept. 1876; to Calzado (from Madrid) 15 Feb. 1875, *Correspondencia*, pp. 59, 23–4.

21 Sierra in *La Tribuna*, 5 Jan. 1874 (*Obras*, vol. 4, p. 377)

22 Sierra in *La Libertad*, 14 Feb.1878 (*Obras*, vol. 4, pp. 141–3).

Scientific politics was basically the application of the now generalised positivism of Henri de Saint-Simon and Auguste Comte to Mexican political life. With the Díaz regime, argued *La Libertad*, Mexico was moving from the 'metaphysical' to the 'positive' (or scientific) stage of history. The abstractions of the 'old' liberals of the Reforma generation, manifest in the Constitution of 1857 — the rights of man, universal suffrage, the unicameral legislature, the weak executive — were giving way to 'facts', to a 'practical liberty' under a strong government dedicated to economic development within a reformed constitution. Revolutionary violence was a thing of the past. Although the term 'scientific politics' was drawn (though indirectly) from classic French positivism, its corollary 'conservative-liberalism' was drawn directly from the experience of Emilio Castelar and by extension from the 'conservative' Third French Republic. Castelar was not a positivist, in fact positivism was just entering Spain in the 1870s; yet Justo Sierra and his *La Libertad* colleagues saw Castelar's eclectic ideas as compatible with scientific politics of positivist inspiration. 'Castelar', wrote Sierra, 'has condensed into a few words the new phase of democratic evolution. We are entering, he says, into the scientific and experimental period. The epoch of vernal dreams has passed.'[23]

In its first two years *La Libertad* was awash with mentions of Castelar. His *correspondencias* appeared regularly (as well as in *El Monitor*), his speeches were reprinted, and his comings and goings in and out of Spain closely followed. In one lengthy article, *La Libertad* announced that 'for liberalism in Latin America, Castelar is something more than a friend and a brother; he is an apostle'. His visions of 'constant evolution, energetic but peaceful, toward the triumph of democracy' are not 'at all foreign to our programme'. Like him, we look to the formation of 'a great Conservative Party', more addicted to 'practical liberty' than to 'liberty declaimed', and we are 'profoundly convinced that positive progress rests on the normal development of a society, that is, on order'. Castelar's methods, in his words, were 'to obtain radical ends through conservative procedures … a strong government within the laws placed at the service of the modern spirit'.[24] Drawing from Castelar's 1873 rhetoric, *La Libertad* insisted repeatedly

23 *Ibid.* (*Obras*, vol. 4, p. 142). Castelar was not a philosopher, but his philosophical orientation appears to have been toward French eclecticism and spiritualism, an effort to reconcile idealism (mostly of German origin) and materialism (or positivism). Hennessy identifies a strain of 'Hegelian historicism' in Castelar's thought, which would have been compatible with French spiritualism. See *Federal Republic*, p. 80.

24 Sierra in *La Libertad*, 14 Feb. 1878 (*Obras*, vol. 4, p. 141); *La Libertad*, 9 April 1878. From 9 May 1878 to 21 March 1879 *La Libertad*'s subtitle was *Periódico liberal-conservador*.

that the Liberal Party must be transformed from a party of revolution into *un partido de gobierno.* In extolling 'conciliation', *La Libertad* referred in July 1879 to Castelar's new (and ephemeral) Possibilist Party, comparable to the Opportunist Party in France, both efforts to implement the doctrine of conservative-liberalism.[25]

Although the term conservative-liberalism may seem a mere exercise in semantics, a confusing manipulation of traditional terminology, it involved in Mexico, as it did in Spain and France, a reconciliation of traditional political positions which was at the heart of political discourse, not only in 1878, but throughout the entire *Porfiriato.* The label 'conservative' was identified in Mexico with clericalism, foreign intervention and treason, and because Justo Sierra and his colleagues considered themselves heirs to the heroic liberal Reforma, they were first of all 'liberals'. In fact, anyone with political aspirations after 1867 had to be a 'liberal', however much interpretations of the term might differ. In short, with the launching of *La Libertad* and its programme of conservative-liberalism (or scientific politics), liberalism in Mexico was being transformed, not abandoned. One could be a 'conservative-liberal', but not a 'conservative'. In looking to the experience and ideas of Emilio Castelar, and by extension to those of the Third French Republic, the *La Libertad* group was aware of the uniqueness of the Mexican situation. As Justo Sierra noted, conservative-liberals in Mexico are more fortunate than were the Spanish republicans, because we can pursue similar objectives without having to change our form of government.[26] After 1867 the liberal republic in Mexico was secure.

As we have noted, the influence of Castelar in Mexico was reinforced by the experience of the Third French Republic, which for the Mexicans had important points of comparison with that of Spain. Following the demise of the empire of Napoleon III and the declaration of the Republic in 1870, France, like Spain in 1873, became the battleground between monarchy and republicanism and between the conservative republic and radical socialism and federalism — the Commune of 1871 in France and cantonalism in Spain. Mexicans followed the events of the early 1870s in France closely, hostile to the 'anarchy and weakness' of the Commune and fearful of the threatened restoration of monarchy. In 1874 Justo Sierra, writing in *La Tribuna*, saw France as epitomising 'the diverse elements that struggle for predominance in the world'. By the late 1870s France had weathered

25 The manifesto of the *posibilistas* (Madrid, 1 February 1879) covered an entire page of *La Libertad* on 2 April 1879.

26 Sierra in *La Libertad*, 14 Feb. 1878 (*Obras*, vol. 4, p. 142).

the storms of left and right, the republic was secured, and the editors of *La Libertad* saw France as 'the model of what common sense and good judgment can do to consolidate a nation.'[27] *La Libertad*'s French heroes were the conservative-republican leaders Adolphe Thiers and Jules Simon. They were also heroes for Emilio Castelar.

Adolphe Thiers was a former adherent of the July Monarchy of 1830–48 and a fierce opponent of Napoleon III, who turned republican and emerged as president during the turbulent period 1871–73. When he died in May 1877, Justo Sierra dedicated a long poem, 'France', to Thiers, which ended: 'The tomb of a monarch [Maximilian] separated us; the tomb of a republican unites us.'[28] Jules Simon was a philosopher who became minister of instruction during the Thiers presidency and who was then briefly premier in 1876–77. *La Libertad* took special notice of the appearance of his book, *Le Gouvernement de M. Thiers*, published in 1878, and referred to Simon as 'a great conservative'. Under Thiers and Simon, it added, France had renounced 'political utopias', had adopted an 'eminently conservative constitution [1875]', and as Castelar had tried to do in Spain, turned the liberal party into a 'party of government'.[29] After his resignation in 1874, Castelar studied French politics closely and incorporated commentary into his *correspondencias* to Mexico. He also wrote to Thiers (in French), and after his death in 1877, told Calzado that Thiers was 'the essence, indeed the quintessence, of the French genius, the most French of those born since Voltaire'.[30] In 1879 he added a 150-page [!] 'prologue' to a Spanish edition of Thiers' history of the French Revolution, first published in 1822–23. Though Thiers was then a monarchist, his history became the classic defence of the revolution taken as a whole, for him a critical stage in the progress of liberty; and the work had great durability throughout the nineteenth century.[31] Castelar regarded the conservative republicanism of Thiers the statesman as the realisation of the positive ideas of the revolu-

27 Sierra in *La Tribuna*, 1 Jan. 1874 (*Obras*, vol. 4, p. 372); Jorge Hammeken y Mejía in *La Libertad*, 5 Sept. 1879.

28 Sierra's poem dated Oct. 1877 was printed in *La Libertad*, 3 Sept. 1878 (*Obras*, vol. 1, pp. 381–5).

29 *La Libertad*, 27 Sept. 1878, 10 Nov. 1878; also 6 June 1878.

30 Castelar to Thiers (from Madrid) 21 Dec. 1876, *Correspondencia*, pp. 66–7; to Calzado (from Bordeaux) 15 Sept. 1877, *ibid.*, p. 76.

31 Castelar, 'Prólogo' (dated 14 Nov. 1879) to A. Thiers, *Historia de la revolución francesa*, 4 vols. (Barcelona, 1877–79), vol. 1, pp. 1–clx. On Thiers' history, see Alphonse Aulard, 'Thiers historien de la révolution française,' *La Révolution française*, *66* (Jan.–July, 1914), pp. 492–520; (July–Dec. 1914), pp. 5–29.

tion, as depicted by Thiers the historian. Castelar's orientation toward French experience formed an important part of his influence in Mexico.

Emilio Castelar's name was invoked in the polemical exchange between *La Libertad* and *El Monitor Republicano* in late 1878, a debate principally between the 'new' liberal Justo Sierra and the 'old' doctrinaire liberal, José María Vigil. Vigil defended in *El Monitor* the democratic and egalitarian features of the Constitution of 1857 against the attacks upon them by Justo Sierra and his colleagues, which included arguments for strong government, even the notorious call by Francisco Cosmes for 'honourable tyranny'. In the midst of the polemic, *La Libertad* queried *El Monitor*, long the principal outlet for Castelar's *correspondencias*, if it was truly in agreement with 'the eminently conservative spirit' of a recent speech by Castelar, printed in *El Monitor* without commentary. On another occasion, *La Libertad* challenged *El Monitor*, saying that a full response to your attacks on 'our conservative-liberal programme' can be found in your columns by Castelar, 'a man for whom you profess profound respect and whose ideas you have accepted without discussion'.[32] *La Libertad*'s challenges drew no response from *El Monitor*, perhaps reflecting the fact that the generalised liberal and democratic component of Castelar's thought and his mesmerising rhetoric had become a fixture in Mexican public life, quite apart from the specific political inferences that could be drawn from them. *El Monitor*, which remained the steadfast proponent of doctrinaire liberalism, generally critical of the Díaz regime, continued to publish Castelar's *correspondencias* until early December 1896, three weeks before the cessation of the newspaper. *La Libertad* had long since stopped publication, though the assumptions of its programme, drawn in part from the ideas and experience of Emilio Castelar, remained a guide to policy until at least 1900.

The influence of Castelar on the editors of *La Libertad* group was also enhanced by strong personal ties. Justo Sierra's father-in-law, Dr Martín Mayora, was a leading member of the burgeoning Spanish colony in Mexico City, and he took part in the planning and construction of the Spanish cemetery and in the reconditioning of the elegant Spanish Casino. He was also administrator of the Casino for many years. However, the closest tie was between Spanish-born Telésforo García and Emilio Castelar himself. The two were close friends before García emigrated to Mexico in 1865, and the tie remained close until Castelar's death. García was a wealthy entrepreneur as well as a journalist-intellectual, and he travelled frequently to Spain, where he held property. He was one of the patrons on whom Castelar depended; for

32 *La Libertad*, 1 Oct. 1878; 21 Nov. 1878.

example, the dining-room furniture in Castelar's Madrid residence was owned by García. Castelar had even hoped to live with García in his last years. In his eulogy on Castelar in 1899, Justo Sierra mentioned a 'hundred or so letters' he had seen from Castelar to García.[33] These personal ties merely punctuated what was a general tone of hispanofilia in *La Libertad*, a sentiment that persisted among members of the liberal establishment throughout the Porfiriato.

Although *La Libertad* continued till 1884, its years of political and intellectual strength were the first two, 1878–80, during the shaky first administration of Porfirio Díaz, when its 'new liberalism' was forcefully articulated. As we have noted, they were also the years when the ideas of Emilio Castelar had their greatest impact. After 1880 both Mexico and Spain settled into a period of political stability, guided by a comparable doctrine of conservative-liberalism. In Spain, the principal architect of this stability was Antonio Cánovas del Castillo, whose Conservative-Liberal Party attempted to reconcile the formerly antagonistic elements in Spanish political life under the tolerant monarchy of Alfonso XII and the regency of his widow, María Cristina. In Mexico, likewise, political reconciliation of former enemies within the liberal establishment became a central objective of the Porfirian regime. Republic versus monarchy receded as a point of ideological contention on both continents. Although he had long been a close friend of Cánovas del Castillo, Castelar was still a convinced republican in the early 1880s, and the Mexico newspaper *El Siglo XIX* reprinted with satisfaction a Castelar article praising Mexican stability and progress under republican institutions. Castelar's text led *El Siglo* to comment broadly that his was the spirit generally prevalent in the Spanish press: 'nothing but fellowship and congratulation for the spectacle of internal peace and great advancement on the road of solid progress presented by our republic'.[34] In subsequent years Castelar came to accept constitutional monarchy, guided by the alternating ministries of Cánovas del Castillo's conservative-liberals and Práxedes Sagasta's liberals. In 1892 Castelar told the visiting Colombian Quijano Wallis that he rejected the notion that monarchy necessarily meant despotism and republic liberty: 'More than a republican, I am a democrat.'[35]

33 On the Spanish colony, which grew from 2,000 in 1876 to 12,000 in 1911 (estimates vary), see T.J. McMahon, 'The Spanish Immigrant Community in Mexico City during the Porfiriat,' (PhD dissertation, University of Notre Dame, 1974). On Castelar's furniture see *Blanco* y *Negro. Revista ilustrada* (Madrid), 30 May 1899. See also Llorca, *Emilio Castelar*, pp. 313, 316. For Sierra's comment, see *Obras*, vol. 5, p. 266. It should be noted that Sierra ended his life as minister plenipotentiary to Spain in 1912.

34 *El Siglo XIX*, 16 Jan. 1882.

35 Wallis, *Estudios, discursos* y *escritos varios* (Paris, 1908), p. 102, quoted in Posada-Carbó, 'Emilio Castelar', p. 16.

At the same moment Justo Sierra, leader of the Liberal Union in Mexico (soon to be the *científicos*), announced that finally the Liberal Party had become 'a party of government'. Castelar's vision of 1873 was seemingly being realised across the sea.

Justo Sierra's eulogy of 1899 probably best epitomises the generalised fame of Castelar in Mexico, long after *La Libertad* evoked his specific ideas and experience as a model for its programme. In grandiloquent prose that was truly Castelarian, Sierra extolled Castelar's oratorical power, unequalled throughout the ages, from the Pnyx and the Forum of the Ancients to Westminster and the Palais Bourbon. However, Castelar's was more than political oratory, said Sierra, it was also a transmutation into 'oral music' of all of history — philosophy, art and science. 'This incalculable power of converting all expression into music and all rational discourse into a symphony' also was evident, added Sierra, in the letters from Castelar to Telésforo García. To be sure, Sierra emphasised Castelar's heroic and forceful efforts to save the Spanish Republic of 1873 from 'cantonalist anarchism' and 'the black hand of carlist absolutism', efforts for which he was later condemned. By resigning, Castelar was not a 'great apostate' to the republican cause; he was, as history will tell us, a 'great patriot'. In tune with the times, Sierra also praised Castelar's 'treaty of permanent peace with constitutional monarchy, in exchange for universal suffrage'. In doing so, Castelar rejected 'jacobinism' (like Justo Sierra himself and his fellow *científicos* of the 1890s), and pursued his own true course. Sierra concluded his panegyric, predicting immortality for Castelar. He will be a future symbol of Hispanic solidarity in two worlds; and his presence will be for us 'the Holy Grail in which the heroic blood of our ancestors will boil up, and in which will live eternally the two supreme passions [*amores*] of the Latin faith: the love of the law [*el derecho*], and the love of the ideal'.[36]

Though Sierra's vision of the immortality of Castelar and his legacy soon became dim and ultimately faded from view in the twentieth century, his great significance in Mexico and throughout Spanish America during his own century is worthy of recognition after the *año de Castelar*, which was celebrated in Spain in 1999. And in Mexico itself, is it not possible that the stunning rapprochement of the 1930s between republican Spain and revolutionary Mexico can trace its origins to the powerful words and deeds of Spain's great republican of the 1870s?

36 Sierra, 'Panegírico de Emilio Castelar'.

CHAPTER 7

Lisandro de la Torre: un orador argentino

Carlos Malamud

En la segunda mitad del siglo XIX, cuando los medios de comunicación no habían alcanzado todo su poder mediático y distorsionador de la realidad, el parlamento, allí donde funcionaba, era el ámbito político por definición. La prensa escrita, la única existente por aquel entonces, se convertía en caja de resonancia de todo cuanto ocurría dentro del recinto parlamentario. Dado el peso determinante que las distintas realidades locales tenían en la vida política, la posibilidad de obtener una amplia publicidad dotaba a la labor parlamentaria de un gran atractivo ante la presencia y el protagonismo que podía trasladarse a escala nacional. Pero para que eso ocurriera, para poder brillar en el parlamento y convertirse a la vez en un atractivo para los cronistas especializados que cubrían todo cuanto ocurría en el congreso, había que ser un buen orador y, como bien sabemos, no todos los políticos lo eran. En numerosas ocasiones la habilidad del parlamentario pasaba por su capacidad para ver incluido el texto y los comentarios de su discurso en los periódicos del día siguiente. Era la época en que la fama de Emilio Castelar recorría todo el continente americano, siendo muchos los políticos de la región que peregrinaban a las Cortes de Madrid para escuchar a don Emilio.[1]

Lisandro de la Torre, el gran político rosarino, impulsor de la Liga del Sur (LS) y posteriormente del Partido Demócrata Progresista (PDP), en los momentos en que se desempeñó como diputado fue capaz de combinar hábilmente la brillantez en el uso de la tribuna de oradores con la agresiva denuncia de la gestión del oficialismo. Precisamente, su gran dominio de la oratoria fue una de las palancas que le permitieron situarse en muy pocos años en el primer plano de la política nacional, pese a representar a un pequeño y modesto partido regional de la Provincia de Santa Fe. En efecto,

1 Véanse los capítulos de Eduardo Posada-Carbó y Charles A. Hale en este libro. En mayo de 1999 se conmemoró el centenario de la muerte de Emilio Castelar. El Congreso de los Diputados de España organizó el 24 de mayo de 1999 un ciclo de conferencias a cargo de Carlos Darde ('Emilio Castelar y el parlamentarismo de su época'); María Cruz Seoane ('Emilio Castelar y la oratoria de su época') y José Antonio Pascual ('Lenguaje y poder').

en su visita a Argentina en 1910, Georges Clemenceau se sintió muy impresionado por la fama y la personalidad de de la Torre y auguró 'que era el hombre para dirigir en un futuro los destinos del país'.[2] Bastantes años más tarde, en 1970, el diario bonaerense *La Nación*, haciéndose eco de una opinión generalizada a principios del siglo XX, lo definió como 'el más grande orador parlamentario de su época'. Esa misma fama le permitió, en 1914, convertirse en el principal dirigente del PDP, la mayor operación del conservadurismo liberal argentino para intentar frenar, aunque sin éxito como terminó demostrándose, al radicalismo en ascenso de Hipólito Yrigoyen.[3]

El trabajo que aquí se presenta tiene un doble objetivo: analizar algunos mecanismos políticos del siglo XIX, especialmente aquellos relacionados de una u otra forma con el uso de la palabra, y simultáneamente analizar el uso del discurso (que no un análisis del discurso) por parte de Lisandro de la Torre (que también fue un notorio publicista), valorando en su justa medida el papel que la palabra tuvo en su carrera política. Para ello nos centraremos en aquellos períodos de su vida política más próximos al siglo XIX, como fueron los años previos a la fundación de la Liga del Sur, ocurrida en 1908; el proceso que condujo a su primera elección como diputado nacional (1912–16) y su primera campaña presidencial (1915–16). Esto implica dejar fuera algunos momentos estelares en la carrera política (y oratoria) de de la Torre, como sus famosos debates parlamentarios en torno a la anulación de la Constitución de la Provincia de Santa Fe (1922) y el más sonado debate 'de las carnes' (1935),[4] que terminó con el asesinato en el Senado de la Nación del senador electo del PDP Enzo Bordabehere y que le valió a de la Torre el apelativo de 'fiscal de la Patria' o el de 'solo contra todos'. Refiriéndose a aquella ocasión, Raúl Larra, uno de sus principales biógrafos, señalaba que:

> Junto al exacto dominio de la materia implícita, esgrime don Lisandro una habilidad dialéctica que enmudece a todos sus adversarios. Mientras sus contrincantes se empequeñecen, él se agranda en la polémica. Todos se llaman a silencio luego de los chicotazos rezumantes de sarcasmo e ironía con que el líder rosarino corta alguna interrupción. Nadie es capaz de enfrentársele. Y él domina la escena

2 Raúl Larra, 'Prólogo,' en Lisandro de la Torre, *Obras de Lisandro de la Torre* (en adelante *Obras*), 6 vols. (Buenos Aires, 1954), vol. I, p. 7.

3 Carlos Malamud, 'El Partido Demócrata Progresista: un intento fallido de construir un partido nacional liberal-conservador,' *Desarrollo Económico*, no. 138 (1995).

4 Carlos Malamud, 'Lisandro de la Torre y el debate de las carnes,' *Anuario del IEHS*, vol. VII (Tandil, 1992).

> con un señorío y una elegancia que contrasta notablemente con el apabullamiento de sus contendientes.[5]

Tampoco se puede olvidar su segunda campaña presidencial, en 1932, cuando encabezó la alianza formada por el PDP y el Partido Socialista, lo que supuso su retorno a la política activa después de algunos años de reclusión en su cordobesa estancia de Pinas. En esa ocasión desplegó toda su artillería dialéctica en torno al avance del totalitarismo en el país y en la defensa de las instituciones liberales y democráticas. También se puede mencionar el debate en torno a la ley de represión del comunismo y la discusión (escrita) en torno al cristianismo y al fascismo que mantuvo con monseñor Francesci, una discusión de muy elevado nivel intelectual

En el mencionado debate en torno a la Constitución de Santa Fe, de la Torre se mostró con su mejor estilo, con un amplio dominio del tema en cuestión (en este caso el derecho constitucional, especialmente en todo lo referente al poder de las Asambleas Constituyentes y su carácter soberano). Sus citas constantes de los principales constitucionalistas argentinos, González Calderón y Montes de Oca (ambos defensores de la anulación), se complementaron con otras alusiones frecuentes a la jurisprudencia y a algunos académicos norteamericanos. Como solía hacer ante cada intervención parlamentaria de envergadura, de la Torre evidenció una vez más un profundo estudio y preparación del tema del debate y de los antecedentes citados en el mismo por sus contrincantes, de forma de atacarlos en su propio terreno. Su estilo directo se manifiesta en la siguiente frase:

> Creo … que los doctores González Calderón y Montes de Oca han estado profundamente equivocados, y atribuyo su error a una circunstancia que es especialmente funesta cuando se trata de interpretaciones de derecho público: la unilateralidad. Han mirado la medalla por una sola cara y se han guiado por la opinión de un autor notable, sin duda, pero tendencioso y anticuado, como si fuera la opinión prevalente hoy en Estados Unidos, cuando sucede precisamente lo contrario.

Instantes después se produce el siguiente intercambio de palabras, que vale la pena reproducir en su integridad, al mostrar cabalmente el estilo agresivo y avasallador de de la Torre, un estilo que en algunas circunstancias era poco respetuoso con el adversario:

> Sr. González Calderón (GC): Y en la de Cooley, sr. Diputado, por mi parte.

5 Raúl Larra, *Lisandro de la Torre. Vida y drama del solitario de Pinas* (Buenos Aires, 1942), p. 217.

Sr. Lisandro de la Torre (LDLT): No lo ha citado, ni Cooley dice eso.

GC: Lo he citado.

LDLT: Ha citado a Jameson, pero no a Cooley. Lo habrá mencionado de paso, pero una cosa es mencionar y otra es citar. Yo necesitaría cotejar la cita. El autor a que me refiero es el juez de Chicago, Juan Alejandro Jameson, que publicó una obra erudita titulada 'Convenciones Constituyentes', durante la guerra de secesión … El dr. Montes de Oca lo llama autor clásico, confundiendo — séame permitido decirlo — el talento y la erudición con la imparcialidad, y afirma que su opinión es decisiva; lo que no sería exacto, ni aun cuando el dr. Montes de Oca no hubiera truncado las citas de Jameson para hacerle decir lo que no dice. Básteme, por ahora, antes de usar de las propias palabras de Jameson para definir el alcance de su libro, decir que sus opiniones extremas no son seguidas por nadie; que ningún tribunal de los EEUU ha dictado resoluciones fundadas en ellas y que ninguna constitución de los Estados Unidos posterior a su libro muestra las huellas de su influencia. Y cuando eso sucede en la propia patria de Juan Alejandro Jameson, en la República Argentina, a medio siglo de distancia, se destroza una constitución como una tira de papel inútil porque el dr. Manuel Augusto Montes de Oca, truncando una cita de Jameson, ha dicho que las convenciones deben estar subordinadas a las legislaturas, hasta cuando las reglamentaciones que les impongan sean absurdas.[6]

En sus debates parlamentarios, de la Torre arrinconaba permanentemente a sus rivales, acosándolos con constantes interrupciones y chicanas, de modo tal que les impedía hablar en numerosas ocasiones o, en el mejor de los casos, les cortaba el hilo argumental. Su retórica era acompañada de una gran profusión de citas, que dejaban clara la profundidad de sus lecturas y la preparación sistemática de los temas que tocaba en sus discursos, un extremo que puede comprobarse en el catálogo de su biblioteca. Por otra parte, y dada la permanente rivalidad que a lo largo de su vida política lo enfrentó con Hipólito Yrigoyen, habría que dejar constancia en este punto de las diferencias de estilo entre la retórica ilustrada y directa de de la Torre con la más florida y a su vez más vacía del líder radical.

6 Lisandro de la Torre, *Obras*, tomo I, pp. 56–8, debate parlamentario del 22 de septiembre de 1922.

El ejercicio de la política a fines del siglo XIX

En las últimas décadas del siglo XIX la política seguía siendo básicamente política local. La incompleta integración del conjunto de las regiones que conformaban la Argentina, así como del mercado nacional, repercutía directamente en el ámbito de la generación y transmisión de las ideas. A finales de la centuria esta situación ya estaba en vías de superación gracias al impacto positivo que había tenido la considerable expansión de la red ferroviaria,[7] a la implantación del telégrafo y, todavía en menor medida, al teléfono. En lo que a nuestro tema respecta, es evidente que estas circunstancias afectaban directamente a la circulación de la prensa escrita que, como la política, era en gran medida prensa local o provincial. Pese a ello, circulaba un elevado número de periódicos, especialmente en las grandes ciudades, como Buenos Aires, Córdoba o Rosario, que colaboraban a crear una audiencia nacional interesada en la política y su actividad.[8] Si bien la mayoría era de asociaciones de todo tipo o se lanzaban con fines coyunturales o electorales y por tanto tenían una vida efímera, había otros, como *La Nación* o *La Prensa*, en Buenos Aires, o *La Capital*, en Rosario, que eran permanentes.[9] A finales de siglo, con la consolidación de periódicos de este tipo, que tendían a considerarse 'independientes', los políticos se encontraban con la necesidad de conquistar sus páginas, algo que no ocurría décadas atrás cuando la prensa era básicamente partidista.[10]

Por eso, es importante señalar que las imágenes que se transmitían de los políticos, lo que equivalía a decir su éxito o su fracaso, eran las que propagaba la prensa escrita. Es indudable que la imagen dependía en buen grado de la utilización de la palabra, hablada o escrita. Pero la imagen o la palabra a veces eran insuficientes y en caso de no bastar, la palabra se apoyaba en la fuerza.[11] La relación entre las guerras civiles, las asonadas y las

7 Entre 1870 y 1913 se construyeron casi 33.000 kms. de vías férreas, ver Roberto Cortés Conde y Ezequiel Gallo, *La formación de la Argentina moderna* (Buenos Aires, 1967), p. 47.

8 Andrew W. Robertson, *Political Rhetoric in the United States and Britain, 1790–1900* (Ithaca, NY, 1995), cap. IV.

9 Sobre la prensa argentina ver Ricardo Sidicaro, *La política mirada desde arriba. Las ideas del diario* La Nación *(1909–1989)* (Buenos Aires, 1993) y Laura Ruiz Jimenez, 'Estados Unidos y Gran Bretaña en la prensa diaria de Buenos Aires, 1926–1945,' tesis doctoral inédita, Instituto Universitario Ortega y Gasset-Universidad Complutense (Madrid, 1994).

10 Robertson, *Political Rhetoric*, p. 164.

11 Vale la pena recordar uno de los versos del *Himno a Sarmiento*: 'Por ver grande a la Patria tu luchaste/ con la espada, con la pluma y la palabra'. Es más, en numerosas ocasiones, la palabra se comparaba con una espada afilada o aguzada.

revoluciones con las elecciones es algo indudable en esta época. La política, su ejercicio, como los duelos o las revoluciones, era una cosa de hombres, aunque las mujeres no estuvieran excluidas de los diversos ámbitos de actuación. El duelo se había convertido en un importante mecanismo de ascenso social y en un instrumento válido para forjar imágenes de virilidad, razón por la cual era corriente ver a políticos y periodistas implicados en este tipo de actividades. De la Torre se batió en duelo en dos oportunidades a lo largo de su vida política, siendo el más conocido el enfrentamiento a sable con Hipólito Yrigoyen que le costó una cicatriz en la barbilla y explica su utilización constante de la barba.

De modo que las imágenes o metáforas *bélicas* constituían una parte importante de los combates o las justas dialécticas: 'aclarados estos antecedentes, voy a avanzar ahora resueltamente sobre las trincheras del adversario'.[12] También el reclamo del machismo y de los atributos viriles era una constante prácticamente omnipresente en las discusiones políticas, aún entre quienes, como de la Torre, lo hacían de forma algo más matizada que muchos de sus contemporáneos:

> La falta de partidos enerva la vida pública y extingue las virtudes viriles de los ciudadanos. En todas las sociedades del mundo, cada vez que se han relajado la autoridad y la disciplina de los partidos, se han visto aparecer especies parasitarias de políticos positivistas, que hacen de las conveniencias personales el único objetivo de su actuación.[13]

De la Torre y la política

El desembarco de Lisandro de la Torre en la política nacional, a partir de 1912, una vez consolidada su posición como líder máximo de la LS, fue precedido por su etapa como joven dirigente radical. Ahí está su participación en las revoluciones radicales de 1890 y 1893 y sus contactos con los máximos dirigentes partidarios. Recuérdese su temprana incorporación a la Unión Cívica (UC), y luego a la Unión Cívica Radical (UCR), de la mano de Aristóbulo del Valle y de Leandro N. Alem, a lo que hay que vincular el hecho de que fuera uno de los grandes impulsores del radicalismo en Rosario, su ciudad natal. Estas circunstancias explican por qué numerosos objetivos impulsados por los radicales en la década de 1890 fueran posteriormente incluidos en la plataforma de la LS. En los años que nos ocupan, muchas de las actitudes del líder rosarino sólo pueden interpretarse en relación y como respuesta a la política revolucionaria y abstencionista del radicalismo yrigoyenista,

12 Lisandro de la Torre, *Obras*, tomo I, p. 146.

13 Lisandro de la Torre, Discurso en San Luis, 13 de marzo de 1916, *Obras*, tomo V, p. 42.

a tal punto que en 'Una página de Historia' escribió: 'Excluido del comicio por la violenta arbitrariedad del gobierno, no le quedaba al Partido Radical otro recurso que el de lanzarse a una revolución justificada'.[14]

Algunos años después veríamos a un de la Torre subyugado por el gobierno local de los EEUU, a tal punto que las referencias a la situación de ese país o a políticos norteamericanos, como Wilson abundaban en sus discursos.[15] Esto se observa en la *Petición de Reformas* presentada por la LS a la Legislatura Provincial de la provincia de Santa Fe en mayo de 1909, con continuas alusiones a la realidad política estadounidense. Así, por ejemplo, se menciona la Constitución de Oklahoma, la última sancionada en EEUU, que recogía el derecho de peticionar (con la única solicitud del cinco por ciento de los empadronados).[16] En parte esto se debe a los dos viajes realizados por de la Torre a EEUU, entre 1900 y 1903, pero también a que en su experiencia recoge una vieja tradición argentina, de la que ya Alem había sido partícipe.[17]

14 Lisandro de la Torre, 'Una página de Historia,' en *Obras*, tomo I, p. 23. Se trata de la respuesta dada por Lisandro de la Torre, en junio de 1919, a la acusación de 'traidor al radicalismo' formulada por el diputado Francisco Beiró.

15 Véase *La Capital*, 20 de enero de 1913.

16 LS, *Petición de reformas constitucionales y legislativas presentada a la H. Legislatura de la Provincia el 18 de mayo de 1909*, Rosario, 1909, p. 4. Enrique Thedy, en 'Indole y propósitos de la Liga del Sur,' *Revista Argentina de Ciencia Política*, vol 1 (1911), reproduce con bastante similitud lo expuesto en la *Petición*.

17 Alem, en su correspondencia señalaba que: 'Nuestro partido tiene por principios la honradez administrativa, la libertad de sufragio, la autonomía provincial, el castigo al fraude y la malversación. Este programa hará la felicidad nacional. Pronto sancionaremos un Estatuto, imitando el que rige los grandes partidos en Norte América. Mientras tanto, es necesario que todos se convenzan de esta verdad: que el pueblo es el único artífice de su destino. La aurora de un nuevo día nos alumbra, se ha dicho con entusiasmo, pero también es necesario recordar que la aurora no es más que un episodio, una etapa, un momento: el despertar del día. El pueblo argentino debe velar por que esa luz de esperanzas continúe iluminando con claridad el paisaje de la patria'; Julio Aramburú: 'Historia de los partidos políticos argentinos,' en Leandro Alem, *Mensaje y destino*, tomo III (Buenos Aires, 1957), p. 155. Melo señala que uno de los efectos de la revolución del 90 fue la introducción de la organización de los partidos políticos estadounidenses, con convenciones que elegían candidatos y sancionaban estatutos y programas y comités que dirigían la acción electoral. En 1888 James Bryce escribió *The American Commonwealth*, un estudio sobre los partidos políticos. La obra llegó a Argentina cuando se formaba la Unión Cívica. Dos de sus lectores fueron el juez Virgilio Tedín y José N. Matienzo, que decidieron influir sobre los partidos políticos para que adoptaran la organización de EEUU. Tedín estaba vinculado a la Unión Cívica y mantenía relaciones de amistad con de la Torre. El nuevo partido decidió que una convención compuesta de delegados elegidos popularmente (de capital y provincias), en número igual a su representación en el Congreso, eligiera los candidatos para presidente y vice; Carlos R. Melo, *Los partidos políticos argentinos* (Córdoba, 1945, 1a ed., 1943), pp. 28–9.

Los ataques delatorristas al caudillismo, que asocia a ejecutivos fuertes, son constantes y paralelos a su defensa de 'los ejecutivos de índole puramente administrativa', en la línea del *self-government*. De ahí su defensa, a veces algo idealizada, de las democracias de base anglosajona, como las de Estados Unidos, Canadá, Australia o Nueva Zelanda. Los valores que éstas tenían se contraponían de forma clara al estilo sudamericano, o incluso centroamericano, de gobernar y hacer política:

> El sistema de Centro y Sud América inviste al ejecutivo, desde luego, de la función y de la fuerza policial, mientras sucede lo contrario en el otro sistema. Así, un gobernador de los Estados Unidos, que desempeña su mandato sobre millones de habitantes, no puede destituir, ni dar órdenes a un modesto comisario de campaña y resulta inferior en el poderío a cualquier mandatario argentino. La policía descentralizada, responsable ante los jueces, y muchas veces responsable ante el jurado popular, pone al jefe del Poder Ejecutivo en la imposibilidad de ejercitar presión sobre los habitantes.[18]

A esto hay que sumar el carácter de lector de Tocqueville y admirador de Sarmiento de de la Torre. En el discurso de presentación de su partido, y aludiendo claramente al caso santafesino, decía: 'Tomad una Constitución cualquiera de un Estado Americano: policía, justicia de paz, instrucción primaria, caminos, etc., todo eso es el resorte local', mientras que en Argentina, 'donde se cree y se repite a diario que practicamos las instituciones americanas', tanto la administración como la política provincial se

18 Lisandro de la Torre, Discurso en Córdoba, 27 de Febrero de 1916, *Obras*, tomo V, pp. 37–8. Previamente de la Torre se había manifestado en términos similares en el Congreso de la Nación, el 17 de enero de 1913, en ocasión de un debate parlamentario sobre la intervención federal a la provincia de Salta, aludiendo al triunfo electoral de Woodrow Wilson: 'el incomparable profesor de política de la Universidad de Princeton, tan sabio y elocuente como virtuoso. Y yo pensaba, no sin emoción, en su gran libro "El Estado", en aquel capítulo, sobre todo, en que estudia lo que llama la dispersión o difusión del Poder Ejecutivo, y me halagaba la ilusión de creer que las hondas perturbaciones a que asistimos de continuo, provocadas por la omnipotencia de los ejecutivos provinciales, habrán cesado el día en que un escritor argentino, hablando de Buenos Aires, de Córdoba o de Salta, pueda decir lo que Woodrow Wilson de Alabama y de otros estados de la Unión; que el Poder Ejecutivo no está desempeñado por un ciudadano con el título de gobernador del estado; que el poder ejecutivo se compone del gobernador de estado, del secretario de estado, del tesorero de estado, del contador de estado, del procurador general, del superintendente de educación y del "sheriff" de cada condado,' *Obras*, tomo V, p. 225.

hallan bajo 'la centralización del Poder Ejecutivo y la sumisa burocracia'.[19] De la Torre pensaba que había que buscar la raíz de los males argentinos en la centralización creciente de los gobiernos provinciales, que engendraba oligarquía. Si bien la LS era un 'partido de ideas y de libre discusión', hay que tener en cuenta que su fuerte impronta ideológica no desdeñaba los intereses económicos como substrato de apoyo político.[20] Posteriormente, en su primer discurso en el Congreso de la Nación comparó la legislación argentina con la de los EEUU, insistiendo en los temas de la educación primaria, la justicia y el gobierno local.[21]

El programa de la Liga del Sur desarrollaría en buena medida las concepciones federalistas y comunalistas de de la Torre, previamente expuestas en su tesis doctoral y sobre ellos volvería el líder rosarino una y otra vez en sus discursos, como se observa en los ejemplos que a continuación se mencionan. Por ello, el partido prestó gran atención a la política municipal rosarina, pero también a la de otros distritos. También dedicó especial atención, dada su raigambre municipalista, a la elección de comisiones de fomento en la campaña. Era una vieja reivindicación de la LS.[22] Para de la Torre el localismo no era un defecto de Rosario sino de Santa Fe, 'que se ha asignado una situación privilegiada y no se resigna a volver a la igualdad',[23] ya que no se ha formado una agrupación de ideas regionales, sino que el programa de la LS es para toda la provincia 'y si aún no se ha constituido la Liga del Norte para los mismos objetos, es porque estamos al comienzo de la campaña'. Había comités liguistas en Gálvez y San Jorge y adherentes entusiastas en Rafaela, Coronda, Esperanza, San Carlos, Sunchales y aún en Tostado. '¿Eso es regionalismo? ¿Qué cláusulas del programa de reformas de la Liga piden un beneficio exclusivo para el Sur? Ninguna.'[24] Desde el primer momento de la Torre negó que la constitución

19 Discurso de Lisandro de la Torre, 29 de noviembre de 1908, Rosario; *La Capital*, 30 de noviembre de 1908 y 'Los grandes argentinos. Dr. Lisandro de la Torre. Homenaje de sus correligionarios y amigos' (Rosario, 1916?), Archivo del Partido Demócrata Progresista, Rosario.

20 Natalio Botana, *El orden conservador. La política argentina entre 1880 y 1916* (Buenos Aires, 1977), p. 316.

21 *Diario de Sesiones de la Cámara de Diputados*, 1 de junio de 1912.

22 'Manifiesto de la Liga del Sur al pueblo de la Provincia', 21 de septiembre de 1913, en *La Capital* de la misma fecha.

23 Carta de Lisandro de la Torre a S. Gómez, 15 de julio de 1910, en Severo Gómez, *La cuestión del día. La Liga del Sur y el gobierno de la Provincia* (Santa Fe, 1910), p. 16.

24 Carta de Lisandro de la Torre a S. Gómez, 20 de julio de 1910, S. Gómez, *La cuestión del día*, p. 26.

de la LS tuviera un objetivo separatista y que por el contrario buscaba la integridad de la provincia.[25]

Sin embargo, de la Torre señalaba que el tema de la capitalidad era más complejo:

> Hostilizados el Rosario y el Sur, en todas formas por los hombres que gobiernan; privados de personería para la defensa de sus intereses en el orden nacional; despojados de la mayor parte de sus rentas; sin educación y sin obras públicas se ha producido un sentimiento lógico de reacción contra la capital en Santa Fe. Hay que observar que es de ese hecho aparentemente nimio que deriva todo. Establézcase el gobierno propio de los distritos rurales y a la autonomía municipal para las ciudades. Devuélvanse a las comunas con la mayor parte de sus rentas el cuidado de la educación, de la justicia, de la policía, de las obras públicas locales y el asiento de la capital carece de importancia; así se explica que Nueva York, Chicago y Filadelfia no echen en la balanza el peso de sus millones de votantes para atraer a su seno la capital. Pero acusarían un desconocimiento de los hechos y de las instituciones los que entendieran que eso puede crear un precedente en Santa Fe, foco de centralismo y de irritantes absorciones. Estos hechos han obligado a colocar la cuestión en los términos en que lo hace la Liga del Sur. Su programa dice que una justa autonomía pudo eliminar del debate la cuestión de la capital. Y es de indudable verdad. Pero como la autonomía no existe, ni hace nada presumir que se conceda el Sur plantea la contienda en las condiciones indispensables para el triunfo.[26]

Ya por aquel entonces, y ante la crisis evidente del Partido Autonomista Nacional (PAN), de la Torre pensaba en un partido que trascendiera el limitado marco local. Años más tarde, cuando presentó en el Congreso de la Nación un proyecto de ley de régimen municipal en las provincias destinado a disminuir el poder de los gobernadores tenía como punto de referencia el sistema político nacional.[27]

En su discurso en el acto inaugural de constitución de la Liga del Sur, de la Torre señaló:

25 Carta de Lisandro de la Torre a Frugoni Zavala, Rosario, 3 de diciembre de 1908, en 'Los grandes argentinos. Dr. Lisandro de la Torre. Homenaje de sus correligionarios y amigos' (Rosario, 1916 ?), Archivo del Partido Demócrata Progresista, Rosario.

26 *Ibid.*

27 N. Botana, *El orden conservador*, p. 316.

No son los hombres los únicos causantes de situaciones como la que ha provocado este imponente movimiento de la Liga del Sur. Cuando los pueblos olvidan, en sus instituciones, los principios esenciales de la democracia, cuando permiten que de absorción en absorción las leyes mismas constituyen una red de acero que aprisiona la libertad, no es lógico esperar gobiernos justos. He ahí la razón porque este nuevo partido difunde claridades y esperanzas desde sus primeros pasos y da alientos a la certidumbre de que estamos en el comienzo de una gran jornada. Las malas leyes se remueven con tanta y mayor insistencia que los malos hombres, pero una bandera de reformas justas, hondamente encarnadas en el espíritu público es al final un torrente que nadie detiene. He ahí nuestra misión: hacer de esta fuerza que nace el torrente de mañana. Concentremos en esta bandera de autonomías y derechos comunales la base esencial de nuestras reivindicaciones. Si el Rosario y el sur de Santa Fe carecen de representación y de influencia cuando se discuten en los altos cuerpos del Estado sus intereses más vitales; si los impuestos son excesivos y se aplican con irritante injusticia en perjuicios del sur; si la representación política es desproporcionada y cuando se eligen los primeros mandatarios del Estado una minoría numérica usurpa la mayoría del colegio electoral; si todo eso sucede, es porque no se vota, porque la opinión no tiene medios de gravitar sobre el gobierno; porque la fuerza es la última razón de todas las arbitrariedades que imperan.[28]

La campaña presidencial

Tras la reforma electoral impulsada por el presidente Sáenz Peña y la imparable ascensión del radicalismo, las fuerzas políticas liberales y conservadoras se lanzaron a la formación de un partido nacional, aunque tras la retirada, por enfermedad, del presidente se quedaron huérfanos de la protección oficial, ya que el presidente en ejercicio, Victorino de la Plaza, no compartía los puntos de vista reformistas. De la Plaza era un convencido de la virtud de la vieja política y de los métodos tradicionales. Fue en esta coyuntura de cambios y transformaciones en que se consolidó la figura de Lisandro de la Torre primero como líder del Partido Demócrata Progresista (PDP) y posteriormente como candidato del mismo para enfrentarse en las elecciones de 1916 a Hipólito Yrigoyen.

28 Discurso de Lisandro de la Torre del 29 de noviembre de 1908, Rosario; *La Capital*, 30 de noviembre de 1908. También en 'Los grandes argentinos'.

A lo largo de la campaña de la Torre optó por lanzar un mensaje centrado en la necesidad de renovar y regenerar la vida política nacional. Para ello era necesario contar con un sólido sistema de partidos, estructurados en torno a un programa o plataforma política y dotado de medios de dirección permanentes (comités y convenciones) que permitieran superar el caudillismo propio de la política argentina. Este mensaje tenía un doble destinatario. De una parte, las viejas estructuras panistas, ejemplificadas en la figura del nuevo presidente, de la Plaza, y en Marcelino Ugarte. Por la otra, el radicalismo de Hipólito Yrigoyen, encarnación, según de la Torre, de los vicios más tradicionales de la política criolla.

En un reportaje publicado en *El Día*, de Montevideo, Benito Villanueva dijo que el PDP se había creado sobre las bases del PAN, lo que era básicamente cierto, aunque teniendo en cuenta la incorporación de otras fuerzas provinciales, como la LS. Para de la Torre, los elementos prestigiosos que pertenecieron al PAN y apoyaban situaciones provinciales demócratas progresistas, así como los demás componentes del PDP, entendieron desde el principio que había un nuevo partido y desde ese perspectiva, de acuerdo con las ideas democráticas del programa, antepusieron la corrección de los procedimientos políticos a las maniobras electorales que garantizaran el éxito.[29] En este sentido, eran continuas las alusiones de de la Torre a la frontera que separaba la vieja política de la nueva. Mientras el PAN era el reflejo del pasado, el PDP simbolizaba el futuro y por su mensaje y sus métodos debían reflejar el cambio, que según él entendía, se había producido en la política argentina.

Tras la convención nacional del PDP, que debía elegir la fórmula con la que la nueva agrupación concurriría a las elecciones, comenzaron los rumores para debilitar a los designados y anarquizar al partido, con el argumento de concentrar a las fuerzas conservadoras y tener mayores posibilidades de éxito frente al radicalismo. En el fondo de la discusión estaba la figura del gobernador de la Provincia de Buenos Aires, Marcelino Ugarte, que como algunas otras figuras políticas de primer nivel, maniobraba arteramente con el fin último de convertirse en el presidente de la República. Posteriormente, el PDP propuso una concentración 'de verdad, que fue rechazada, alrededor de nombres independientes y prestigiosos', como los de Drago y Bermejo. Ante la persistencia de rumores sobre la aparición de nuevas fórmulas, de la Torre se preguntaba: 'Se ha dicho ... que alguien elabora tal o cuál fórmula presidencial exponente futuro de la concentración conservadora. ¿Qué partido nacional auspiciará tal fórmula?'

29 *La Prensa*, 8 de enero de 1916.

Insistía en la equivocación de Villanueva y que el cuento inacabable de la concentración conservadora debía concluir de acuerdo con la 'historia de los organismos políticos y ese fin no podía ser otro que la subsistencia de los más nuevos y fuertes y la transformación de los más débiles y gastados'. Según su opinión, la situación política se polarizó en la lucha entre radicales y demócratas progresistas, las únicas fuerzas actuantes a escala nacional y los otros grupos debían inclinarse a uno u otro lado. De la Torre no tenía problema a renunciar a su candidatura 'para dar paso a soluciones prestigiosas',[30] pero la salida exigida por sus rivales implicaba la renuncia de valores por los que de la Torre había luchado toda la vida. Sin ellos, no se hubiera movilizado tras el proyecto del PDP, ni lo hubiera impulsado como hizo.

En enero, de la Torre fue a hacer campaña a la provincia de Santa Fe. En esa ocasión Julio A. Roca (h) proclamó las fórmulas de la Torre — Carbó y Thedy — Martínez Zuviría, para gobernador y vice. Sus viajes a Santa Fe, su provincia natal, fueron constantes y desde allí iba a las provincias limítrofes.[31] Pese a que la proclamación de la fórmula evitaba una nueva vuelta atrás, continuaban los conflictos internos en el PDP, ante la posibilidad de que sus electores modificaran su postura en el Colegio Electoral, que era el responsable último de la elección presidencial y dada la gran discrecionalidad de los electores de votar por quien quisieran. Roca no participó de la proclamación de la candidatura en San Luis, por haber viajado a Córdoba. Por eso, de la Torre lo acusó de cuidar sus intereses políticos en detrimento de los partidarios y tras una conversación telefónica entre ambos, Roca renunció a la presidencia del Comité Nacional.[32] Pese a las enormes dificultades que encontraba en su camino, el PDP proseguía su marcha. Desde Santiago del Estero y Tucumán, llegaban adhesiones a la fórmula. De la Torre criticó el hecho de que un mes después de la proclamación, los que se opusieron 'no han producido acto alguno positivo, tendiente a proponer al país otra fórmula mejor o peor'. Mientras tanto, Ugarte mantenía sus aspiraciones presidenciales. Ante ello, la respuesta de de la Torre fue que la tentativa de una nueva 'Concentración', urdida en el Senado, 'sobre la base deleznable del extinguido "bloque" no marchará'.[33]

En la proclamación de su candidatura, en Córdoba, de la Torre recordó su fe en los programas y que por ello y por encima de todo prefería la obra de un partido ('iniciada en la propaganda doctrinaria, proseguida en la con-

30 *La Prensa*, 13 de enero de 1916 y *La Nación*, 13 de enero de 1916.

31 *La Prensa*, 17 y 21 de enero y 17 y 19 de marzo de 1916.

32 De Julio A. Roca (h) a Lisandro de la Torre (s/f), Archivo General de la Nación, Fondo Julio A. Roca (h), Leg. 2, Doc. 145.

33 *La Prensa*, 25 y 27 de enero de 1916.

sulta al pueblo en los comicios y culminada en el recinto parlamentario') a las reformas promovidas desde el gobierno por un hombre superior. Comparó la defectuosa organización provincial argentina (ejecutivos fuertes o caudillescos, apoyados en la fuerza policial) típica de América Central y del Sud, con la de EEUU, Canadá, Australia y Nueva Zelanda. En alusión directa a los radicales, se preguntaba si: '¿Puede llamarse partido a aquel que elude la proclamación de sus candidatos, o la realiza en las vísperas mismas de las elecciones? … Sólo un partido provincial, el conservador de Buenos Aires, sostiene la conveniencia de realizar la elección de electores de presidente sin presentar candidatos. Y cuando esa actitud es señalada sin discrepancias, como un error en abierta contradicción con los programas políticos de la época, he ahí el partido radical que después de muchas otras coincidencias sugestivas, coincide también con el partido conservador en su doctrina política, y desertando la convención, lo que implica desconocer la soberanía popular, entrega sus destinos al capricho de círculos oligárquicos.'[34] Un discurso posterior mantiene la misma tónica: 'Los partidos son los instrumentos necesarios para el ejercicio de las instituciones libres. El desprecio por la política es una prueba de ignorancia y de falta de patriotismo.'[35]

La campaña se cerró en el Frontón Buenos Aires el 29 de marzo. De la Torre protestó contra la postura partidista y reaccionaria del Ejecutivo, apartado de sus deberes, obligaciones y compromisos.[36] La situación se agravó por la intervención federal a la provincia de Corrientes y la actitud del Ejecutivo en San Luis, tendientes a debilitar las posiciones del PDP. En un discurso respaldó el 'gobierno parlamentario', o de gabinete responsable. También fue proclive a reformar la manera de designar los senadores, siguiendo el modelo de EEUU, que se había cambiado por haber sido 'una fuente de corruptela en el orden estatal y federal'.[37]

Durante toda la campaña, de la Torre, asumiendo una cierta institucionalidad de su condición de candidato, respetó la figura de de la Plaza, pese a los constantes ataques del presidente.[38] Sin embargo, su actitud

34 *La Prensa*, 28 de febrero 1916 y *La Nación*, 28 de febrero 1916 y en L. de la Torre, *Obras*, tomo V, pp. 33–40.

35 Lisandro de la Torre, Discurso en San Luis, 13 de marzo de 1916, en *Obras*, tomo V, pp. 41–2.

36 *La Prensa*, 30 de marzo 1916.

37 'Crónica y documentos: Discurso del Dr. Lisandro de la Torre al PDP,' *Revista Argentina de Ciencia Política*, enero 1916.

38 En un discurso en Corrientes, el 20 de marzo de 1916 dice que de la Plaza 'ha demostrado conocer sus deberes de magistrado y apreciar la gravedad del momento que atraviesa la República', L. de la Torre, *Obras*, tomo V, p. 45.

cambió la semana previa a las elecciones, cuando ya todo estaba perdido y la ingerencia del presidente y de su ministro del Interior fueron demasiado evidentes. Ante esa situación era imposible fingir una pretendida neutralidad y el tono del discurso expresa claramente la amargura que lo acompañaba en esos momentos, cuando estaba claro el hundimiento de su proyecto: 'Durante más de un año se ha trabajado disimuladamente desde arriba, por detener la organización y la marcha del PDP. Los planes para arrebatarle las presidencias de las cámaras, las tentativas para organizar un núcleo parlamentario regresivo, con el papel de partido político encargado de resolver la cuestión presidencial, las intrigas para conmover y desquiciar las situaciones demócratas de Córdoba, Salta, Corrientes, San Luis, la protección oficial a todos los cismáticos y el repudio de todos los hombres que mantenían situaciones independientes, todo eso emanaba sistemáticamente de la casa de gobierno por los conductos subalternos del Ministerio del Interior y Agricultura.'[39] Tras la elección, sus juicios contra de la Plaza fueron más contundentes, y si bien mantuvo sus críticas contra Ugarte, aunque tildaba de 'franca' su postura, su acritud contra el presidente aumentó. En carta a su amigo Martín Aldao señalaba que en los primeros tiempos del PDP, 'y mientras Plaza no intervino — intervención que nadie pudo prever — hubo sinceridad' por parte de los dirigentes conservadores, para concluir que si bien la actitud de Ugarte fue mezquina, no fue la peor. 'Más despreciable mil veces me parece de la Plaza, el colla hipócrita y traidor por naturaleza, que, movido por rencores seniles, ha atizado todas las intrigas oculto detrás de Vidal y de Castañeda Vega.'[40]

Pese a que los plazos se extinguían, se continuó negociando en torno a la elección presidencial y a la actitud que asumirían los elegidos para participar en los colegios electorales. A mediados de mayo se anunció la renuncia de Ugarte y de la Torre para facilitar el acercamiento de sus seguidores, aunque ya era demasiado tarde y todavía quedaba pendiente la designación de nuevos candidatos. En la reunión del Comité Nacional del PDP, a principios de junio, Roca consideró que el acuerdo con los conservadores de Buenos Aires estaba más próximo por las renuncias de de la Torre y Carbó. Si bien se planteó la fórmula Rojas–Serú como alternativa, los delegados de Catamarca y San Luis manifestaron que votarían por de la Torre–Carbó, ya que tenían un mandato imperativo para hacerlo.[41]

39 Lisandro de la Torre, *Obras*, tomo V, pp. 49–50.

40 Carta de Lisandro de la Torre a Martín Aldao, 10 de agosto de 1916, *Obras*, tomo V., pp. 55–7. Más matizada resulta la opinión de Carlos Ibarguren, *La Historia que he vivido* (Buenos Aires, 1977), pp. 382–7.

41 *La Prensa*, 18 de mayo, 2 y 11 de junio de 1916 y *La Nación*, 2 de junio de 1916.

El 9 de junio se supo que tras una intensa discusión, de la que dependía el triunfo del candidato de la UCR, los radicales santafesinos votarían por Yrigoyen y el 10 la concentración propuso, con la oposición del PDP, las candidaturas de Rojas y Semprún. A último momento se negoció que los electores del PDP, del Partido Conservador de Buenos Aires y de los partidos provinciales antirradicales designarían una fórmula común para votar en los colegios electorales, encabezada por Bermejo. La fórmula sólo se proclamaría en caso de tener mayoría absoluta o que los radicales disidentes de Santa Fe se abstuvieran y que el Congreso Nacional tuviera que decidir, pero eso nunca llegó a producirse. De la Torre no quería hacer causa común en la derrota con los seguidores de Ugarte y de la Plaza. Antes de la reunión de los colegios electorales, los conservadores convocaron una asamblea en el Teatro Güemes para debatir la fórmula presidencial. No se invitó a los representantes demócrata-progresistas de Santa Fe y Capital Federal y los convencionales de San Luis, Tucumán y Catamarca se abstuvieron de concurrir. Tras el fracaso de la reunión, que constituyó el núcleo inicial de lo que más tarde se llamó la 'concentración conservadora', Roca dimitió como presidente del PDP, junto a los vicepresidentes primero y segundo. Fueron muchos los que en ese momento dieron por disuelto al partido, aunque no se había tomado ninguna resolución orgánica en ese sentido.[42] El 11 de junio se reunió el Colegio Electoral. Yrigoyen tuvo 152 votos, Rojas 104, Justo 14; de la Torre 20 con la minoría tucumana y Carbó los ocho de Santa Fe.[43] El suicidio de las fuerzas liberal-conservadoras se había terminado de consumar.

El triunfo de Hipólito Yrigoyen abría un nuevo período en la historia argentina y consolidaba el descalabro del PDP, que desde entonces nunca volvió a ser lo que fue y concluyó como un partido minoritario, limitado a la provincia de Santa Fe y la Capital Federal. Cuando se habla del fracaso del PDP y de sus causas se acude a las ambiciones presidenciales de de la Torre y Ugarte. Si bien la intransigencia de uno y la ambición del otro liquidaron el proyecto y permitieron el triunfo yrigoyenista, hay que considerar otras razones. Primero, de la Plaza se oponía a la consolidación del PDP y favorecía una coalición tradicional de partidos provinciales para ejercer cómodamente su papel de gran elector, amenazado por el proyecto delatorrista de que un partido moderno eligiera sus candidatos en una convención. Segundo, la fragmentación de las fuerzas liberal-conservadoras de la Capital Federal imposibilitó formar un eje articulador del nuevo partido.

42 L. de la Torre, *Obras*, tomo V, pp. 7–8 y 91.

43 J.O. Sommariva, *La República Federal, 1912–1936* (Buenos Aires, 1955), pp. 48–9.

Tercero, las diferencias políticas e ideológicas de conservadores, católicos y liberales, con planteos, reivindicaciones y estilos distintos, agravadas por la diversidad de los partidos provinciales 'concurrencistas'. Cuarto, el carácter que unos y otros querían darle al PDP. De la Torre pretendía un 'partido orgánico permanente', mientras que para numerosos líderes conservadores, el partido era 'un estado de transición preparatorio de otras soluciones'. La fórmula del partido permanente también amenazaba la supervivencia de muchos partidos provinciales, un extremo al que se negaban la mayoría de sus líderes, ante el temor de perder poder negociador. Por último, la existencia de numerosos 'presidenciables' (Villanueva, Roca(h), Gómez, Cárcano, etc.) dificultaba cualquier proceso unitario. Natalio Botana sugiere que más allá de los enfrentamientos personales y la intolerancia de los dirigentes, la división en partidos modernos y agrupaciones tradicionales encubría dos visiones antagónicas. Una, la de la práctica política ensayada en numerosas elecciones. La otra, una visión racionalista de la acción política, con un programa ordenado, que marcaba el contraste con las formas tradicionales.[44]

Por otra parte, la principal pregunta sigue siendo por qué un político como de la Torre fue elegido de un modo casi unánime para encabezar semejante proyecto. Es posible que durante un breve momento, especialmente mientras se mantuvo el influjo de Sáenz Peña, se valorara muy positivamente el esfuerzo que el líder rosarino había hecho desde la LS por renovar la política santafesina, pensándose que la experiencia podía ser trasladable a la escena nacional y que ello sería una carta de triunfo para enfrentar a los radicales. El fracaso de la experiencia impidió comprobar en las urnas que hubiera sucedido si de la Torre e Yrigoyen se hubieran enfrentado en igualdad de condiciones.

De todas formas, el discurso de Lisandro de la Torre encarna la realidad de una cierta Argentina que quiso ser y no fue, de una Argentina que apostaba por las instituciones más que por las personas y que intentaba superar de forma positiva los enfrentamientos partidarios, juzgados como estériles por muchos contemporáneos. De alguna manera, esas notas en el discurso vibrante y florido de de la Torre estuvieron presentes hasta el momento de su muerte y fueron uno de los elementos que lo convirtieron en un referente obligado de la política argentina en los años previos al estallido de la Segunda Guerra Mundial.

44 Botana, *El orden conservador*, pp. 322–3.

Selected Bibliography

Alonso, Paula (1997) '"En la primavera de la historia": el discurso politico del roquismo de la década del ochenta a través de su prensa,' *Boletín del Instituto de Historia Argentina y Americana Dr. Emilio Ravignani*, 3rd series, First Semester, pp. 35–70.

Beaujon, Oscar (1981) 'Buenos Aires en la prensa venezolana del siglo XIX,' *Boletín de la Academia Nacional de la Historia* [Venezuela], vol. 64, no. 253 (January–March), pp. 29–60.

Bushnell, David (1950) 'The Development of the Press in Great Colombia,' *Hispanic American Historical Review*, vol. 30, no. 4 (November), pp. 432–52.

Chust, Manuel (1997) 'Construir y difundir. La prensa en la formación del Estado nacional mexicano, 1821–1835,' *Caravelle*, vol. 68, pp. 19–42.

Clément, Jean-Pierre (1997) *El 'Mercurio Peruano', 1790–1795*, 2 vols (Frankfurt am Main: Vervuert; Madrid: Iberoamericana).

Clément, Jean-Pierre and Pons, André (1978) '*Mercurio Peruano* et *Edinburgh Review*: Une analyse libérale de la situation péruvienne à la veille de la guerra d'indépendance,' *Caravelle*, vol. 31, pp. 113–33.

Covo, Jacqueline (1993) 'La prensa en la historiografía mexicana: problemas y perspectivas,' *Historia Mexicana*, vol. 42, no. 3 (Jan.–March), pp. 689–710.

Covo, Jacqueline (1986) '*Le Trait d'Union*: periódico francés de la ciudad de México; entre la reforma y la intervención,' *Historia Mexicana*, vol. 35, no. 3 (Jan.–March 1986), pp. 461–76.

Deas, Malcolm (1993) *Del poder y la gramática, y otros ensayos de historia política y literatura colombiana* (Bogotá: Ediciones Tercer Mundo).

Desramé, Céline (1998) 'La comunidad de lectores y la formación del espacio público en el Chile revolucionario: de la cultura del manuscrito al reino de la prensa (1808–1833),' in François-Xavier Guerra, Annick Lempérière, et al. (eds.), *Los espacios públicos en Iberoamérica: ambigüedades y problemas. Siglos XVIII–XIX* (Mexico: Fondo de Cultura Económica), pp. 273–99.

Díaz, César Luis (1998) 'El periodismo en la Revolución de Mayo,' *Todo es Historia*, vol. 32, no. 370 (May 1998), pp. 76–88.

Donoso Vergara, Guillermo (1987) 'Perfiles del diario *El Mercurio* escritos por don Santos Tornero,' *Revista Chilena de Historia y Geografía*, vol. 155, pp. 9–36.

Earle, Rebecca (1997) 'Information and Disinformation in Late Colonial New Granada,' *The Americas*, vol. 54, no. 2 (1997), p. xxx.

Estrade, Paul (1994) 'Pasando revista a los periódicos cubanos publicados en París en la segunda mitad del siglo XIX,' *Revista de Indias*, vol. 54, no. 200 (January–April), pp. 191–209.

Febres Cordero, Julio (1983) *Historia del periodismo y de la imprenta en Venezuela* (Caracas: Academia Nacional de la Historia).

Figueroa Esquer, Raúl (1998) '*El Correo Español*: la prensa españolista mexicana y el '98,' *Cuadernos Hispanomericanos*, nos. 577–78 (July–August), pp. 87–98.

García Ponce, (1975) *La imprenta en la historia de Venezuela* (Caracas: Monte-Avila Editores).

Goldman, Noemí (2000) *Historia y lenguaje. Los discursos de la Revolución de Mayo* (Buenos Aires: Editores de América Latina).

González, Aníbal (1993) *Journalism and the Development of Spanish American Narrative* (Cambridge: Cambridge University Press).

González-Ripoll Navarro, María Dolores (2000) 'Ocio, lecturas y escritura en la ilustración cubana,' *Revista de Indias*, vol. 60, no. 219 (May–August), pp. 331–43.

Guerra, François-Xavier (1992) *Modernidad e independencias: Ensayos sobre las revoluciones hispánicas* (Madrid: Editorial MAPFRE).

Halperín Donghi, Tulio (1985) *José Hernández y sus mundos* (Buenos Aires: Editorial Sudamericana).

Hample Martínez, Teodoro (1993) 'The Diffusion of Books and Ideas in Colonial Peru: a Study of Private Libraries in the Sixteenth and Seventeenth Centuries,' *Hispanic American Historical Review*, vol. 73, no. 2 (May), pp. 211–33.

Herrero Rubio, Alejandro and Herrero, Fabián (1992) 'A propósito de la prensa española en Buenos Aires: el estudio de un caso, *El Correo Español*, 1872–1875,' *Anuario de Estudios Americanos*, vol. 49 (1992), pp. 107–20.

Jakšić, Iván (1994) 'Sarmiento and the Chilean Press, 1841–1851,' in Tulio Halperín Donghi, Iván Jakšić, Gwen Kirkpatrick and Francine Masiello (eds.), *Sarmiento: Author of a Nation* (Berkeley, Los Angeles, London: University of California Press), pp. 31–60.

Jensen, Larry R. (1988) *Children of Colonial Despotism: Press, Politics, and Culture in Cuba, 1790–1840* (Tampa: University of South Florida Press).

Lacoste, Pablo Alberto (1997) 'Americanismo y guerra a través de *El Mercurio* de Valparaíso, 1866–1868,' *Anuario de Estudios Americanos*, vol. 54, no. 2 (July–December), pp. 567–91.

Mariluz Urquijo, José María (1988) 'La *Gaceta de Buenos Ayres*, 1764,' *Investigaciones y Ensayos*, vol. 38 (July–December), pp. 449–83.

Martínez Riaza, Ascensión (1985) *La prensa doctrinal en la Independencia del Perú, 1811–1824* (Madrid: Instituto de Cooperación Iberoamericana).

Moore, Charles B. (1996) 'Oratoria sagrada y retórica barroca en el "Sermón de Nuestra Señora del Carmen" de Juan de Espinosa Medrano,' *Revista/Review Interamericana*, vol. 26, nos. 1–4 (Jan.–Dec.), pp. 149–65.

Myers, Jorge (1995) *Orden y virtud. El discurso republicano en el régimen rosista* (Buenos Aires: Universidad Nacional de Quilmes).

Núñez, Estuardo (1992) 'Bicentenario del *Mercurio Peruano*,' *Cuadernos Hispanoamericanos*, vol. 499 (January), pp. 59–73.

Pani, Erika (1996) 'Una ventana sobre la sociedad decimonónica: los periódicos católicos, 1845–1857,' *La Palabra y el Hombre*, vol. 99 (July–Sept.), pp. 113–31.

Peralta Ruiz, Víctor (1997) 'La revolución silenciada: hábitos de lectura y pedagogía política en el Perú, 1790–1814,' *Anuario de Estudios Americanos*, vol. 54, no. 1 (Jan.–June), pp. 107–34.

Pérez Vila, Manuel (1988) 'La *Gaceta de Caracas*: testimonio de una época,' *Boletín de la Academia Nacional de la Historia* [Venezuela], vol. 71, no. 281 (January–March), pp. 162–213.

Rama, Angel (1996) *The Lettered City*, translated by John Carles Chasteen (Durham and London: Duke University Press).

Ramos, Julio (1989) *Desencuentros de la modernidad: literatura y política en el siglo XIX* (Mexico: Fondo de Cultura Económica).

Salas, Rubén Darío (1998) 'La prensa periódica de Buenos Aires: consideraciones en torno a la forma de gobierno, 1810–1819,' *Jahrbuch fur Geschichte Lateinamerikas*, vol. 35, pp. 129–57.

Seminario de la Historia de la Educación en México (1997) *Historia de la lectura en México* (Mexico City: El Colegio de México).

Sidicaro, Ricardo (1993) *La política mirada desde arriba. Las ideas del diario La Nación* (*1909–1989*) (Buenos Aires: Editorial Sudamericana).

Silva, Renán (1989) *Prensa y revolución a finales del siglo XVIII. Contribución a un análisis de la formación de la ideología de independencia nacional* (Bogotá: Banco de la República).

Thomas, Jack Ray (1979) 'The Role of the Press in the Chilean Rebellion of 1851,' *The Americas*, vol. 36, no. 1 (July), pp. 59–78.

Vega Jiménez, Patricia (1993) 'Los protagonistas de la prensa: los primeros escritores de periódicos costarricenses, 1833–1850,' *Revista de Historia* [Costa Rica], vol. 28 (July–Dec.), pp. 61–88.

Vega Jiménez, Patricia (1995) 'El mundo impreso se consolida: Análisis de los periódicos costarricenses, 1851–1870,' *Revista de Ciencias Sociales* [Costa Rica], vol. 70 (Dec.), pp. 83–96.

Vega Jiménez, Patricia (1996) 'De periodista a literato: los escritores de periódicos costarricenses, 1870–1890,' *Anuario de Estudios Centroamericanos*, vol. 22, no. 1, pp. 149–63.

Villalobos V., Carlos Manuel (1998) 'Sueños de iluminismo: *La Unión*, un impreso rural de 1891,' *Revista de Ciencias Sociales* [Costa Rica], vol. 81 (Sept.), pp. 81–95.

Vogeley, Nancy (1983) 'Mexican Newspaper Culture on the Eve of Mexican Independence,' *Ideologies and Literature*, vol. 4, no. 17, pp. 358–77.

Printed in the USA
CPSIA information can be obtained
at www.ICGtesting.com
JSHW020750070224
56801JS00001B/35

9 781900 039468